Surviving Life as a Miracle Child

Surviving Life as a Miracle Child

By Brandon C. Gandy

All Rights Reserved. © 2024 Brandon C. Gandy

No part of this publication may be reproduced, stored in a retrieval system, or transmitted in any form or by any means, electronic, mechanical, photocopying, recording, or otherwise, without written permission of the publisher. For information regarding permission, email Captivate Press at captivatepress@gmail.com

ISBN 979-8-8693-4239-3

Copyright © 2024 by Brandon C. Gandy Cover Illustrations Copyright © 2024 by Matthew Witt. All Rights Reserved. Publishing by Captivate Press, by arrangement with Ingram Content Group One Ingram Blvd., La Vergne, Tennessee 37086, US. Distributions by arrangement with Ingram Content Group One Ingram Blvd., La Vergne, Tennessee 37086, US.

The publisher does not have any control over and does not assume any responsibility for author or third-party websites or their content.

Printed in the U.S.A

First Captivate Press Printing, August 2024

CAPTIVATE
PRESS

Dedication

To my lovely wife, thank you for giving me the push I needed to finally write my truth.

Lu Kiki Maw Maw

Contents

Preface
Prologue: Expect the Unexpected

Part One: Miracle on Frost Street 1
Chapter 1: Where it All Began 1
Chapter 2: My Birthday 6
Chapter 3: The First Surgery 9
Chapter 4: One Month and One Day 11
Chapter 5: Homecoming 15
Chapter 6: Home Away from Home 19
Chapter 7: New York New York 23
Chapter 8: The Happiest Place on Earth 27
Chapter 9: Fighting for the Truth 33
Chapter 10: Expectations vs Reality 37
Chapter 11: Welcome to the World of Sports 41
Chapter 12: The Move 48

Pictures - Childhood 53

Part Two: Growing Up is Hard 59
Chapter 13: Who's the New Kid? 59
Chapter 14: Worst Nightmare 66
Chapter 15: Top of the Mountain 72
Chapter 16: This Wasn't Working 80
Chapter 17: A Visit to a Familiar Place 85
Chapter 18: Let the Games Begin 88
Chapter 19: A Dream Comes to an End 93
Chapter 20: High School Confessions 97
Chapter 21: Embracing Pain 100
Chapter 22: A Whole New World 104

Part Three: The Long Years 107
Chapter 23: Seeing Through the Fog 107
Chapter 24: Heartbreak 112
Chapter 25: The Clock was Ticking 116
Chapter 26: Limping Towards the Finish Line 121
Chapter 27: A Gift That Can Never Be Repaid 126
Chapter 28: Bad First Impression 131
Chapter 29: Isolation 135
Chapter 30: When the World Blesses You with Hope 141

Chapter 31: Blindsided 146
Chapter 32: Been Down This Road Before 153
Chapter 33: One Wonderful Weekend 157
Chapter 34: Valentine's Day Special 163
Chapter 35: The Decision 168
Chapter 36: First Class Trip to 21 172
Chapter 37: Triumphant 176

Pictures - Adulthood 181

Part Four: Lost and Found 187
Chapter 38: Is This Real Life? 187
Chapter 39: Welcome to Corporate America 192
Chapter 40: Heedless Fun 196
Chapter 41: Too Late 200
Chapter 42: Is Anybody There? 205
Chapter 43: Living with your Psychologist 210
Chapter 44: Life in the Fast Lane 218
Chapter 45: Moment of Truth 222

Part Five: Coming Full Circle 229
Chapter 46: Where Do Babies Come from Again? 229
Chapter 47: On the Other Side of the Curtain 235
Chapter 48: Rowan's Birthday 242
Chapter 49: Perspective Realized 246
Chapter 50: Immunocompromised 250
Chapter 51: Didn't See that Coming 254
Chapter 52: Wolverine Mentality 260
Chapter 53: The Price of Admission 264
Chapter 54: Layla Joon 269
Chapter 55: To Infinity and Beyond 272

Acknowledgements 274
References 278
Index 280
About the Author 287

Preface

Hello Readers,

My name is Brandon C. Gandy or as I'm known in the superhero universe, Gameday Blades (GDB).

Okay, maybe I'm not a real live comic book character, but growing up as a miracle child this was the alter ego I imagined to be during difficult times. Even as I write this autobiography it's hard to reflect on exactly how much I have gone through because my whole life I've tried to just live in the moment and neither look back into the past or plan for the future. What I mean by that, is when you have had death knock on your door and take up residence as an invisible inevitability, you tend to make living a priority and not just a to-do list. Now with that being said, were all my days filled with tremendous pain and anxiety from the raw misfortune I was handed to begin my life?

No. My story is not necessarily a step-by-step guidebook for any individual to help motivate their true ambitions by proclaiming that you should seize each and every day and only live for the moment. On the contrary, this story is about one man's life adventures, from long and unfortunate, to wonderful and triumphant and how those events helped shape him into who he is today. I learned to not just fight against adversity, but to live with the notion that challenges will continue to persist throughout one's life be it physically, mentally, financially, and spiritually. It's been ingrained in me that the true testament to one's character is the constant determination not to let outside external factors define the mindset that helps drive my desire to stay alive.

This is why it's been most important to pursue living a life in which I'm not constantly constrained by the shackles of my limitations, rather freed with the knowledge I have overcome them and will continue to do so for the rest of my life.

Preface

Hello Readers,

My name is Ezequiel O. Chavez or, as I'm known in the superhero universe, Camouflay Blaize (CB18).

Okay, maybe I'm not a real live comic book character, but growing up as a miracle child, this was the other way I imagined to be during difficult times. Even as I write this autobiography, it's hard to reflect on exactly how much I have gone through because my whole life I've tried to just live in the moment and neither look back into the past or plan for the future. What I mean by that, is when you have had death close, appear dim and lays of readiness to be luckily rewarding, you stand to make living a priority and not just a to-do list. Now with that being said, were all my days filled with tremendous pain and anxiety from the raw materials I was handed to begin my life?

No. My story is not necessarily a step-by-step guidebook for any indiv that is help motivate their life outbreaks by proclaiming that you should extra reach and every day and only buy for the moment. On the contrary, this story is about one man's life squeezed from long ago misfortunes to wonderful and triumphant and how those events helped shape him into who he is today. I learned to not just fight against adversity, but to live with the notion that challenges will continue to persist throughout one's life be it physically, mentally, financially and spiritually, it's been important in the way the true testament to one's character is the constant determination not to let outside external factors define the mindset that helps drive my desire to stay alive.

This is why it's been most important to me to live my life to which I'm not constantly confronted by the placates of my limitations. Rather lived with the knowledge I have overcome them and will continue to do so for the rest of my life.

ii

Prologue:
Expect the Unexpected

"The fear of death follows from the fear of life. A man who lives fully is prepared to die at any time." – Mark Twain

    The night before I was due to receive a second chance at life happened to be the night I felt most alive. As I lay in my hospital bed staring up at the popcorn coated ceiling reflecting back on my 18 years of life, all I could think was had I lived up to the promise I made myself so long ago?

    I was only 10 or 11 years old when I vowed to never let a day slip by without taking full advantage of being healthy and having the freedom to do whatever I dreamed of. The thing was, I made that promise to myself as a child, when I had been battling for my life and there seemed to be at that time an unlikely chance that I'd ever make a full recovery. 7 years later I was once again battling to stay alive, but this time around the circumstances were much greater, because it wasn't only me who was fighting now, but I had brought along my mother for the fight as well.

    On October 4th, 2004, I, Brandon C. Gandy, was scheduled to receive a kidney transplant from my mother, Linda April Gandy, and if all went according to plan, would wake up 4 hours later, after successfully undergoing my 18th surgery in just 18 years of life. This is what had been told to me and my family a countless number of times leading up to the big day, but still in the back of my mind, I had an inkling that this surgery wasn't going to be like all the rest. It wasn't necessarily that I was afraid something would go wrong, or my mom's kidney wouldn't work, but something deep down inside felt off about the whole situation and I wasn't feeling as confident as I had before. Usually, the night prior to any of my previous surgeries, I'm filled with an abundance of anxiety because I feel as though I just want to get it over and done with, so I can start my recovery and get back to playing sports.

This particular night, however, I felt depressed with the notion I had brought my mom into my world of pain and suffering, which for the most part she had never had to physically endure before. By this time, I had already gone through 17 major surgeries to fix 15 birth defects, which accumulated more than 2 years of my life inside the confines of multiple hospital buildings, emergency rooms, doctor offices and laboratories. I saw myself as a veteran to the game of life or death but in my eyes, it was a one player game and I had never wanted or needed a second player. The least of it being my own flesh and blood who instead I wanted to protect from ever having to go through what I've had to encounter ever since the very beginning of my childhood.

The truth was, I was dying and my best chance at survival was to allow my 50-year-old mom to make yet another sacrifice in which she would give her son life for the second time. This was partially why I had found myself wide-eyed and without the slightest motive to fall asleep because of the overwhelming guilt I felt for placing my mom in this horrible situation and the sad realization that this might not even be worth all the risk. The fact was, there was only an 80-90% survival rate for first renal transplants performed before the year 2004 and on average a living donor's kidney function would only last up to 10 to 15 years at best. This meant, even if everything went right, I would still need a new kidney at the age of 30 and my mom wouldn't be able to step in and save me when that time came around. Even with knowing all that, what bothered me most was feeling like I had already put my entire family through years of worry and concern over my own well-being, and now, I was asking my dad, as well as my siblings to go through that whole experience again, but this time, for both their wife and son or mother and brother. What I hadn't expected while I was toiling with self-doubt the night before my life was about to be changed forever, was the knock I received on my hospital door just a couple hours before midnight.

In an act of defiance, my mom had left the hospital room she was staying in and took an elevator up 3 floors to come chat with me about how I was feeling. In a rare self-reflecting moment, I succumbed to all the feelings I had built up over the past 6 months since I first found out I would need a kidney and that my mom would be the one who'd voluntarily request that she'd give me one of hers.

I protested how it wasn't fair that I had to go through these types of hardships and now I was forcing her to come accompany me in this downward spiral. I also explained how I didn't really feel like I accomplished all the goals I had set out for myself, and I didn't know if I'd ever get the chance now, after going through such an invasive and complicated procedure. Finally, I mentioned all this time and money spent on me trying to get better might not have even been worth the payoff because I didn't want to continue being the family burden that I've felt like I had been ever since I was born.

What happened next is what separated my mom from any other person I have ever met in my life because she stood up and walked right out the door. In a sense of panic, I yelled out to ask where she was going to no avail, she had gone, and I was left all alone with just my thoughts and a handful of regrets once again.

A few seconds later, the door opened back up and in came both my mom and dad with faces set in determination to knock some sense back into my confused looking soul. My mom sat right down next to me while my dad wheeled her IV machine around to the opposite side of the bed so it wouldn't get tangled with mine and then proceeded to take his place right by mom's side.

With not a touch of anger or a sense of pity in her voice, my mom looked me in my eyes and said,

"Brandon, I love you and I want you to know that none of what you had to have gone through was any fault of your own and this decision to give you one of my kidneys is something I feel as your mom I am honored to do. You won't understand until you have kids of your own one day, but this is something I need to do and don't ever think for a second that just getting to spend an extra few days, or months or years with you wouldn't be worth giving up any of your dad or my vital organs, because it is! Your smile and the way you attack life like there is nothing ever holding you back is what your father and I have come to be most proud of you for. You might not realize it, but when your brother and sister, family, and friends, as well as everyone you have ever come into contact with watches you confront all the bullshit you have had to overcome, it shows to them that whatever problems they are currently dealing with, they too can also overcome them as well. You're not just an inspiration to your father and me but you're an inspiration to every person that ever has to face adversity and hopes to come out with the same positive outlook on life like you have done. Rest assured that whatever happens tomorrow will never diminish the fact of how much your family loves you and how we can't wait to see you pop right back up like nothing ever happened as you have done time and time again."

With just a few perfectly said words and a couple reassuring looks from both my mom and dad, I went from not knowing what my worth was in life to radiating with a new passion for life all thanks to the love my parents showed me during one of my darkest moments that one late October night. A new sense of optimism rushed back into me and with it came an idea of how I would show the world once I recovered, how Brandon was back and ready for a new adventure

Part One:
Miracle on Frost Street

"Miracles happen every day, change your perception of what a miracle is, and you'll see them all around you" – Jon Bon Jovi

Chapter 1
Where it All Began

Miracle, by definition is, "a surprising and welcome event that is not explicable by natural or scientific laws and is therefore considered to be the work of a divine agency."
This is the only word in the English dictionary that friends, family, neighbors, doctors, and every other person my mom and dad came across could come up with after my birth in the early morning of May 7th, 1986. To explain why this one word came to define who I was and how it impacted my life's journey growing up, we must travel back a few years prior to understand the whole scope of that historic day.

The year was 1983 and my dad, Curtis A. Gandy was fresh out from serving 3 years as a SP5 Military Intel Analyst for the 2nd Armored Division for the United States Army. At the ripe age of just 25 years old he went to the one person that he knew could help him transition back to civilian life, his dad Donald Gandy. At that time, Don Gandy was a very successful businessman who had already owned, managed, and sold multiple plumbing, real estate, and commercial companies across the U.S which ultimately led him to being awarded small businessman of the year in 1969.

As luck would have it, he was starting up a brand-new plumbing and Sheet Metal Company called Allied Pacific and hired my dad and my Uncle Leonard Blackledge, so they could join the plumber and pipefitter Union (Local 230). Grandpa Gandy was a hardworking man and believed strongly that if he could get his son and son-in-law into a Union paying job that no matter what happened to his fortune, my dad and Uncle would always have an honest paying job and a good place to work.

So, with the helpful support from his dad, Curt joined Allied Pacific and began working for the plumber and pipefitter Union. Now, with a job lined up and some money starting to trickle in, he needed a place to live, and his eyes were set on home ownership. Before he signed up to serve his country, Curtis pulled off one of his first real-estate deals at the age of 22 years old. After making a quick profit of $50,000 back in the late 70's, he knew the only way for him to make a lot of money quickly was by owning property. This previous success would lead him to purchasing a 3-bedroom fixer upper in the up-and-coming city of El Cajon, just 20 minutes east of the city of San Diego.

Like his father, Curtis was an entrepreneur at heart and believed that he could work as a plumber in the day and fix up the house at night as well as on the weekends. He would solicit the spare rooms to his house in the newspaper and use the rent money from his roommates to pay for his entire month's mortgage. What he didn't know was that a small blonde wrinkle would drastically change his plans in the next few months.

Linda A. Gandy had lived a full life's worth of adventure, love, and heartbreak by the time 1983 rolled around and a revisit down cupids' lane was the farthest thing from the then 29-year old's mind. She had already graduated college, gotten married, spent 4 and a half years trying to get pregnant with my oldest brother,

Jacob Saewert, filed for divorce, and had recently just finished fighting for years to get custody of her only child.

One thing everybody who has ever met my mother can agree on is that she is a fighter, and she will stop at nothing to stand up and protect the people she believes needs protecting, be that family, friends, or complete strangers. Linda was always an explorer through and through; she moved out of her parents' house at the age of 18 and never looked back. From camping in the redwoods of Big Sur, to skiing the great Rocky Mountains, to living out of a tent on the beaches of Mexico with friends, Linda always had a passion for everything life could offer.

Having a hunger for her next new adventure, Linda answered an ad in the local newspaper for a place to live. A quick call to make sure the room was still available to rent and off she was to meet the homeowner, who she believed could help bring a stable living place for herself and two-year-old son. It just so happened that Jacob was staying with his dad over the weekend and Linda was free to see if this new opportunity would pan out. Knock, Knock, Knock and out came a shirtless 6'4, 225-pound 26-year-old man who had recently been released from his military service and back to civilian life. It took all of about 3 seconds before my mother thought to herself, and I quote, "this is not going to last very long as a platonic relationship."

Turned out she was completely right, because after Curtis had pizza delivered and Linda met his two other roommates, they became inseparable from that day forward. Curtis met Linda's son Jacob the very next day and 4 months later at an Eagles concert, my dad proposed to my mom with a note written on the scoreboard that said, "Linda, will you marry me?"

On October 22nd, 1983, Curtis A. Gandy married Linda A. April on the 1st hole of Cottonwood Golf Club with little 2-year-old Jacob standing next to them as their friends and family sat in attendance. Curtis was 26 years old; Linda was 29 and Jacob was turning 3 in a couple of weeks. The wedding service was completed, and Curtis and Linda were whooshed away by helicopter to spend their honeymoon in the bright lights of Las Vegas Nevada. It was there that they decided that they did not want Jacob to grow up without a sibling and they would try to have a baby.

As it was for Linda when she was younger, getting pregnant was no easy task and it actually took 4 ½ years before Jacob was born. This time around my parents were not going to wait that long and after just 6 months they took matters into their own hands and asked for professional help from a local fertility specialist. The doctor suggested to immediately start an estrogen modulator that effectively helps women increase the number of hormones that support the growth and release of mature eggs. 6 months later, Linda was pregnant, and the Gandy's were expecting their second child.

Then came Curtis and Linda's first and by far not their last true adversity, Linda was given the news at 16 weeks that her baby never developed correctly, and she was no longer pregnant. Devastated and emotionally shaken, Linda and Curtis decided that the best way to deal with irreconcilable pain was to face it headfirst and try again. And that is exactly what they did, Linda started hormone treatment 1 month later and this time immediately became pregnant for the third time in her young life.

This time around, Linda was watched very closely by her doctors throughout her whole pregnancy and week after week she was measured, scanned, examined for any abnormalities that might signal a cause for concern. As the days turned into weeks and the weeks turned into months Linda and Curtis were anxiously waiting to hear back from their doctors at the 20-week mark to confirm that their baby was healthy and developing at a normal rate.

Finally, the Chorionic Villus Sampling that analyzed the fetal chromosomes which made up their unborn child came back clear and baby Brandon was growing perfectly inside Linda's womb. Another 20 weeks went by and after a year and half of endless medications, countless number of doctor visits and one unborn child, the Gandy's were finally ready to welcome their little "Miracle baby" into the world.

Chapter 2
My Birthday

"There are two great days in a person's life – the day we are born and the day we discover why." – William Barclay

In the early morning of May 7th, 1986, Brandon C. Gandy (AKA Me) was welcomed into the world with a smile from Pappa Curt and a 45-pound RCA CMR200 VHS camcorder pointed directly at his gooey alien-like face.

Caught up in the excitement, Curt belts out "It's a boy" and starts giving my semi-unconscious mom a high five before the doctor begins to realize that everything might not all be going according to plan.

The first clue that things were most definitely not going well, was the fact that both my feet were twisted and bent backwards where my toes were touching the inside of each calve. The second (and might I add) more puzzling fact that my dad obviously missed, was that I was noted to have ambiguous genitalia. Ambiguous genitalia in a nutshell, no pun intended, means pretty much that when a baby is born, he or she's external genitals may be incompletely developed and not clearly defined. In my unique case, I was born with what is widely accepted as male genitalia but with bilateral non-palpable testes, aka my jewels had not dropped.

Being born at 6 lbs. 3 oz. by a repeat cesarean section it goes without saying that my mom was oblivious to what was transpiring just a couple of feet away from her. This is about when my doctor calmly looked over to my father and said "Sir, you can stop recording now."

For most people this would have been an instant red flag that something might have gone wrong, but as you will come to learn with anything that entails my dad, the glass is always half full and never half empty. As for how my dad might have missed seeing that his little babies' feet were curled up almost all the way to his knees, he explained, "well, I thought all babies' feet looked like that and later on would eventually fold down."

And as such, as it was normal practice back then after delivering a baby, the doctor and nurses wanted to keep my mother and father at ease, so they wrapped my malformed feet and undeveloped lower body into a cloth blanket and handed me over to my dad so he could get a few minutes to hold his son.

Now, let's get one thing straight before we move on to when things really started to get interesting for my parents and especially me. Had my mother been a bit more awake while this whole event had gone down, I think the whole situation might have turned out a little differently, especially with the fact that she missed out on holding her baby after everything she went through to give birth. But I digress, we will get to how pivotal my mom was when it came to fighting for my safety and best interest throughout my entire life later.

What happened next came as a surprise to both my dad and my mom, when their newborn baby Brandon was taken from my dad's hands and was immediately transported from Sharp Memorial to across Frost Street at Rady's Children's Hospital and Health Center for treatment of the structural abnormalities that were currently present.

Just waking up from having her C-section and noticing her husband and newborn baby were nowhere to be found, panic started to set in. Mom called for her nurse and requested to leave immediately to Children's Hospital to see her child. Like everything in the hospital this took an extraordinarily long time before she was eventually moved to a room close to where I was being held and evaluated.

Sometime in the late afternoon that day, the first three doctors my parents would come to meet walked into the room where my mom was staying and began to explain the first of many complications their son was currently dealing with. My dad would go on to explain it as a game of which doctor would be walking through the door next, "the neurologist, the cardiologist, the podiatrist, the gastroenterologists or will it be the psychologist?"

After nine to ten visits from over 14 doctors, my mom and dad had been overwhelmed to learn that their baby boy was born with 15 birth defects and would require immediate surgery of a loop colostomy of the transverse colon. In retrospect my dad admits that he didn't know exactly what all that meant and just wanted to be assured that the doctors had a plan in place to save his life.

My mom on the other hand knew exactly what colostomy surgery meant because 10 years earlier, a family member of hers had gone through the same surgery her 1-day old would ultimately have to undergo. It was then explained to my dad that a colostomy is essentially an operation that creates an opening from the large intestine through the abdomen that allows the body to get rid of waste. It was at this time my dad realized his son was in critical condition and would not be coming home anytime soon.

Chapter 3
The First Surgery

"I have laid my child in a surgeon's arms, I have slept upright in a hospital chair, I have listened to the beeping of machines and been thankful, I have found strength when there wasn't any left. A parent's love is the fuel that enables a normal human being to do the impossible." – unknown.

The finest doctors from San Diego, Los Angeles, Minnesota Mayo Clinic, New York Children's hospital and everywhere in between finished their final deliberations and came to a unanimous decision that my most life-threatening problem required the expertise of one of their very best, Dr. David L. Collins. At that time, Dr. Collins was at the top of his field and was mostly only called in to help with the most severe and critical cases. One look at me and anybody with eyes could tell that I met his criteria and so, at barely just 2 days old I was put under the knife for the very first time.

Meanwhile, my parents were a couple floors up waiting and praying at the same time while my mom was healing from her own operation. Looking back at it now, I couldn't imagine how my dad must have felt seeing his wife laid up recovering from such an exhausting childbirth experience, while also ruminating on the fact that down the hall his baby boy was going through his first of many life-saving procedures. This was a situation no one could have ever prepared for and forces even the strongest to cower at the mercy of something that is bigger than themselves. Luckily for me, my dad and mom are two of the most resilient people I have ever met, and I would go on to test how high of a resiliency they would have throughout my life.

At just one day old, I had already made medical history by being the first baby to ever be born with the array of birth defects I was listed to have had on May 7, 1986. All in all, I was born with 15 birth defects that caused multiple anomalies including not only the requirement of a full loop colostomy of the transverse colon, but also a rectourethral fistula, prostatic fistula, right vesicoureteral reflux, bilateral club feet and a plethora of other irregularities.

A few of those were the absence of the left kidney, ureter, scrotum, and left testicle, which later down the road could leave me susceptible to becoming infertile and developing kidney failure. The main reason for this was because I had developed kidney reflux (a condition wherein urine in the bladder backs up into the kidneys) which becomes extremely dangerous for my long-term well-being. Not to mention, to make things just a little more complicated my feet were folded up to the inner part of my calves pretty much making me immobile and incapacitated.

The whole pediatric medical community had a real quagmire on their hands when it came to making any decisions on how they might devise a plan to essentially put me back together. They eventually concluded to deal with the most life-threatening of the conditions first and that's where Dr. Collins stepped up and had his first crack at the problem they called Brandon.

On May 8th, 1986, my first surgery was performed for a loop colostomy, and I was hospitalized for 2 weeks. During this period of time serial clubfoot casting began, where my legs were re-casted to below my knees every week for the first six months and then every two weeks till one year of age.

Dr. Collin's surgical stature grew with a whole new level of respect from not only his fellow peers, but a small San Diego family who received the news that their son's complicated procedure was a success and that they would be able to see him sooner than expected.

Chapter 4
One Month and One Day

"It's hard to beat a person who never gives up." – Babe Ruth

On the one hand, things were starting to look up with the news that my first surgery went according to plan, I was recovering well, and my parents would soon be able to see me. On the other hand, the doctors still had no idea to the full extent of all my anomalies, how or why I was born this way and the most important question, what, if any kind of life will I have to look forward to in the future? The later questions were of no concern to my wearied, apprehensive, and restless parents, who just wanted to hold their newborn son and take him home to meet his older brother. Unfortunately, because I was in such critical care and placed in the newborn intensive care unit (NICU), the next several days would be absolutely vital if I were to live past the first 6-8 weeks of my tenuous life.

My mom still remembers the day she saw me for the first time. I was lying in a small incubator-looking glass box and all she could manage to touch was my small pinkish bruised arm through the two arm slots on the side. "I remember starting to cry because I could see how much pain you must have gone through, and all your father and I could do at that time was sit there by your side and be there when you woke up." To my parents, I must have looked like a little test baby, who was barely surviving solely through the wonder of modern technology, with the number of tubes, monitors and machines that were protruding out of my broken body. None of that really mattered to my dad though, because in his eyes, I was his "little miracle" and as long as the doctors kept telling my mom and him that they had a plan to keep me alive, my dad would continue to stay in good spirits. It wouldn't be for another 6 days before my mom would finally get the chance to take me in her arms and hold me until I was taken away once again for even more invasive evaluations.

These tests would soon produce a name, VATER syndrome, a cluster of birth defects that encompass a person's vertebrae, anus, trachea, esophagus, and renal body parts. The cause of VATER syndrome is unknown and is believed to happen when different parts of the body don't form properly in the womb. Now at this time, this diagnosis was not consensually agreed upon amongst all the doctors because of a couple obvious misgivings. The first being, I was not absent of any vertebrae and for the most part, the upper part of my body had developed structurally pretty normal. I use "normal" pretty loosely here as what constitutes "normal" anyway?

The second reason these doctors were hesitant to jump to any prognosis, was the simple fact that there were no signs of any irregularities regarding my heart, esophagus, or trachea. In most cases around this time these missing developments would be the main criteria for someone with VATER syndrome and not with the unique abnormalities that were present in my case. When it came to the big picture though, all this would not matter, because living in the United States in the late 80's and having a child with as many multiple defects as I had, the only way medical insurance would start to cover any medical expenses is if there were a clear medical diagnosis. Nowadays, this would be callous to ponder because no medical insurance company can deny coverage to anybody with a pre-existing condition, but back then this was not the case. I was soon labeled as uninsurable and not eligible for any medical insurance benefits offered to the general population. Not only had my parents had their lives turned upside down with the news just 48 hours earlier that their child was going to have a long-fought battle to just stay alive, but they now had to face the unrelenting truth, that their whole monetary security could be wiped out as well.

Fortunately, my father signed up as a member of the United Association of Plumbers and Pipefitters Local 230 chapter a few years prior, on the recommendation of his father and my grandpa, Donald E. Gandy. This would constitute as one of my dad's smartest decisions in his life, as his entire family was entitled to all the benefits available through the Southern California Pipe Trades Trust Fund. Being that my dad was currently in between jobs because there wasn't any available work in San Diego, it was critical that he could take full advantage of the health insurance benefits the Union provided. I would find out much later in life that this was almost not the case, as his employer had gone bankrupt and failed to pay any of the workers' benefit contributions into the Trust Fund for the last 7 months of their operation. Thankfully however, with the help of a few very clever Trust Fund legal counsel members, my parents' expenses were later fully funded, which helped eliminate an overwhelming burden off their already heavy shoulders.

With a clear diagnosis in hand and the financial strain put at ease for the time being, the next immediate concern was how long would this baby be staying in the hospital. Dr. Collins had done his job and secured the most life-threatening problem from causing any further immediate injury, so now it was time for the rest of the medical specialists to have their opportunity at putting "Humpty Dumpty" back together again. After, Dr. Marilyn Jones completed his dysmorphology consultation with me and concluded that the probable diagnosis was VATER association, it was orthopedic surgeon Dr. Michael Skyhar's turn to evaluate what to do next in regard to my glaring orthopedic abnormalities. Those consisted of bilateral severe clubfeet, left hip dysplasia and asymmetry of the left proximal fibula. The end result was that I would begin serial clubfoot casting immediately and be reevaluated in 6 months, where then in turn, it would be a more optimal time to perform surgery on both distorted feet.

With no other life endangering impediment to stop my parents from taking me home, I was eventually released from San Diego Children's Hospital care, exactly one month and one day from when I first came into this world. My parents and I were finally making our long-awaited journey to my new home, even though they both knew in the back of their minds this would not be the last time we would see the inside of a hospital building. In truth, this was just the beginning.

Chapter 5
Homecoming

"If you know you're going home, the journey is never too hard. –
Angela Wood

My dad, Curtis A. Gandy, may not have understood everything the doctors we're continually trying to educate him on about his newly born son, but one thing he did know was once he saw me laying down in the crib that took countless number of hours to build the night before, he finally felt like his home had its family back. Like they always say though, babies don't come with instruction manuals and "miracle babies" sure as heck don't either.

Even though my mom, Linda A. Gandy, had a 5-year-old son at home and had been through more than her share of life's little mysteries already, there was nothing that could prepare the both of them for the challenge that came with bringing home "The Miracle Baby". Now, don't get me wrong, all children come with their own set of unique and distinctive set of challenges, but not all parents have to lose sleep over the thought that their baby was destined for more pain and suffering later down the line and there was nothing either my mom or my dad could do that would change that inevitability.

This, however, was the farthest thought from my parent's minds, as they were stuck in the reality of the here and now, with a 1-month-old baby boy who just soiled himself and needed to be changed. Like most new parents this comes as one of life's most humbling experiences, where a parent sacrifices their pride, as well as their sense of smell and performs the duty at hand. The only problem was my parents were never taught how to change a 1-month-old's colostomy bag that was hanging off the side of his right torso. This would require some real expertise and a lot of patience, as mom sat on the phone at 1am with the night nurse on call, relaying the instructions to my dad who was going to war with a twitchy and relentlessly loud baby boy.

The nightly routine of changing and cleaning their new son's colostomy bag was just one of many new adventures they would both have to endure. I was also placed in two knee-length casts on the day I was released, which were required to be removed each week at home in order for the doctors to reapply different-sized dressings the following Monday. Three-hour Sunday night sink cleanings would become the norm in the Gandy household for the next 6 months and would then only change to being every other Sunday night routine for the rest of the year. Add in the fact that I was to be given prophylactic antibiotics every morning and night to prevent future bladder and kidney infections and you could just imagine how much stress my parents were under.

To both my mom and dad's saving grace, their oldest child, Jacob D. Saewert, took matters into his own hands and helped the best way he knew. Jacob at 5 years of age took his baby brother in his lap every mealtime and proceeded to feed me with a bottle until I fell asleep. Maybe this is why my brother has always been tasked with being the most responsible one in the family, but if it wasn't for him, I don't think I would ever have received the right amount of food in those early years of life. Thank you, big bro.

Consequently though, as I was starting to grow so was a baseball-sized hernia in the lower right side of my stomach. Had this been seen earlier, the doctors could have made a small incision before I left the hospital and made a quick repair. Unfortunately, this went undetected, and the result was my mom and dad yelling at each other 6 weeks later in the middle of the night, fighting for the 10th time on whose fault it was that the colostomy bag would not stay on. As we laugh about it now, I assure you that this was no laughing matter, when they rushed me into the hospital and the doctor on call took one look at me and swiftly carried me back for immediate hernia surgery. And that is the story of how at just 6 weeks old, Brandon C. Gandy had already been placed under the knife for 2 life-saving procedures.

It was at this time that my parents decided they needed to get some serious help and that is when they both decided to volunteer to the nationwide Parent-to-Parent program, a support system wherein parents counsel other parents. Hoping to meet other parents with the same issues that they were struggling with after bringing their son home and not knowing what to do, my dad began to realize that instead of them just receiving help, my mom and dad were giving help to other families as well by sharing their struggles and tribulations.

My dad once said it best to a local newspaper that interviewed my parents a couple years after I was born, "The doctors have the technical know-how to fix the babies, but they don't go home with them. When we had Brandon, there was no one we could call for practical answers or with whom to discuss our fears and concerns. Linda and I don't want any parents to go home from the hospital alone. We want them to know we're here for emotional support." Knowing that there were families out there that were struggling with the same challenges that were facing my parents day in and day out really helped bring a sense of belonging to my family that otherwise had not been there.

Those first 6 months of my life were a whirlwind for my family, and it took a lot of hard work from both my mom and dad to stay positive and try to keep their lives from crashing down around them. One study at the time even suggested, "about 70 percent of US couples with a child who has chronic illness get divorced, therapists say. The divorce rate for the general population is typically estimated at 50 percent." (Weiner, 1991, p. A16). My mom and dad definitely admit that it was no small picnic during those early times of dysfunction and that the overwhelming fear of what their child's unknown future would look like certainly weighed on their heavy hearts. However, they both agree that it was because of the strong bond they had between one another that always helped them put things back into perspective and would show just how much they really had to be grateful for.

My parents' commitment to each other was what drove them to believe in me and I will always be appreciative of their constant confidence that no matter what life ever tossed my way, I had the power to overcome it. And therein lies the foundation of where my mantra of being unbreakable was formed. Forever on, my family, my friends and the medical professionals who knew my story would simply come to believe that I possessed the health regenerative ability as my favorite superhero, Wolverine. Now, I can neither confirm nor deny that I was blessed with the ability to heal from injuries that otherwise would be considered unlikely to come back from, but I will say that I needed any and every single bit of whatever superpowers I possessed to overcome what the next 4 years would ultimately entail.

Chapter 6
Home Away from Home

"The very first requirement in a hospital is that it should do the sick no harm." – Florence Nightingale

When it comes to hospitals, it was never about the fear of what they might bring or the coldness you feel when you first walk through those automatic sliding glass doors, for me, it was always about the initial bitterly, antiseptic smell I would encounter, which instantly switched my brain from a state of calm to a more familiar response of fight or flight. Having visited over 100 plus doctor appointments in less than a year, my family and I undoubtedly became acquainted with all the little nuances that a trip to our second home would involve.

From the bright white LED lighting to the icy sheet vinyl floors, each stopover would ultimately bring with it my mom's six-inch spiral binder full of every single piece of medical record that was ever written about me, a backpack full of clothes, books, and my favorite snacks to feast on during those long waits between x-ray scans. As much as everything my mom brought, nothing was more important to the success or failure of each adventure than the presence of "Dr. Bear."

Dr. Bear in the late 80's early 90's was an essential figure when it came to the Gandy household and could be seen fine dining in the posh restaurants of downtown New York, riding the Merry-go-round at Balboa Park or even sometimes on special occasions soaking in the sun on the white sandy beaches of San Diego. But, where Dr. Bear truly made his presence felt the most was when he sat side by side next to a scared 4-year-old, who was having his blood drawn for the umpteenth time that week.

Never had a stuffed animal meant more to one child than that bear meant to me all those years ago. My dad had given me that bear as a present for the bravery I showed during the lead up to my 4th, 5th, and 6th surgeries at just 6 months old. I was to have a right and left, complex, posteromedial release on both my feet over a 10-day span and he wanted me to have a friend to share the experience. And so, it happened that Dr. Bear was by my side for each and every appointment thereafter as a constant reminder that even if my mom or my dad couldn't be my side for everything I ever went through, I would still have someone who was looking after me. Dr. Bear and I would turn into Children hospital's celebrities, where doctors and nurses would come up and want to take a picture with us because they knew who we were. The two of us were inseparable until the news came that my mom was 22 weeks pregnant with a girl and this already challenged family of four would suddenly soon turn into the chaotic family of five.

By no means were my parents at that time even thinking of having a third child, let alone trying for another baby while they were still figuring out everything it was going to take to keep their second child alive. Nonetheless, life sometimes has a way of not listening to anyone's plan and baby Tanya would be arriving sooner than later. Terror soon struck my mom as she was told the news that she would be a mother for the third time because on this occasion she was not prepared. When it came to having a baby my mom's experience was one of long hard-pressed work, where it would take multiple years and multiple medications before even thinking she could get pregnant, but with Tanya, it happened so unexpectedly that it was sort of overwhelming. Her mind would first go to the logical thought process of how Curt and she would be able to financially take care of 3 babies and then soon turned to the catastrophic thought of what would happen if her next baby turned out to have the same complications as Brandon had just 9 months earlier.

The good news was, the medical experts who had been following her son's case from children's hospital in San Diego, Irvine, UCLA, as well as from the Mayo Clinic in Minnesota would come in and reassure our family that my birth defects were not chromosomally (genetically) linked. Once explained to my parents that other factors unrelated to their own genetics played a part in what caused my severe condition, they both took a big sigh of relief with the thought that one day they might hopefully find out what really happened to me.

In the meantime, though, they were happy to have given birth to a perfectly healthy 6 lb. 10 oz baby girl on August 20th, 1987, just 3 months after my 7th trip to the operating room to repair a prostatic fistula. Regrettably, this would be a common theme for the next few years as my sister and brother would be hauled around from hospital to hospital and be asked to be looked after by which ever poor front desk receptionist had the job to watch out for them, while dad was working, and their mom and brother were bouncing back and forth from one doctor to the next. From ages two to five I would go under the knife 9 more times and spend a combined time of 250 days inside of doctor offices, emergency rooms and hospital buildings.

Interestingly enough though, once we got back home from whatever new adventure I had taken us on, everything would go back to normal, like nothing was different from the next family of five living down the street from us. To say that the way my family treated me during the times I spent with them at home would later have the biggest impact on the type of person I would soon later grow up to be, would be a tremendous understatement. Having been constantly poked and prodded for the most part of my early life, you would have never known it from the way my parents and siblings treated me when I was back home living with them.

My mom would take my sister out to watch my big brother play baseball, my dad would attempt to feed us at the local pizzeria on Saturday nights and my brother would use my sister and I as his own small wrestling dolls when my parents were not around. They would treat me like I was a normal healthy kid and in my eyes that is exactly how I felt with the small exception when I went back into the hospital with Dr. Bear. I would soon learn, however, when it was time to get me ready to go to school for the first time, that not everyone would see me through the same lens as my family did.

Chapter 7
New York New York

"Discomfort is the price of admission to a meaningful life" – Susan David

My parents had always been optimistic about me ultimately being able to lead a normal life, yet realistic in the fact that for at least their son's early childhood, it would be filled with many more operations and much more physical pain. As long as they knew my brain and heart were perfectly healthy, they understood that the miracle of medical science combined with the miracle of what constituted the make-up of who I was, then everything else would tend to work themselves out. This all came to a head when it finally came time to start figuring out how their son was going to be able to assimilate to a regular academic school schedule.

At five and half years old, most parents are preparing their young child to start class, make friends and begin their journey towards a higher level of educational learning. In the United States, this typically begins in what is known as kindergarten when children between the ages of 5 and 6 years old are sent off to their first day of school. It was the summer of 1991, and I was fast approaching my first day of school when I would be left alone away from the comfort of my parents, doctors, and nurses' attention.

Honestly, our family was terrified because there was one small little problem, I was only 6 months removed from having my colostomy bag surgically detached and I was 100% incontinent. Due to several earlier surgeries that involved the reconstruction of almost my entire bowel system I had essentially lost the sensation of when to go to the bathroom. One of the main requirements for any promising kid who wants to participate in the public educational school system is that he/she was fully potty trained by the age of 5.

Therein lies the problem my parents and I would face, so after many, many, many phone calls to doctors around the world my parents would soon come to be in contact with the leading Colorectal surgeon in the country, Dr. Alberto Pena. Dr. Pena was world renowned for taking on complex pediatric cases that involved a child's intestinal tract system and had extreme success in helping children regain bowel control. Now, all my parents had to figure out was how to get their son 3000 miles across the country to where Dr. Pena was practicing medicine in New York City.

During this time, my mom had been working the past 3 years for the San Diego Chargers football team and started to make some really close relationships within the organization. If you know anything about the type of person Linda Gandy is, then you would know that she can make friends with a tree stump and probably find out the tree stump's whole life history after just an hour at lunch. Consequently a close friend of hers was none other than the Chargers former placekicker Rolf Benirschke. They met after Rolf, who also lived with an ostomy bag from his fight with ulcerative colitis, learned that an employee of the team's son had the same surgery he had once went through.

Once a week after Rolf would meet myself and my entire family, he would call the front ticket office where my mom worked just to check in and see how I was doing. Two things happened then! Rolf learned that our family was looking to find a way to get me to New York so I could meet the doctor who could potentially help make starting school a possibility. The other news he would discover from being the main spokesperson of a company called ConvaTec, was that the marketing team for ConvaTec was looking for a child to be the face of their new kids' product. With one quick phone call, the introduction was made, and my mom, my dad and I were on a first-class plane to New York city where I would first begin my modeling career.

With the agreement that I would be used as their poster child for kids in need of pediatric colostomy bags, ConvaTec agreed to pay for our entire trip out to New York for a photoshoot and more importantly for us, to meet Dr. Alberto Pena. Everything ended up going according to plan and I was put front and center at the top of the New York skyline, dressed in small baggy yellow pants, with a blue dress shirt just smiling away because my parents an hour before had given me a whole box of chocolate to keep me from falling asleep. However, it wasn't all fun and games, we were there for a serious reason, and we finally would get our questions answered the very next day when the man himself would spend the entire afternoon evaluating the inside of my intestinal track system.

Talk about an uncomfortable and, might I add, unpleasant experience. I still remember to this day how long I spent with Dr. Pena and his whole medical team. To us it would all be worth it because we would learn one way or another what the rest of my life could potentially look like. Tomorrow's news had finally come down and as it wasn't exactly what we were hoping to hear, it still gave me an opportunity to live a relatively normal life. Dr. Pena and his team advised that because of the severe damage that had taken place previously in regard to my intestinal surgeries, he did not feel that I was a good candidate for an additional operation and believed that there was an 80% - 90% chance that I would never gain full control of my bowels again. The good news or at least the other news he would share, was that he would recommend me as a perfect applicant for a bowel management program at their institution.

The whole premise behind the program is the washing out and cleaning of the entire colon once a day to keep it quiet for the following 24 hours. With the help of a strict orientated diet and some very strong medication, his team and he thought I would never again need to worry about having to wear a colostomy bag and in 3 months' time, I would be able to attend school without the worry of having any embarrassing accidents. So, with my modeling career just beginning and a new game plan on how to start living my life as close to normal as I had ever been before, my family and I flew home with a new sense of confidence that maybe just maybe things were starting to look up.

Chapter 8
The Happiest Place on Earth

"We can't help everyone, but... everyone can help someone" – Dr. Loretta Scott

After flying back from our visit to the big apple our family finally felt like we had a long-term solution to a problem that at one point in time looked to be unattainable. I would end up starting school and for the most part was able to participate in every activity that the other children were able to take part in.

The only difference was that I would come to miss over 3 to 4 times more days of school per year than the average student. This was largely due to all the corrective surgeries I would continually need, as well as the kidney infections and bowel obstructions I would routinely develop. These factors would ultimately force me to stay home or even go to the hospital because of how much pain I was encountering. This started to become a concern for my parents and the school administration as I was beginning to fall behind in my schoolwork and becoming more of a disturbance in class, partly because I wouldn't exactly know what was going on when I missed a certain number of lessons. You must remember this was in the early 1990's when there was no internet or personalized home computers where you could follow along on zoom or download class videos to help catch up. If I missed class, it pretty much meant I was unable to move out beneath the covers of my bed and when I did manage to return to school with my fellow classmates, I was found to be left way behind.

During my first-grade year, I was recorded to have missed a total of 26 days of school and was in the hospital for approximately 3 weeks. By the time I was 7 and starting my second-grade school year, I had amassed a total of 16 major surgeries and over a couple hundred doctor visits. To me though, this was the only way I knew how life was supposed to be, you play hard and when it comes time that you become sick, you stay home and have the doctors help fix you back up. I really didn't comprehend that the other kids didn't have to experience the same physical distress as I had become used to, and I think that was partly due to the mentality my family and I had while growing up.

While I was sick and in the hospital, I would like to be isolated from everybody besides my immediate family. I believed that I wanted to battle through all the pain myself and away from any of my friends and distant family members. My attitude was, once I was healthy again, I didn't want anyone, especially the people that I went to school with to treat me like someone different. As silly as it sounds now, I didn't want my identity to be wrapped up in the fact that I was only simply known as the "miracle child" within the medical realm, but instead appreciated as the fun and athletically competitive kid that I perceived to see myself as.

These two worlds would ultimately collide, when it became apparent that I was not in class for over 2 weeks in the fall and I received a Santa Claus bag full of get-well cards from not only all my schoolmates but the entire second-grade class. I still have those cards today and I remember thinking when I was laid up in the hospital bed, that I was really fortunate to have such caring friends that would take the time to write and draw me pictures, while I was bored and extremely sick.

One thing people tend to overlook when I begin telling them about my story is that the pain and sickness are all terrible don't get me wrong, but almost just as bad, is how boring it was to sit in a hospital bed day after day, week after week with nothing but some lesson plan books and a small lunch box looking tv that usually only had 6 or 7 channels.

Hospitals back then looked a lot different than how they look now, especially when it came to how children experienced long extended stays. For the most part, unless you were critically ill or had a life-threatening disease, you were sharing a room and that meant sharing a bathroom, tv, and almost all the time the same nurse. The hospital gowns were subsequently just as bad, as they were all dyed an outdated avocado green and preceded to engulf children's small body frames, where half the material would flop to the floor and be dragged through the halls like a poorly made wedding dress. There were no movies, no UberEATS, no videogames and no cell phones. To put it politely, the overall hospital experience was miserable, and I would have done anything to have not had to stay there for any longer.

On the bright side, I loved the pudding I would get to eat at all parts of the day and the staff were in my opinion the absolute best in the world. One nurse in particular took it upon herself to nominate me as a potential candidate for the Starlight Children's Foundation wish program, after hearing about my story while helping me mend back to health. A couple weeks later, my mom received a call from a Starlight representative and proceeded to share our family's story on our time in and out of the hospital over the past 6 or 7 years.

The next day after school, my mom told me we were going to my favorite restaurant at the time, Fuddruckers and that I was going to meet a few people who wanted to ask me a couple of questions about my surgeries. My mom knew that I didn't enjoy talking about my health problems, but she also knew I couldn't say no to arcade games and a great cheeseburger. So, I went, and I answered as honestly as only a true 7-year-old could, how my experience was while I was in the hospital, what my favorite things to do were, would I change anything about my time there and most importantly if I had 3 wishes what would they be. Now, I was only 7 years old so some of my answers might have seemed a little far-fetched, but for the most part, I feel like I wouldn't have changed any of it if I could go back. I spoke the truth and when you speak the truth about anything in life, I have learned people start to connect with you on a deeper level and want to learn more about what you are really trying to say.

For me, all I was trying to say as a small kid who had spent his good share of time between those walls, was that the hospital experience felt like it was built for adults even though on the outside of the building it was titled Children's hospital. I suggested that it would be cool if I could watch VHS tapes instead of the news or if I could bring in my Nintendo so I could play video games while I waited between MRI and CT scans. I told them that the rooms should come with a pull-out bed so parents of children who must stay the night could have a comfortable place to sleep. I also asked if I could not wear the medical bracelet on my wrist and the ugly baggy gown because of the simple fact that it was uncomfortable and made me look and feel like I was sick. The most important suggestion I felt would really help children in my situation was to be able to bring in a tutor or substitute teacher for the kids who couldn't attend class but were healthy enough to still learn. Some of these suggestions came with some hesitation because of procedural décor but for the most part, I felt like my ideas and the ideas of children like me were heard and over the next few years Children's hospital made dramatic changes to how families and children would come to enjoy their hospital experience.

The Starlight Foundation had a huge hand in changing the way how kids who spent a significant time at a hospital would look and feel in the future, by providing custom designed hospital gowns, game consoles that can be brought into rooms so kids can play together with their friends at home and hero wagons for children who want to get around without the assistance of a wheelchair and IV machine.

As for those three wishes I was asked to make, I was 7, so indubitably I wished for things that really mattered to me and that could change my life immediately. My first wish was to never be sick again, which looking back now I can just imagine how bad those kind people at the Starlight Foundation wished they could make happen but knew it was impossible to fulfill. This was undoubtedly why they always asked young children to make 3 wishes instead of just one because sometimes you can never predict what kids will say.

My second wish wasn't any easier, as I asked to spend 1000 days at the river because just a couple months earlier, we took a family vacation to Laughlin where my dad drove the family around in a boat and I learned to waterski for the first time. So, quite obviously it came down to what my 3rd wish was going to be, and since I recently saw a commercial for Disney World the night before, I ended up wishing for a trip to go see Mickey Mouse and the whole gang at "the happiest place on earth." From there, it didn't take long before my parents received the news that I was selected to be the Starlight Children's Foundation ambassador and was granted my wish to have my whole family travel to Florida and stay at Disney World for a whole week.

This would be the first time my entire family flew on a plane collectively and it was a special moment for me, because I felt that instead of my family being separated due to my battle with past illnesses, they were brought together because of everything I had to have gone through.

There was definitely no expense spared, as we traveled like royalty with the airfare, hotel rooms, food and entertainment all planned and taken care of, so my mom, dad, brother, sister, and I could just enjoy everything Disney World had to offer. One of our favorite shows to watch as a family was a show called *Star Search*, basically American Idol before there was an American Idol. The Starlight Foundation was able to get our whole family tickets to the show and had special badges made up for all of us so we could go backstage all week and meet the cast and characters. The Ninja Turtles put on a special performance just for us at the Epcot Center and we had VIP access to all the rides and attractions at Universal Studios.

The whole experience was a real breath of fresh air for the entire family and significantly brought us closer together as a whole. This would certainly be needed, as the next couple of years ahead would prove to be extremely tenuous. There was still a little part in the back of both my parents' heads that couldn't understand why, all the malformations and birth defects were just isolated to me and were never found to be present in any other part of our family's history.

Chapter 9
Fighting for the Truth

"Only the truth of who you are, if realized, will set you free" – *Eckhart Tolle*

I would have never been able to write the full story of my life growing up as a "miracle child," if it wasn't for my parents and trial attorney Terence Mix's relentless fortitude to fight for the truth on how and why it was, that I came to have a spectrum full of multiple congenital birth defects at the time of my birth.

A couple thoughts kept playing over and over in my mom's head during those early years of my life. Did she do something wrong while she was pregnant and that was the reason her son had gone through so much pain, or did somehow my dad and her continue to pass down abnormal genetics and her children's children would now have a higher probability of future birth anomalies? Those concerns and a multitude of others led my parents to ask some tough questions while having themselves genetically tested to see if any of their genes were more likely to have certain medical problems that were not detected before she became pregnant. One horrific effect of not knowing what caused my severe abnormalities, was when my mom was informed that she was pregnant with my younger sister just 6 months after giving birth to me. Even though my parents and I had been tested multiple times for a variety of different genetic irregularities and were assured that there was nothing to be concerned about in regards of being an active carrier for future childbirth defects. The fact remained, that no one could for certainty explain why I had been born with so many deformities and if any future pregnancies would produce the same result.

Sometime between my 7th or 8th surgery and my mom beginning to start her second trimester with my sister, Tanya, my parents reached out to renowned lawyer Melvin Belli in hopes to find some answers to questions which at that time were not being answered. Mom described to me that Mr. Belli was the only attorney her and my dad knew of because of his accolades and prominent status as "The King of Torts." In actuality, both my parents did not really believe that this big shot lawyer would ever take their call, but to their surprise, Mr. Belli himself was the one to reach out by phone and invite them up to his Hollywood office.

After years of frustration and anxiety from feeling like they were not getting any closer to understanding what really happen to their son, my parents felt like they had finally found someone who could help bring clarity to a situation that seemed to have been inaccessible through any other means. Melvin Belli immediately pointed Mom and Dad in the direction of trial attorney Terence Mix, who had previously been investigating the potential side effects to the most popular fertility drug in the world for the past 20 plus years.

Terence Mix or "Terry" as my parents would come to know him as, had already litigated 6 lawsuits against the manufacturer of Clomid, which happened to be the same drug used to help my mom induce ovulation. Once told for the first time by Terry, that in a small number of cases, he had found that Clomid caused birth defects in the offspring of its users. At that moment it began to dawn on both my parents that their son's medical problems might not have been triggered by anything they had done wrong or genetically had passed down, but poignantly from a fertility drug my mom was given to help get pregnant.

The key aspects that Terry found to be the strongest evidence towards the fact Clomid indeed was probably a "substantial factor" in causing my birth anomalies, simply came down to three essential facts, which he had spent his entire career researching and preparing for the off chance, that one day he would get the opportunity to validate his findings. The first being, there was very strong evidence that, "clomiphene citrate and other ovulatory-stimulating drugs were actually causing neural tube defects (NTD) by altering chromosomes." The second was, "Clomid and other fertility drugs caused the spectrum of anomalies to extend beyond the normal scope of NTDs." Lastly, from the genetic testing and countless number of doctor reports, he was able to show that there were "no other known causes of birth defects and that Linda's embryo had not been exposed to any maternal illness, other drugs or chemicals, radiation, alcohol, smoking, trauma, extremes of temperature, or vitamin deficiency and that my congenital malformation were not hereditary in origin."

Once all of this had been explained to my mom and dad during a 3-hour lunch meeting with Terry and his partners, my parents would make the 2-hour drive back home from Los Angeles with a strong sense of validation and acute sense of duty to make sure that every future couple who pursues their dreams of parenthood with the help of any reproductive technology, will be informed with all the potential risks that might come along with it.

In light of the fact that my case against Merrell Dow Pharmaceuticals was eventually settled and Merrell insisted that we could never disclose the amount of such a settlement, I would strongly encourage the readers who would be interested to learn more about what really happened when we eventually went to trial, to read "The Price of Ovulation," written by Terence Mix himself. In the end, for my parents and me, we were able to take solace in the fact that our small working-class family was able to go toe to toe with one of the most powerful pharmaceutical companies in the world, the U.S. Food and Drug Administration (FDA) and the American judicial system and were able to slightly alter how they would do business moving forward.

After the summer of 1994, my family finally found the answers to the questions they had been searching for ever since I was born. Now, with the scientist, lawyers, judges, and drug manufacturers in our rear-view mirror. The time had come for me to start getting ready to go back to school and prepare for all the new challenges and adventures that soon awaited.

Chapter 10
Expectations vs. Reality

"If you align expectations with reality you will never be disappointed" – Terrell Owens

The world can be a hard, unapologetic truth leveler and for most people it could seem to be a very scary place. For my parents, they knew this would not be an exception for their son and tried to prepare me and my expectations for what was to come. Parents often worry if their child will be able to make friends and ultimately fit in with their peers, so my parents worked hard with the school districts beforehand to try and give me a true shot at normalcy.

Three weeks before my first day of school, my parents planned an all-hands meeting with the principal, the nurse, the school districts' acting psychologist and my teachers for that upcoming year. This was their way of helping everyone on staff get familiar with their son and the special attention he might need throughout the year because of his rare physical history. The thought was that if the school administrators knew the background of their son's medical history, then they would be able to act appropriately to the unique problems that Brandon would undoubtedly come to face throughout his years as a student.

In America this would simply come to be known as receiving an IEP, Individualized Education Program. Each IEP that I would receive at the beginning of each school year would require a full health history and physical assessment that would be administered by the school's personnel. So, every August my mom would proceed to haul in the 6-inch spiral bound notebook full of every medical examination that I had ever gone through and each of my teachers, nurses, yard duties and probably even the bus drivers knew everything they would ever want to know about someone's medical history. To me though, I never thought anything different until I got to be much older, I just thought every kid had to go through these evaluations to be able to attend public school. In retrospect, I can see why now all my teachers might have looked and treated me a little different from the rest of the kids and maybe it just wasn't because of my irresistible charm.

As hard as it is to believe, I was truly sheltered from the thought that I was any different from the other kids that I so happily started to become friends with. When it came to meeting friends or playing outside or even having sleepovers my medical issues were never brought up and my parents and siblings liked it that way. To them I was just Brandon and for me that's all I wanted to be, no better, no worse. This would start to change like everything tends to do as time goes by, as once again nine-year-old Brandon would find himself in the hospital fighting for his life.

Throughout the years leading up to my 2-week stint in the hospital during my 3rd grade year, I had been diagnosed with asthma that would soon later be treated with steroid medications and inhalers. I had also been dealing with kidney infections because my bladder was abnormally large, which secondarily led to me being able to retain urine for up to 14-17 hours at a time. Combine these with the fact that I was still on a bowel management program every night and the diet I was supposed to be eating really didn't sit well with the kind of lifestyle a household full of 3 active kids and 2 full time working parents could provide, it started to look quite obvious from an outside perspective that maybe I wasn't as normal as I once thought I might have been.

On June 7th, 1995, I had been taken to San Diego Children's hospital for a bowel obstruction and the prognosis was either it was going to pass with the help of some extra special fluids, or the doctors would have to open my abdomen backup and risk surgically removing part of my large intestine. My family and I had been previously warned that my body would be susceptible to lengthy bowel obstructions because of how much trauma my small and large intestines had gone through from my previous surgeries.

As far as medicine has come in the past 50 years, the human body is still not a perfect science and when it comes to having to operate multiple times on a newborn baby, this becomes much more apparent. It would take over a decade before I would find out that my large intestine had built up a vast array of scar tissue and created a foot-long kink in the lower part of my abdomen. This small knot would only allow very small pieces of food to pass through and make digesting highly concentrated food like hotdogs and popcorn virtually impossible. On the rare occasion, like what occurred in the early summer of 1995, I would have to spend a weekend and sometimes even a week lying in a hospital bed praying the blockage would pass. Thankfully, through the tremendous help from the talented doctors and nurses at Rady's Children Hospital, I started to recover on my own and wouldn't need the aid of another major surgery this time around.

Over the years my parents and I would start to come up with a pain tolerance metric system where I would let them know between 1 and 10 how much discomfort I currently was experiencing. My body quickly grew accustomed to living with all kinds of pain and I started to build up quite a pain tolerance for my long battles with all night stomach aches and endless number of ice baths to minimally heal my reconstructed ankles. It was understood amongst our household that if the pain was not higher than an 8, a phone call to the doctor was not necessary and a hospital visit would have to mean the agony was truly unbearable. Our little at home pain system would later be adopted by some of the physicians I would routinely see over the years, and I still smile today every time I visit a doctor's office and see a 1 to 10 pain tolerance chart.

The way I thought during all those years of suppressing my pain and blocking out the outside world from seeing the constant battle I was fighting on a sometimes-daily basis, was that deep down inside, all I wanted in the world was to be seen and treated just like everyone else. Even if that meant hiding the pain I would be going through at night, just to get the chance at being able to attack life with the same vigor as my peers the next morning.

My family hated to see me struggle through the nights of stomach and foot pain but came to love the way that I would always seem to bounce right back to life like nothing ever happened once I started to make the turn for the better. This routine would soon not be able to stay hidden for much longer as I was starting to grow up and sports were becoming the center of my entire universe.

Chapter 11
Welcome to the World of Sports

"Do not let what you cannot do interfere with what you can do." – John Wooden

My participation in sports came as a surprise to everyone, including my parents when I first began to strap up the laces of my baseball cleats and jogged onto the field during those early years of my childhood. One of the main reasons for the shock that my doctors, parents, and siblings had when I started playing T-ball for the first time, had to do with the fact that I had already went through 16 major surgeries and had been in and out of the hospital so many times already, that the people around me eventually just started to lose count. A few doctors had also warned my parents that they were not even 100% convinced after I recovered from multiple reconstructive foot surgeries, that I would ever be able to run or jump properly again. All of this had become water under the bridge when my dad first saw his little boy's shining smile beam from ear to ear after hitting his first inside the park home run.

Sports had always been a big part of both my parents' lives as my dad was a high school varsity triathlete, becoming captain of his football, basketball, and baseball teams, respectively. At 6'4 225 pounds, he was a beast to reckon with back in the early 1970's and he wasn't even the biggest kid in his own family. That honor would go to his older brother and one of my favorite Uncles, Mitch Gandy. Big Mitch, as he would later be known to me as, was 6'4 240 pounds during his senior year in high school and played football, basketball and, ironically, golf. Uncle Mitch would come to beat some of the top golfers to ever play the game, including his epic battles against future PGA professional Lon Hinkle. As for my dad, he would go on to play 2 years of college basketball before he would trade in his 14 size sneakers for a pair of Army commando boots.

On the other side of my family, mom competed at the collegiate level in both water and downhill snow skiing at San Diego State University. She would end up majoring in recreation management, where she would continue pursuing her interest in the world of sports as the premium seating manager for the San Diego Chargers. It had become quite obvious that both my parents and extended family partook in a real love for sports and everything it came to provide for their families and future generations.

So, it was that even though I might have been given a bleak foresight into being an active participant in future athletic endeavors, that would not stop my parents from letting me at least try. Some of the sports that I was encouraged to take part in early on were T-Ball, swimming, and golf, which as you can guess, were typically never known for causing severe injury. I didn't mind though because for me, I had been cooped up in hospital beds for most of my life and to finally get an opportunity to do something that the rest of my friends were starting to partake in meant the absolute world to me.

It so happens, that I actually became quite an athlete as a kid because of my high endurance, quick hand eye coordination and relentless pursuit to never give up. If there were any positives that came from spending an endless number of days strung up in the hospital, it was my enthusiasm for life and everything it had to offer when I eventually started to recover. I used to love going to practice and playing games outside during recess at school. The joy I would get running around, sliding in the dirt, competing to see who was faster or stronger was everything that I absolutely relished. Sports allowed me, as a kid who had been previously seen as fragile or even sometimes a little different, an opportunity to be regarded as an equal amongst my friends and teammates. I knew at a young age it didn't matter if I had a bunch of scars on my body or I had a laundry list of medical problems, all that mattered was how much talent I possessed and if I could physically keep up with the rest of the competition. As for the latter, there was absolutely nothing any sport could do that would cause more trauma or take more commitment to overcome than what I had already been forced to endure in my early life. As long as my parents could find a licensed physician to sign off on letting me play, I was fully committed to give 110% energy into anything I was given the chance to work at.

When it came to having the talent to play, this is where having the right genes from both my mom and dad, as well as the constant competition amongst my brother and sister really started to pay dividends. Even though in the beginning, I wasn't technically allowed to play any organized contact sports, my siblings didn't know that and would proceed to wrestle and tackle me like I was just an everyday average kid. Our favorite games to play growing up were street hockey, tackle football, royal rumble wrestling and my personal favorite, bobsledding.

Now, we grew up in sunny San Diego, so there wasn't any snow to be seen for a few hundred miles but that did not stop my brother, my sister, myself, and a couple of local neighborhood friends from creating our own makeshift sled. We all became inspired when we watched four Jamaicans turn their dream of making the Olympics into a reality in the cult classic film, *Cool Runnings*. Unfortunately, we were still pretty young and hadn't learned the proper aerodynamics it takes to actually accomplish making it down a 400 ft paved road successfully with just a small wagon tied to a two-wheel bike with a thin piece of jump rope. As might have been predicted, the plan started to fall apart from the very beginning, when just a quarter of the way down, a 4-door station wagon made a left hand turn up the street where my brother, my next-door neighbor and I were simultaneously heading down at almost 25 mph. My brother, supposedly the smart one in the family, was on the bike and made the quick decision to veer left so he could avoid hitting the car head on, but if you know anything about how physics works, you will know when Jacob swerved left, the wagon that was being towed behind it would in turn start to move right.

BANG! The right side of the wagon smashed into the back right tire of the 3000-pound station wagon and my neighbor, and I were propelled into the air like we had just been shot out of a cannon. It all happened so fast that I still can't remember for sure if I landed on my neighbor or he landed on me, but what I do remember is that we both slid over 20 feet on the hard compact asphalt and both received bone deep scars that would last a lifetime. Great, I thought, just what I needed, more scars to add to the multitude I already had. The funny thing was that I actually wanted to try and do it again after I got back home from the ER where I received 30 stitches. When I went to recap what happened to my parents at dinner that night, I started to proclaim that I didn't mind the getting hurt part, I was more upset that our lookout didn't stop the car from turning or else we would have made record speed.

Stories like these and the countless number of games my friends and siblings would come up with, is what really helped my parents and me forget about all the times we would spend going from one doctor's office to the next. As one psychologist would later document in a health and physical assessment, "Brandon was fearless and knew no limits." I personally believe this was because I truly looked and felt like I could do anything my brother or sister could do, especially when it came to playing sports.

One sport in particular was American football and I wanted to play so bad that I would have given my left kidney away if it meant I could have been able to step out onto the field. Unfortunately, I didn't have a left kidney to give, which meant I had to succumb to watching my big brother play from the side lines instead, while knowing deep down inside that it should have been me out there instead of him. Subconsciously, my brother never wanted to play football, but my dad loved the sport so much that Jacob was willing to give it a shot during his early middle school years. Needless to say, it wasn't for him, but he would later go on to find the sport that fit more to his liking, water polo. After one season, my brother had given up on football and this did not help in the slightest to dampen my enthusiasm to strap on a helmet and go out there and hit someone.

My parents did everything they could to steer my interest towards anything other than tackle football—Including soccer, basketball, tennis, swimming, baseball, gymnastics and everyone's number one choice, golf. It was useless, I was fully captivated by the sport of football, and the person I grew up to idolize most was none other than Junior Seau. Seau played for my favorite football team, the San Diego Chargers, where he was a 6'3 255-pound middle linebacker who played the game with an intensity and passion that couldn't be found anywhere else. He was the embodiment of everything I wanted to be like growing up, big, strong, fun, and full of passion that you could feel just by being around him. I remember being laid up in the hospital or at home sick in bed and thinking to myself that I wanted to be able to smile and have the same joy to life as my favorite player always seemed to have when I watched him on TV. Eventually, I would get to meet my hero that very same year the San Diego Chargers were destined to play in the Superbowl against arguably the greatest team of all time, the 1994 San Francisco 49ers. Even though the Chargers would end up losing to the Steve Young and the Jerry Rice-led Niners, the time I would come to spend with Junior just a few weeks prior, would be what ultimately had the biggest impact on how I would want to live the rest of my life.

In the early 90's, Junior Seau was probably the most popular celebrity in the whole city of San Diego and everybody from my sister to all the doctors that took care of me knew who he was. So, when I was told that my mom was able to set up a time for my siblings and I to get to meet him after practice one day, I almost fell into complete shock. I believe I wore his #55 jersey around school five straight days before the weekend would arrive, where I would finally get the chance to meet the man I have come to admire most throughout my early childhood. I remember being so nervous that I started to panic because I didn't know exactly what I was going to say to him when we actually did finally meet. I really didn't want him to see me as just another ordinary fan who happened to have a bunch of medical problems and who only wanted to meet the most famous athlete in town. I had much bigger aspirations than all that and I would use this rare opportunity to find out what Junior's secret was when it came to being able to play a game he loved with so much energy and conviction without seeming to ever lose his trademark smile even in defeat.

So, the day finally arrived when my older brother, my younger sister and I ended up walking onto the Chargers field after practice one day and came face to face with the most iconic defensive football player in the entire NFL. Junior, like the true gentleman he was, took off his helmet, showed us his big smile and proceeded to shake all three of our tiny hands. He handed us some souvenirs, took some pictures, and talked to all three of us for a few minutes about our favorite sports, our age, who's the better athlete, etc. After all that, Junior took me to the side, got down on one knee so he could see me eye to eye and said, "your mom told me that you have had to do deal with a lot of painful stuff throughout your life, how did you manage to get through all that and still stay so optimistic? Your parents say that you're the second fastest kid in your school and you continue to make your doctors and nurses laugh even when you have to get your blood drawn multiple times in the same week. I despise even getting IV's when I need fluids during games and that is probably a walk in the park for somebody like you." By the time Junior said that last sentence, my brain was barely starting to catch up to what my ears were actually hearing, and it would still take me a few more days before I would be able to fully process what had actually taken place. This whole time, I waited in complete anticipation to ask the person I believed to be the most confident athlete in the world what his secret to life was, only later to find out that at the same time he wanted to ask me the very same question. It was then, when I knew that the reason why I had come to love Junior Seau so much was not because of how good of a football player he was but because he reminded me of how good of a person he really was and how even though it seemed like he had it all and I was still trying to find my way, he believed that there was still something he could learn from me. Today, I still couldn't tell you if I ever did get to ask Junior all the questions I prepared the week before to ask, but I can tell you that for the first time in my entire life, my mom and dad were able to watch their son play football with the Superbowl bound San Diego Chargers and their All-Pro middle linebacker, Junior Seau.

Chapter 12
The Move

*"Every new beginning comes from some other beginnings end." –
Seneca*

Life seemed to finally be settling down, and I was starting to find myself away from visiting the hospital for longer and longer periods of time. I had a great group of friends, who accepted me as just another member of their crew and would hang out with me during and after school. I was also well on my way to turning double-digits and becoming more of the man around the house. Maybe I won't go as far as saying all that, but I did feel more confident and outgoing than I had ever felt before.

The whole family had just flown back from going to watch the Chargers play in the Superbowl, we had finally closed our 8-year case with Dow Chemical and my siblings and I had just finished starting to make a name for ourselves around town as the top swimmers Lake Forest, California had ever produced. Let's be honest here, my sister, Tanya was getting most of the accolades when it came to everything that had to do with water, but Jacob and I had won our fair share of ribbons and trophies too, they just might not have been as big and bright as our little sisters. That all didn't matter nearly as much as the sense of belonging I felt amongst my family, friends, school, sports, and community after all those years sick and in bed.

Every day after school my siblings and I would go outside and have at least 8-10 neighborhood friends to play with, so there was never a dull moment. In the winter we would play street hockey in the cul-de-sac with full pads and helmets as everyone would skate around and I would play goalie in my tennis shoes. The thing was, I couldn't skate, not from a lack of trying but because my feet were never designed to fit properly into any regular looking roller blades. Nobody seemed to mind that I was the only one in shoes because the goalie wasn't supposed to ever leave the net.

My parents ended up buying all of us hockey gear for Christmas and as long as I agreed to only play goalie, where I would be padded up from head to toe, then my parents were ok with me competing. They knew I would never be able to play any sort of organized roller or ice hockey because I could never skate or else I don't think they would have ever been so nonchalant about me getting smacked by a flying puck the whole time.

As a family, we would also frequently travel up to the mountains of Big Bear, Mammoth and Lake Tahoe to go skiing and sledding. I ended up frequently getting in trouble because I would find myself on lifts that would take me to the top of the mountains, whereby that time, my only option was to ski down black diamond runs and jumps with the most experienced of snowboarders and skiers. My punishment was always a 100+ word essay on why I should always listen to my parents and not put my sister or my life in danger.

Mom and dad never used physical punishment like pinching, ear pulling or spanking to punish me. My siblings and I personally believe that was because deep down inside they didn't want to cause me any more pain than I had already endured earlier in my childhood. What they came up with instead, I would argue, would turn out to be much worse because of the time and energy it would take to write why we were sorry and what we'd do differently next time. In hindsight, I guess I should thank them for all those essays they made me write because without all that practice, I don't think I would have ever wanted or been able to write this autobiography.

Summers brought swim competitions at Lake Forest Beach and Swim club and long hot days at the beach digging massive man-made underground Jacuzzis while also riding the waves like we were Kelly Slater. However, what my brother, sister and I looked forward to most was our annual trip to Laughlin, where my dad would drop his boat into the water, and we would ride up and down the river until the sun came down. There was no better feeling in the world than when dad decided to push the boat up a notch and my siblings and I would start to skip along the water in a small inflatable innertube that was being dragged from behind. I would come to cherish those family vacations because that year in the late summer of 1996 my world was about to be flipped upside down.

    As we returned home from another amazing trip, all tan and full of memories, my parents would ask for us all to meet in the living room for a Gandy family meeting. Usually when it came to having a full Gandy family meeting it would include my dad, my mom, my brother, my sister, and myself sitting around the living room, with no music or TV and talking about what sports we would like to play in the upcoming year or which movie we all wanted to see in the theaters that night. This had probably been partially why I was so caught off guard when my dad announced that we would be moving from our home in Orange County back down to where my mom and dad first met in San Diego.

    I knew that my dad worked in the commercial plumbing industry, and we had moved around before from one job site to the next, but we had always seemed to stay in Orange County or close to it. This time was different, we were leaving the place where I had grown up for the past 6 years and more importantly where I found my friends and sense of security. In just a few short words, my parents were able to strip away the long hard years I fought for a sense of belonging and had traded it in for a bigger house 100 miles down the highway.

    I wouldn't know at the time, but I'd later find out that my dad had been offered a job to work in San Francisco with his same company and that he would have to leave Lake Forest if he wanted to remain working for them. At the same time, his dad was terminally ill with lung cancer and needed help running his company while he tried to recover in the hospital. These two major factors would be what ultimately swayed my parents to leave the security and safety of their current lives and start all over in a small town just North of the city of San Diego called Carmel Mountain Ranch.

My Grandpa had played a big part in my dad's life, from teaching him how to shoot a basketball when he was a kid, to helping him enlist into the army, as well as giving him his first start in the plumbing industry when my dad first returned home from serving as an Army Specialist. Dad felt like he owed Grandpa a lot for where he was in life, so when it came time for when Grandpa Gandy needed my dad's help in return, he was "sure as heck" not going to let him down. What my Grandpa had been masterminding for the past 3 years before he fell ill was a residential community property development, where he would own 180 single family residential homes on the shores of the Colorado River, just outside Laughlin. The plumbing, sewers, electrical and streets had already been put into place and one of the last hurdles he was trying to overcome was assembling a loan for $400,000 to finish a bridge that would connect his housing development over to the Indian casino on the other side. This is where my dad was asked to step in while my Grandpa was out of commission and see if he could help rescue what my Grandpa had been working on for so many years before.

With little to no experience in garnering any financial housing development loans, my dad was tasked with an almost impossible job. Luckily for my parents, my mom had been working for the Chargers part-time for the past 6 years and was able to start working full time when we moved back to San Diego. This would help sustain my family financially while my dad and grandpa worked on making the Mojave Shore project a success. Unfortunately, this would leave my siblings and me pretty much on our own to figure out how we were going to adjust to having both our parents busy at work and no real friends to keep us occupied. We were left with no other option than to pack up and try to rebuild our lives as the new kids in town and life was going to start getting a lot more complicated for the entire Gandy family again.

52

Pictures
Childhood

"Parental love is the only love that is truly selfless, unconditional, and forgiving." – Dr. T.P. Chia

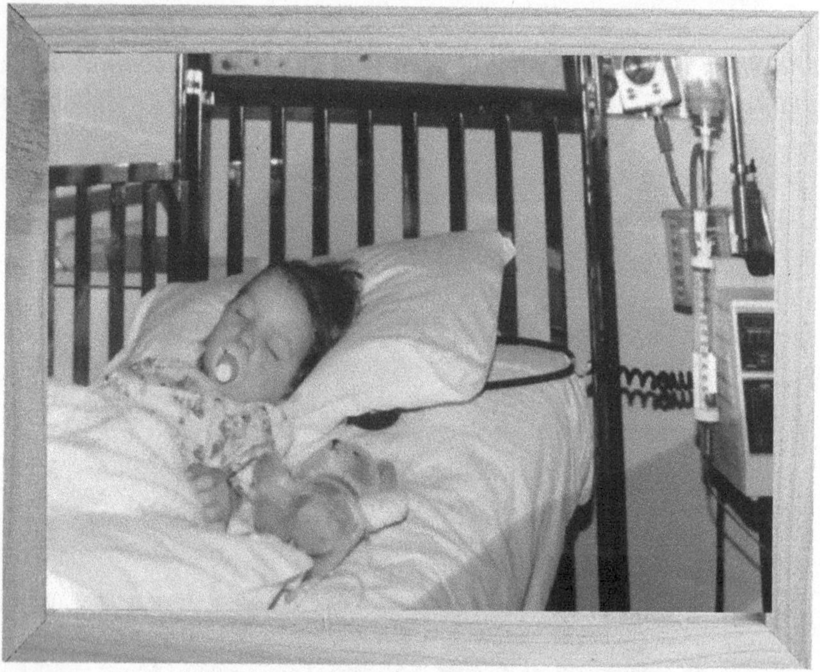

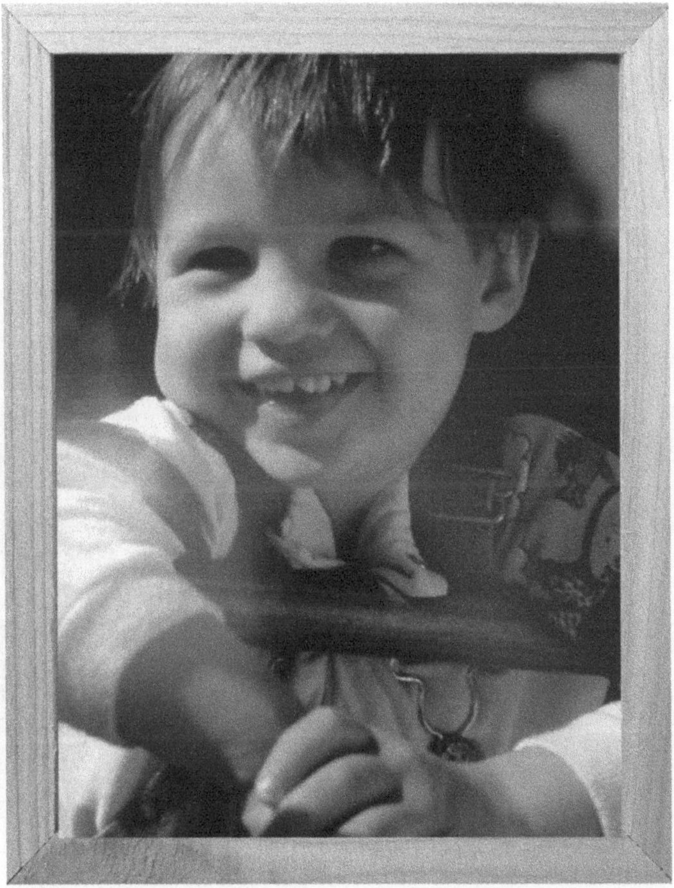

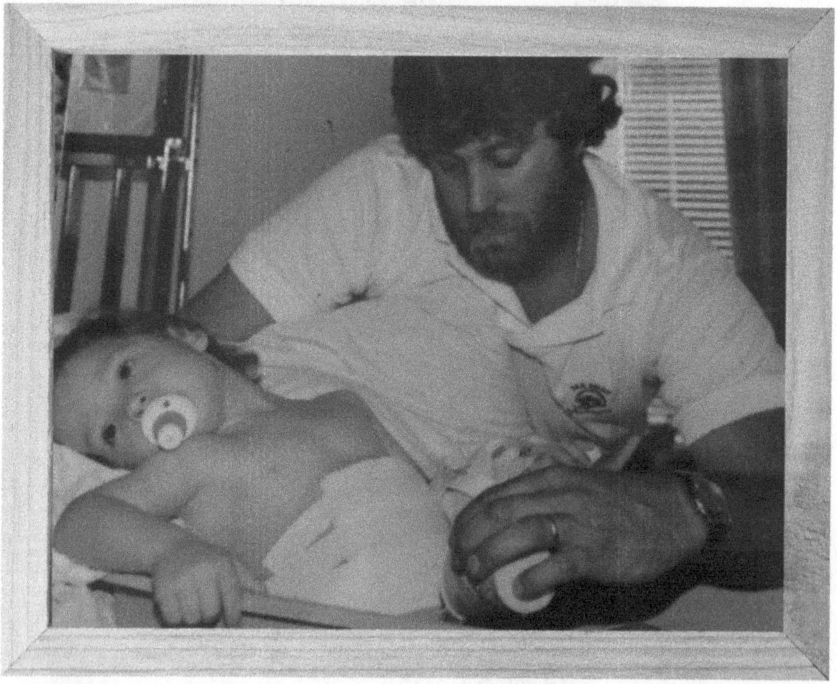

57

Part Two
Growing Up is Hard

"The only reason a true friend won't be there to pick you up is because they are lying beneath you from trying to break your fall."
– Tommy Cotton

Chapter 13
Who's the New Kid?

It's hard to remember a more difficult time in my life where I had felt as lonely and isolated from any sort of true friends than those first 6 months of my 4th grade year, after moving down to San Diego from my old home in Lake Forest, CA. On the very first day, my siblings and I walked up to a 2 story, freshly painted white 4-bedroom house, and were asked to run inside and look around to see which room we all wanted for ourselves. As my brother and sister proceeded to shove me aside so they could fight for the room of their choice, I slowly picked up my small cardboard box out of the car, which was filled with my whole life's possessions inside, including a piggy bank filled with $67 worth of chores' money, my baseball glove, a box of 1980's baseball cards and the one thing that actually really mattered to me, Dr. Bear.

I already knew that my brother was going to get the biggest room because he was the oldest and my sister was eventually going to get the only room with a full bathroom attached because she was "the princess," so that left me the smallest room in the upstairs corner of the house. In my mind, there was no need to clammer upstairs and fight over which room I was going to get when the outcome had already been rigged at the start. I will say, the house was absolutely beautiful and if there was one thing you should know about my dad, it's that he would do just about anything to make my mom's dreams become a reality.

One of those dreams was to one day live in a 2-story white painted house with vaulted ceilings, just like this one. Even if it meant stretching my father's budget to the limit, he wasn't about to let the opportunity go by where he could make my mom's wishes come true. I would come to admire this quality about my dad later in life, when it came apparent to me that he really didn't care much for any of the material possessions he ever bought or purchased throughout his life but instead, only really cared for the joy and happiness it would bring my mom when he was able to provide them for her.

As soon as the last bags were unpacked and the boxes were unloaded off the moving truck, my brother, sister, and I ran outside and started to scope out our new surroundings. Since we were all new to town, we were essentially all looking for the same thing, where were all the kids to play with? Back in Lake Forest, we had just moved from a house on a cul-de-sac where we were inundated with families with kids all around my same age, so there was never a real problem finding someone to hang out with or have something to do. As for this new house, we lived on a thru street in the middle of a neighborhood that had recently just been developed around a local golf course and there were not as many families with small children occupying the houses around our nicely newly built home. That did not deter my mom from driving around the entire neighborhood that very same day looking for any children who might be playing outside and interested in making friends with her 3 bored children.

After a few strolls up and down the streets of Carmel Mountain Ranch, we finally met a family with 2 young girls that were close to Tanya's age and their dad, Steve Pelton. Steve would go on to be a life-long friend of my parents and our family and I can honestly say that to this day I have not genuinely met a nicer man in my entire life. Unfortunately, this was about the only family we were to meet in our neighborhood that late summer before we were to begin the school year in just a few weeks.

Leading up to the start of my 4th grade year, my mom enrolled me into a traveling soccer team called the Vaqueros, which she heard was one of the top programs in the area at that time. She knew that I excelled at soccer back in Orange County because I never seemed to tire and surprisingly pretty quick. I loved the sport and was eager to get the chance to meet new friends and play a game that I felt I was pretty good at. Everything worked out to plan as I was able to play a game that I was passionate about, and I was quickly able to meet new friends because everybody on the team was essentially considered the "new kid." This would also be where I would first meet one of my close friends still to this very day, Jamie Boyle.

Jamie's family was born in England and moved to the States back in the late 80's, so Jamie was destined at a very young age to be a superstar when it came to the game he called football. In the beginning though, it would take some time before Jamie and I would become such good friends, simply due to the fact that almost everybody was from a different part of the city and didn't know who attended the same school and who didn't. This would mean, sometime in the late part of August I would begin the first day at my new school without knowing any of my fellow classmates and having no friends to help me transition into my new environment.

Like always, I was given a full health history and physical assessment a couple of weeks prior to my arrival, and it was shown to provide evidence that I had no hesitation in speaking my mind or becoming friendly with anybody. Actually, the assessor would go on to say, "Brandon is a zealously hyperactive kid, who needs no extra motivation to find something to do." With that being said, deep down inside I actually felt quite lonesome after the move because I had lost a part of my identity, as well as my comfort system amongst the friends that I believed to have known the real me.

    I was only 9 years old, and I had no clue how to formulate the words that I was feeling at that time, but I do remember now that I was struggling with severe anxiety from the thought of having to make new friends and if the children around me would be able to understand and accept all my physical dissimilarities. It became even harder for me to cope with the new change when I learned that my older brother would be attending a completely different school from my sister and me because he was 5 and half years older and would be starting his first day in high school. My one saving grace would come in the fact that my 8-year-old younger sister would also be joining me on our adventure at Morning Creek Elementary school and I could always rely on her to hang out with if I couldn't find any friends of my own. However, it would soon come apparent that because of how big the size of the school we were attending was, there would be 2 separate break and lunch periods. The 1st, 2nd and 3rd graders would begin recess at 9:30am and start lunch at 11:15am, while the 4th and 5th graders would begin recess at 10:00am and lunch at 12:00pm. This basically meant that Tanya and I would not get to see each other during school because she was in 3rd grade, and I was in 4th grade. This would result in becoming the ultimate letdown for me and my self-esteem because there went my last true support system, and I was left completely alone.

    In just a matter of a few weeks, the fun, confident and full of energy kid had somehow lost the spark that he had once developed to help persevere through the troubles and tribulations that haunted him over the many years spent in and out of the hospital. I remember fearing for the bell to ring during those first couple of months at school because I knew that meant I would have to go outside the safety of the classroom and brave the unknown school lunch yard. The lunch tables always seemed to be filled with kids who had their own group of friends and were not in the business of looking to bring in a small legged, scarred up, bucktooth new kid from the OC. So, I would sit and eat alone next to the trash cans where the blackjack bees would continue to swarm over the half drank soda cans that yes, were still being served to young kids in the late 90's.

I used to cry when I read the notes my mom would leave for me on a napkin in a brown paper bag because she would always have some kind of encouraging message for me each and every day. "You're going to do great and show those kids how a real soccer player kicks a ball" or "Have fun and know your mom and dad always love you." As much as I would grow to cherish these little messages, I had felt at that time I was just letting them down because I wasn't happy, and I didn't know how to make it better.

Then came the day where I was walking around the playground by myself like usual, and two older 5th graders came up to me and began to make fun of the way I looked and physically pushed me to the ground. That was it, I immediately ran to the health office, called my mom to come pick me up because I wasn't feeling good and continued to cry the entire drive home begging to never have to go back to school again.

When it came to the physical pain and countless number of medical procedures I had to endure during my early life, my family and I felt like we knew exactly how to handle and overcome any situation that was presented to us, but when it came down to tackling the psychological side of dealing with anxiety, depression, and the constant fear of being bullied, we had been left in disarray. It wasn't until my parents decided to take matters into their own hands and ask the school if they had any suggestions on how to acclimate their son to his new surroundings in a more helpful way.

With the help of some very kind parents and teachers, they devised a plan where before lunch the following day, my teacher would ask the class if there would be any volunteers who would like to show Brandon around at recess and lunch for the next couple of weeks. What I didn't know was that my parents and teachers had already reached out to a few parents beforehand and asked if their child would be willing to introduce me to some of their friends. So, as it happened, three kids would raise their hands and I instantly went from having nobody to call a friend, to having 3 new friends to hang out with outside the classroom. Brian and Travis would play a big role in introducing me to all their friends and picking me on their teams to play kickball and dodgeball during break, but it would be the friendship with my fellow teammate, Jamie Boyle, who really helped bring back the spark that once defined who I really was from the inside. It wasn't just because Jamie seemed to know every person at the school or even that every person seemed to know who Jamie Boyle was, but it was because he chose to become my friend at school, outside of school and on the fields where we would come to compete with each other. We became teammates in the same travel soccer and baseball program that very same year and our families would start to get to know each other a lot better because of all the time we would come to spend with one another traveling from one practice or game to the next. It was because of the foresight of a few parents and faculty staff that really aided in my recovery in finding a new place that I could call home and I am eternally grateful for them, as well as Brian, Travis, and Jamie for accepting me into their inner circle.

    It was due to this act of kindness that I strongly encouraged myself throughout the years to be more inclusive, because all it takes is a simple nice gesture that could change a person's outlook on the rest of their life. The very next year I would go on to repeat what was done for me and show a new kid named Jon Crane around the lunch yard not knowing he would end up becoming one of my best friends for years to come. With my loneliness at school resolved and my health concerns quietly set at bay, I was all set to start making a name for myself in the world of sports, but I still had one more obstacle I would have to overcome, which had been my parents and I's biggest fear ever since I was first born.

Chapter 14
Worst Nightmare

"Worry does not empty tomorrow of its sorrow; it empties today of its strength." – Corrie Ten Boom

Besides the difficult transition those first 6 months at Morning Creek Elementary had on our family, the rest of what San Diego and our new home were able to offer was exactly what the doctor ordered. My parents were both busier than ever at work, my brother had just met his first long-term girlfriend, Tanya and I were both starting to excel in our athletic endeavors and for the most part I was starting to find myself staying away longer and longer between hospital visits. There had been those rare asthma attacks that would randomly flare up here and there, as well as the seemingly monthly bowel obstructions that I would have to continuously fight through, but nothing that required any sort of surgery or more than a couple night's stay at Children's hospital.

The family really started to find their new groove and between hanging out with Jon during and after school, plus playing organized sports with Jamie on the weekends, my schedule as a 10-year-old was quite filled. Jamie and I were just starting baseball season in our first year of majors, which to us, was equivalent to actually playing in the real Major Leagues. The main reason for this belief was because as soon as a child turns 10 years old, they are eligible to participate in The Little League World Series which is held each year in Williamsport, Pennsylvania and televised on ESPN all around the world. From the likes of Padres third baseman Sean Burroughs to 1997 World Series champion Gary Sheffield, it was widely known that if you wanted to make it to the pros, your first crack at it began in Little League and specifically the Majors division.

That being said, Jamie and I were very young when it came to being a part of our first Majors team on an already highly touted CMR Dodgers squad. Our birthdays would not fall until mid-summer that 1997 year, and baseball season had already started in the first week of March. That meant we were both 10 years old and for the most part having to compete against 11- and 12-year old's who had already been playing for 1 to sometimes even 2 years together. Considering I was only about 4 and a half feet tall and weighing a measly 65 pounds, it was safe to say that I was destined to ride the bench for the most part of my rookie season. I didn't mind though, because I knew I had been drafted by one of the best Little League teams in all of North County San Diego and I'd also be teammates with one of my best friends. Playing for the Dodgers was everything I thought it would be, from being given 2 brand new practice and game day uniforms, 2 home and away hats, as well as all the Big League Chew bubblegum and David's Sunflower seeds that we could ever want. I went on to pick the number 5 to put on the back of my jersey for obvious reasons but would have to wait an entire year before I could upgrade it to my favorite number 55, when the kid who currently wore it moved on to play pony league.

There was no greater pride that I felt than when I put on that light blue jersey for the very first time and stood in the middle of the baseball field with all my fellow teammates on opening day, while the National Anthem was sang and the umpire belted out those famous two words, Play Ball. The game went as expected with our team winning by a large margin and then celebrating at the local pizzeria with all the parents and coaches. The parents, coaches and kids seemed to really come together and care for one another early on and for me, that is what I came to love most about being a part of team sports. There was nobody who was left out or treated any differently from one another, be it the best player on the team to the not so best players on the team. We all practiced and played with the same passion and effort that was demanded from our coaches, as well as ourselves and to be honest we couldn't get enough of it. When you have something that becomes the first thing you think about when you wake up and the last thing you dream about before you go to bed, there is no amount of work that you wouldn't want to do to become better at that one such activity. The Dodgers and the team that brought me in as one of their own was that one thing for me. The camaraderie, competition, and weekly pizza parties were everything I ever wanted, and I never wanted it to stop. Then came the day that would end up changing the way I went about living my life from there on out.

    Our baseball schedule was just a little over halfway through its season and we were getting ready to play a home game against one of our top rivals on Thursday night under the lights. As usual, our team would wear our home jerseys that consisted of a light blue jersey, grey and blue hat, blue belt, blue socks, and grey pants. We all loved that jersey because it was an exact replica of what the Major League Baseball Dodgers would wear when they played their home games. In our eyes, we felt like we were just one notch below them, and this was something that could make us look and feel like the real professionals we had revered. Coach Fred had asked all of us to show up an hour before the game so we could get in a good practice and work on a few extra drills that we didn't have time to go over the previous day. Now, usually my nightly routine would consist of taking my medication and drinking a mix of different fluids that allowed the food I ate earlier in the day to pass through my digestive system quicker, so when it came to the following 24 hours, I wouldn't have to worry about going to the bathroom. Unfortunately, every once in a while, I would sometimes forget to take my medications during the night, and I would have to wake up early and take them the next morning. On the very rare occasion that I would miss taking my medication the night before and the morning after, I would proceed to go through the rest of the day risking the chance I could potentially have some serious stomach issues.

This was the kind of unexpected perfect storm that arose on the day of my teams' big game, and sequentially would end up causing me quite some embarrassment, as one of my fellow teammates would go on to obviously point out. Sometime, between batting practice and catching fly balls in the outfield, one of my close friends on the team informed me that I must have slipped in the mud because the back of my pants was covered in dirt. To my horror and without my knowledge that something ever happened, I had indeed shat my pants and was desperately rattling my 10-year-old brain on how I was going to rectify the situation in which I now found myself in. Luckily, I became aware of the crisis early on in practice and most of the other team and parents were not fully in attendance yet. This would allow me to hopefully leave the field without too many people knowing what had happened, and I could go home to change into some new clothes. Once faced with the realization that one of my nightmares had suddenly and without warning come to fruition, my very first instinct was to play it cool and demonstrate how this might have occurred. Without any provocation I began sliding in the muddy grass in front of all my fellow teammates. This might have appeared quite strange to the rest of my teammates and coaches who were taking batting practice just a couple hundred feet away. It probably looked like I was just rolling around in the outfield trying to get my uniform as messy as possible. Thankfully, one of my assistant coaches walked on over and started to scold me for messing around during drills and to go run a few laps around the field before I even thought about having a chance to play in the game. Without even knowing it, that coach gave me the excuse I needed to run off the field and start to devise my plan on how I was going to escape without the notice of my fellow peers. One of the major obstacles in which I had to figure out how to overcome, was the fact that my parents were not at the park yet and wouldn't be for another half an hour. Both my parents were still at work, and I had carpooled to practice with one of my friends on the team. Instead of panicking, I calmly whispered to my assistant coach that I had an accident out of my control and because of the genius foresight that my parents showed a few months prior, Coach Dick, had already been cautioned that this type of situation might occur at some point during the season. Coach immediately went into protective mode and asked me to follow him to his car and away from practice. My heart was still racing because I knew one of my teammates had witnessed what had happened and was concerned, he might spread the rumor that the kid everyone nicknamed "Gandyman" had indeed done the unimaginable. I soon came to dismiss this fear when coach Dick told the entire team, he had forgotten some extra baseballs and a new bat back at home and I was to accompany him to go and retrieve them. In actuality, he rushed me back to his house to get a brand-new pair of pants he had a few extras of, as well as those bucket of balls and new bat he had just purchased for his older grandson a few weeks prior. We returned back to the field just in time before the game was to start and to my surprise nobody on the team noticed that I was wearing a pair of new pants that were just one size too big.

    To this day, I still don't know if the rest of the team ever really knew what happened on that early spring night or if they did hear and were told to never bring it up to me by a couple of our coaches. I do remember, however, being so mortified after that whole ordeal that I decided to stay home from school the very next day just in case by chance my teammates who I would see in class were going to ask me about what really happened. Since it was a Thursday night game and I missed school on Friday, I was able to go all weekend without seeing any of my friends until the following Monday and was hoping everyone had just forgotten about the whole experience entirely. Those 4 nights were probably the worst sleep I had ever had up until that point in my life and that includes all the time I spent in the hospital being woken up every few hours to check my blood pressure and battling nightly pains. I went on to play out every scenario in my head on what exactly the kids at school would say and how I would be perceived amongst my peers going forward. All that pointless worry and discomfort had later been proven to be wasted in vain, because as I returned back to school and soon back to practice later that same night, the situation of me having to leave and return back with a new bat, bucket of balls and a pair of pants that were one size too big was never brought up and seemed to have disappeared from everyone's memory. In the end, everything turned out to be just fine and gave myself, as well as my parents a humbling life reminder that there were still some physical issues that needed to be addressed as I was beginning to hit puberty. In the meantime, I was able to continue enjoying my newly found happiness on a team that would soon come to create some of my fondest memories growing up in San Diego as a young kid.

Chapter 15
Top of the Mountain

"There is no education like adversity." – Benjamin Disraeli

There has never been any doubt that my life has been filled with enough adversity to count for a multitude of different life spans, but the one that took not only myself but an entire teams' determination to overcome was that of the 1998 Yankees. No, not those 1998 New York Yankees, arguably the greatest assembled MLB team in history. Who by no stretch of the imagination had an unmatched surplus of All Stars and Hall of Famers with the likes of Derek Jeter, Mariano Rivera, Bernie Williams, Joe Torre, Darryl Strawberry, Andy Pettitte and David Cone at their disposal. I'm talking about the Carmel Mountain Ranch 1998 10-12-year-old baseball team. It would be this team that I would get my first chance at tasting what it felt like to be on top, but it sure didn't come easy.

It had been just a little under a year ago when the once seemingly unbeatable Dodgers team that I had grown to love playing for was shockingly knocked out of the playoffs during their semifinal game in heroic fashion. As much as I would love to be able to recall the exact details of why and how we lost, my mind has betrayed me and all I really can remember is sitting in the back seat of my dad's 1997 Expedition crying in my hands that there was not going to be a pizza party on this gloomy night. It would take another whole year before the teammates that remained, would get our chance for glorious redemption. Until then, I was fully entrenched in doing anything and everything possible to keep my mind and body as physically distracted from the ghosts of my past, be it from my numerous surgeries to my recent athletic failures, to even my unknown and convoluted medical future. There wasn't anything I didn't want to try now that I was deemed healthy enough to play contact sports. See, once I was promoted from 5th grade elementary school to 6th grade middle school, I began to start puberty a little early. Normally, this would not be such a big deal to the average adolescent besides the slight annoyance they would experience when their voice would crack or the excessive amount of acne that would seem to pop out of nowhere at times. Ah, but for the "miracle child" whose parents and himself were told that there was a chance because of some earlier surgical procedures that were performed during infancy, that little Brandon might not get to experience the typical sort of puberty that most children come to disdain during this ever so delicate period of life. So, in doing so, I had reached a milestone that was once put into question and had changed the entirety of how I would be medically examined going forward.

The fact that my body was able to produce the correct amount of testosterone as a normal growing middle school boy, proved to my doctors and school medical examiners that one, my reconstructive testicular transplant a decade earlier had turned out to be a resounding success and two, I needed no additional restrictions when it came to signing off on my athletic physical endeavors. Well, of course there was still the small issue of only having one functioning kidney, as well as the ungodly amount of built-up scar tissue in my lower abdomen that prevented me from being able to digest food properly.

So, when it was brought to my attention that there would still be a small limit to the types of activities I would be allowed to partake in, I reluctantly gave in. However, not on that initial "Cannot Playlist" was any mention of flag football or wrestling, and in the fall of my first year at Meadowbrook Middle school I had found myself playing middle linebacker for the Mustang flag football team. Mind you, my mom was not so pleased with my decision and would go on to boycott any involvement in both my pursuit of flag football and wrestling. This had been one consequence I was willing to accept if it meant I was able to finally get the opportunity to play out the hopes and dreams I have been transfixed on, ever since I first witnessed my greatest heroes perform on TV.

This is part of the story where my parents can turn to my older brother and sarcastically thank him for all the nights he would sneak me into his room past my bedtime and watch the WCW and WWE Monday Night Wars. I became mesmerized by the high-flying nonstop athleticism that these wrestlers would show and the bravado they encompass when promoting each of their own characters' back story. Over the next 2 or 3 years, before my brother would eventually graduate from high school and move away to college, you could mark down on your calendars in permanent marker that my brother and I would be upstairs in his room quietly imitating each wrestler's patent catch phrases, as well as reenacting their signature finishing moves on one another.

From a very young age I grew to love watching the San Diego Chargers football team and now, with my brother's support, I was growing to love wrestling just as much. "And that's the bottom-line cause Stone Cold said so!" Sorry, I had to throw in one of my personal favorites even though it was actually The Rock who became my greatest inspiration. With the admiration of Jr Seau's enthusiasm for life, coupled with the swagger of Dwayne "The Rock" Johnson's personality, I was determined to play out my childhood dreams if that was going to be the last thing I ever did.

Nevertheless, it came time for reality to set in and I was still only a small 90-pound kid who had never participated in any sort of organized wrestling matches or flag football games. It would take me the rest of the entire 6th grade year to grasp all the concepts and techniques my coaches were trying to teach me before I would be promoted onto the highest level of competition. I am grateful that I did not gain success early on in my football and wrestling career as it might have prevented me from turning back to the sport that my dad first introduced me to all those years before. That sport was, of course, baseball and Jamie and I were returning one year older with a single thought of sweet redemption in our minds.

It so happened, most of the Dodger team from the year before was coming back besides only two players that moved on up to pony leagues. With coach Fred, Dick, and my dad all back to give it a go at the title, we were primed and ready to start the season, but first coach Fred had a surprise for all of us. To rectify the disappointment we all felt after our loss in the playoffs a year before, he was able to raise enough money with the help from all the generous parents to buy all the kid's new uniforms with our names and favorite number on the back. In doing so, he essentially wiped away our memory of the past and provided us with a whole new mindset as proud members of the CMR Yankees.

Can I say for sure whether the psychology around his actions were right or wrong in regard to erasing the previous year's accomplishments, who knows, but it sure did lift everyone's spirits on the team to an all-time high and the heck if you'll ever hear me complain about it. We were all one year older and had one more year of motivation to go out there and do something special. As it went, we proceeded to roll through the competition with the help of dominating performances poured in from our 3 powerhouse pitchers and our unstoppable offense. The regular season would come as just a warmup for us, as we would go 19-0 and never come within 8 runs of ever losing. The true test would come in the playoffs where we would try and right a wrong that we felt slipped through our grasp once before and weren't about to let it happen again. Our team was undoubtedly the odds-on favorite to win the title because not only were we undefeated, but we possessed 9 All-Stars on the same team. Talk about unheard of, it was unimaginable and never before had a CMR Majors team gone undefeated throughout the entire regular season and playoffs, so we had some history to make.

A couple days before our first playoff game, where we were scheduled to pitch our #1 starter, Coach Fred called us over after practice to discuss a matter that he and the other coaches had been debating about for the past couple of days. Supposedly, our team had been selected to compete in San Diego's tournament of champions and were asked to represent CMR in the District 31 championships. The only problem was the tournament began the day after we were scheduled to compete in the Finals in our own league's playoff format if we were able to make it that far. So, like the true players' coach Fred was, he asked for our opinion on what mattered to us more, going undefeated and having a chance at redemption from last year's misfortune or sit our #1 and #2 starters during the playoffs so we could have them eligible to pitch in the District Championships?

The reason the question was even asked was because when it comes to the official Little League Rules you cannot pitch the same pitcher on back-to-back days. This meant if we made the Finals and ended up pitching either our #1 or #2 starters then they would not be able to pitch in the first round of the tournament of champions the very next day. To me, the answer seemed pretty obvious and the discussion amongst all of us might have only lasted less than a half of a minute as we all decided as a team that we wanted to stay undefeated and then go on and win the tournament of champions as well. All our coaches could do after that was just smile and say, "then let's go win it all."

When it came to confidence, our team seemed to be filled to the max with it and we cruised through the CMR playoffs straight to the finals. We would come face to face with the same team who knocked us out the previous year. This time around, there was no contest, as our #1 ace pitched lights out and only gave up 3 hits all game. The woes of the Dodgers past were rectified by the Yankees of that day, who ended up staying undefeated throughout the entire 1998 season and claiming the all so coveted CMR Little League Championship. Next up, the tournament of champions and the true test to see how great a team we really were.

In a surprise move, our team was notified that we had been scheduled to play a double header, in which we had never played 2 games back-to-back on the same day before. We knew it wouldn't be the first game that we had to worry about losing, it would be the second, where we would be locked in battle with the also undefeated Escondido Marlins. What ensued on that unforgettable Saturday night would be remembered by all in attendance and be talked about amongst each other for the rest of our lives. Our tightly knitted group of ballplayers were geared up for our clash under the lights and used that energy to dominate our first game 14-0. The atmosphere couldn't have been more riveting as the two best teams in all of San Diego were to collide and put both their undefeated records on the line. The stands were packed with not just the parents of the kids who were playing in the game, but of all the rest of the teams who were playing in the tournament as well. The stage was set for something incredible to happen, and for each member of my team who were lucky enough to play in that game, it would be the closest experience most of us would ever get to feeling what it would be like to play in the Major Leagues. In that moment, everything else in our lives ceased to exist and we were all focused on accomplishing one mission and that mission was to walk away from that field as the victors and not the losers.

    With the introductions made and the national anthem sung, it was finally time to start the game that everyone had been desperately waiting to see. Boom! With one swing of the bat our best player, Brian smacked the first pitch over the left field fence and gave our team an immediate 2-0 lead over the Escondido Marlins. This would not last though, as the Marlins would rally in the next inning to take a 3-2 lead after scoring a couple runs off our #3 and #4 best pitchers. Our coaches knew that because we were limited to pitchers that specific night, it would come down to whether our offense could muster up enough runs to pull out a win. Somewhere throughout the next several innings we were able to tie up the game and extend the contest into extra innings.

This is where it started to get interesting, because I was due up to bat second and our 2 best hitters were scheduled to hit right after me. Quite simply, in baseball, if a game goes to extra innings, then the first team to score without the other team scoring as well, wins the game. In this case, our team had already shut down the Marlins offense and now it was our turn to try and win the game. As I looked over to my coach down the 3rd base line and saw him sending me hand signals on what he wanted me to do as I was in the batter's box, my head started to draw a blank and I completely forgot everything I had ever learned. Not knowing exactly what to do, I tightened my grip on the end of my bat and prepared myself to just swing at the very first pitch. As luck would have it, I was given a fastball that was coming right down the middle of the plate and I smashed it to the opposite side of the field, where I would round first and slide into second with a double. Now, safely secured as the go-ahead run-in scoring position, with only 1 out and still having our 2 best hitters yet to come to the plate, our chances of squeaking out a win were looking good. Then came the strike out, which left me still stuck on second base, but with 2 outs instead of just 1.
    The gravity of our situation had thickened, and it was up to the guy who had always appeared to be relied upon when we needed something big to happen. Brian stepped into the batter's box with that overly confident smirk he seemed to always carry with him, and I knew right then he was going to end this. Like Nostradamus himself, I was able to gaze into the future and predict the outcome of what was about to be foreseen. Crack, Brian's bat collided with a hanging curveball that soared through the summer night sky and would finally fall a hundred feet over the fence where it would eventually come to rest under the right back tire of his mom's Jeep Grand Cherokee. As I looked up and saw the ball traveling through the air like Haley's comet, I jumped into the air with complete joy knowing that we had just won the game and would advance onto the semifinals the following day. When I finally reached home

plate, I was mobbed by the rest of my teammates as we waited for Brian to round the bases so we could all celebrate together as we basked in the moment in which we had just been given.

We still had a few more games to play before we would eventually be crowned the tournament of champions winner, but it ended up being that game against the other undefeated San Diego team that had ultimately decided who would continue to reign supremacy. In 1998, there had been two Yankee baseball teams that for all inclusive purposes would go down in history in their respective divisions, as the best overall team to ever do it. I was only 11 years old at the time, but it was because of this great success, I had felt I had finally reached the top of the mountain they called life and there'd only be one place left for me to go, unless I was able to find a new higher mountain to climb and fast.

Chapter 16
This Wasn't Working

"Your life does not get better by chance. It gets better by change."
– Jim Rohn

It didn't take long before the novelty of being San Diego's best little league baseball team wore off and I was on to the next bigger and more exciting thing. The main culprit for this was just 2 weeks after winning district championships it was time to get ready for All-Stars and a chance at competing against the best teams in the nation. As a team though we were physically and mentally drained from everything we had put into going undefeated all season long and just ran out of the right amount of focus it would take to continue. Our All-Star campaign never made it out of the California bracket and our season ended one week before the 4th of July. Frankly, I wasn't too upset because we had set out to do what we wanted and that was to win the CMR league championship.

The rest of the summer was all mine, and I was planning on spending it outside and in the sun as much as possible. Jon and I had started becoming closer ever since we first met just a few years back and began hanging out at one or another's parent's house daily. The funny thing about our relationship was that we both knew Jon was the smart and organized one and I was the more outgoing and athletic one. Essentially, we were a perfect fit, as we would soon prove to both our parents upon creating our first business venture together called J&B Lawn Mowing Services. Jon's dad, Russ, used to work on cars as a hobby, and one day we came across a Go-Cart race and Russ offered to help us win.

We were told if we could save up enough money to buy all the necessary parts, Russ would help us build our go-cart to enter in the race. Now, all we had to do was figure out how we were going to make money fast, so we could enter the race before the summer was over. This is where having a smart friend really comes in handy, as Jon knew his neighborhood was full of houses with real grass that needed to be cut at least a couple times a month. He also knew that his parents had a lawnmower and weed whacker that we could borrow if we were able to persuade any of his fellow neighbors who were desperate enough to let a couple 7th graders cut their grass.

Our enthusiasm grew as we printed out flyers and started going door-to-door asking if anyone needed our services for the modest fee of just $10 per lawn. Eureka! After just 4 houses politely saying no, Jon was able to fast talk his way into the home of, ironically, my 7th grade English teacher. Let's be honest, Jon really didn't trust me with any sort of heavy machinery, so that meant he oversaw the mowing of the lawns, and I was subjected to weed-pulling duties. Jon was a good friend though, because after I pulled all the weeds and he finished mowing the lawn, he would call me over and teach me how to use the weed whacker to clean up the final touches.

J&B Lawn Mowing Services had become a huge success and we had turned our one client into 10, and soon found ourselves booked out for the rest of the month. When we were not busy cutting grass, Jon and I loved trading football cards, going to the mall, playing arcade games, and talking about the girls at school who we imagined had crushes on us. That last part took up most of our time because to us, what girl wouldn't like a couple of guys who owned their own business and were in line to purchase their first set of wheels? Life was going well as I was staying healthy and finding new and fun things to do with my best friend.

There was only one hiccup that kept popping up from time to time—having any sort of sleepovers, including traveling alone for sports or spending the night at a friend's house. The reason for this was because I'd have to take medications at night that were time sensitive and would require up to an hour to be administered. I had already missed attending a few slumber parties, as well as 6th grade camp, because of the nightly toll all of the medications placed on my body. Ever since my trip to New York to see Dr. Pena, I have had the same nightly routine, that for the most part, really didn't have an impact on my everyday life—up until now. I was growing up and starting to seek my own independence as a young man who no longer wanted to be tied down by the limitations that his body had set on him so long ago.

The good news, there was a solution, but it would require that I not only have to revisit an old friend 3000 miles away, but likely have to go under the knife for the 17th time before my 12th birthday. It had been just a couple years before that my parents were informed that Dr. Pena, who was still practicing medicine in New York, had just discovered a new bowel management program for children like me. The new discovery involved a surgical operation but had an 80%-90% chance of successfully transforming a person's intestinal track system back to normal. Unfortunately, at the time we were notified of these findings my family had recently moved from Lake Forest down to San Diego and I had just been released from the hospital after a 10-night stay for an intestinal blockage. The last thing my parents or I wanted to do was to go through another surgical procedure that would require me to fly across the country and possibly stay for several weeks or months at a time. Fast forward to the summer of 1998, when my family and I were in a completely different phase of our lives, and we were beginning to actually forget most of my past trauma from the years before. Couple all this with the fact that if I was going to want any chance at living a normal life, I needed to change what I was doing and take the risk.

I can't recall exactly how I was able to convince my parents to fly me across the country just to have yet another surgery that was supposed to be the end all be all to my problems, but I did. This time though, my entire family was able to accompany me to New York with the help and generosity from the Conner's Cause for

Children Foundation. I would also like to mention, if it weren't for the existence of The Ronald McDonald House this exceptionally rare opportunity would have never been possible. Foundations like these truly make a difference in changing peoples' lives for the better and is one of the main reasons my family and I will continue to be eternally grateful for the kindness they showed us when we needed it most. Now, with my parents on board and the funding in place, it was up to me, and the team of doctors led by Dr. Pena himself to make the trip an actual success.

    The plan that was initially presented to us was pretty straightforward and my parents and I really didn't have much of a concern after our visit with Dr. Pena. The new breakthrough program did require 3 months of intense rehabilitation once I got back home to San Diego, but if this is what it was going to take for me to be able to gain full control over how I was going to live the rest of my life, I was ready to make that sacrifice. Before I did so, however, my family and I were able to spend 5 days in the Big Apple enjoying the sights and sounds that only a city like New York could offer. Trips like these would come few and far in between for our family as a whole, with Jacob moving away to college and my sister's and my life beginning to get busier by the day. This is why I always carry a special place in my heart for what the tremendous doctors and medical staff did to improve the quality of my physical well-being and will also hold close to me the time and memories my family and I were able to share during our unforgettable summer vacation.

    The return home is where the real work had begun, and it would take the rest of the summer and most of the fall to fully recover and get comfortable with how I was going to go about living my new life. For the very first time, I was no longer in need of nightly medications, a colostomy bag, or hour-long treatments and instead, was able to finally enjoy my newfound independence as a healthy young boy. I did, however, have to break the news to Jon that I wouldn't be able to continue working our lawn mowing business or be able to enter into the Go-Kart race because of these extended circumstances. Jon didn't seem to mind because we had made a ton of money the month before I left for New York, and he had already devised a new plan on how we were going to spend it.

Chapter 17
A Visit to a Familiar Place

"I guess some things never change" – Tim McGraw

The summer had just come to an end, and I was beginning my 8th grade school year, when my mom informed me that she had a once in a lifetime opportunity for me and a friend. Usually when my mom would say stuff like this, it would entail something that had to do with sports, so I was filled with anticipation of what she was about to say. The news that was delivered rocked my teenage brain into a sense of delirium and it took me a while to realize that I was indeed not dreaming.

I was told that I could pick one friend, obviously Jon, to accompany me on the field to work as water boys for the San Diego Chargers cheerleaders. Not only did Jon and I immediately say yes, but we asked if we could go down to the stadium right away and get our official badges with our picture and name printed on them, so we could flaunt our new status around school. No teenage boy even dreams of becoming the exclusive water boy to their favorite football teams' cheerleaders because it's such a far-fetched idea that it wasn't even worth thinking about. Somehow though, Jon and I had found ourselves in that exact sort of position. My mom knew that I had experienced a lot that previous summer, with all the pain and changes my body was forced to go through. Because of this, I believe she asked her employer if there was anything they could think of that might be able to lift her son's spirits. Well, they definitely found a way to do that, but there was still one more thing Jon and I had to do before we became official employees of the San Diego Chargers.

Since we wouldn't have our weekends available to continue our J&B Lawn Mowing company anymore and our dreams of becoming legendary Go-Kart drivers were no longer a possibility, we decided to retire on top. We went around the neighborhood and informed all of our clients that we were no longer available to work, and we had decided to spend the money on building a real-life size model rocket. Jon got the idea after seeing a flyer for tickets to the Blue Angels air show and thought it would be cool if we could build something that could fly just as high.

We got straight to work, Jon laid out the design and I glued the correct pieces together. Every day after school for the next couple of months we worked together on crafting the biggest and "baddest" looking model rocket any of us had ever seen. Finally, it was launch day and we decided to invite both our families to the highest part of a nearby mountain to witness our great achievement. 3,2,1 blast off! The rocket ascended straight up into the air, climbing at nearly 250 mph where it would eventually reach its peak around 1500-2000 feet. Oblivious to what day it was, Jon and I had just launched a homemade model rocket directly into the path of where the Blue Angels were currently flying. Not only did we forget entirely that maybe we should be on the lookout for other possible planes flying in the area, but we had neglected to recall the very reason why we decided to build a rocket in the first place. All of our hearts skipped a beat while we looked up and prayed that somehow the pilots of these enormously fast jets wouldn't notice what looked to be a missile heading straight for them.

Thankfully, the planes flew right on by without a care in the world and our 6-foot-tall model rocket safely fell back down to earth, where it would never be found again. Two lessons we learned that day, one, never launch a rocket into the sky if you are not 100% sure of what you are doing and 2, the Blue Angels usually fly around 8000 feet in the air and were never in any real danger from our little pet project. To this day, I still have not found out if it was due to all the stress I had gone through after almost bringing down a U.S. fighter pilot, or the more likely possibility of having scarfed down a pile of fatty foods a few hours after, that landed me back in the hospital for a 6-day staycation.

These sorts of earlier common occurrences were supposed to be gone since I flew to New York the prior summer and entered Dr. Pena's medical program. To say my family and I were completely distraught over the fact a bowel obstruction the size of a softball was causing a consistent level 8 pain inside my stomach, would most definitely be an understatement. We were convinced after everything we had gone through to end the nightly battles against pain, we thought these dilemmas were put behind us. To our dismay, some of the scar tissue that had been left over from years before had remained and was too risky of a procedure to try and fix. Reality soon hit and we would be forced to come to terms with the news that I would more than likely be plagued with having to live with these types of episodes for the rest of my life. For my family and I, this had been a tough pill to swallow, because we were told that the medical professionals who we had grown to rely on for so long, finally ran out of any fresh ideas for a long-term solution.

When it came to how many intestinal blockages I would have to endure throughout the rest of my childhood, the numbers were said to be too astronomical for anybody to be able to put an accurate number on. This is why I had made a deal with myself while lying in a medical bed for the umpteenth time that year; as soon as I was to be released from the hospital, I would do everything in my power to live the rest of my life as actively as possible. I had come to the conclusion at that point; I could no longer depend on what tomorrow was going to be able to offer me.

Chapter 18
Let the Games Begin

"The beauty is that through disappointment, you can gain clarity, and with clarity comes conviction and true originality" – Conan O'Brien

I had just started to enter into my teenage years, where I would be blindsided by the diagnosis of chronic intestinal pseudo-obstruction (CIP) and the knowledge that I would forever have to live with severe abdominal pains. Not only did I have to overcome being born with 15 birth defects, as well as having to go through 17 major surgeries but now I was destined to live the rest of my life with the fear that I could find myself back in the hospital for weeks at a time. I felt defeated and completely helpless to change what seemed to be an endless cycle to an illness that was deemed incurable. If it were not for my family's constant support and earnest pursuit to get me back to having the life we had all grown accustomed to living, I couldn't say for sure if I would have ever been able to pull myself back up from the knock-down I had just been handed. It was one thing to make a promise to yourself while you are sick with no hope of ever feeling better, but it is a whole different scenario when you do start to feel better and now it was time to actually honor what you had once proclaimed.

Regrettably, this did not come as easy for me as it once had so many times before. I couldn't say for sure if it was solely because this time around, I felt I was told for the first time that there would be no end in sight, or if part of my frustration and anger stemmed from just growing up as a teenage boy. Either way, something had changed inside me after those couple of weeks spent in the hospital and I was determined more than ever to figure out who it was that I wanted to be.

My last year before moving on to high school, I found myself falling behind in school and getting into more and more trouble, which was out of character from how I was raised. To me it was like I just noticed that I was given a raw deal in life, and I was no longer going to let anybody, or anything determine how I was going to live my life from here on out. What I mean by this is I wanted to start doing what the other kids (that I believed to be cool) were doing, which was snowboarding, skateboarding, going to parties and having girlfriends. Previously, none of these sorts of things ever sparked my interest, well besides maybe the whole girlfriend thing, but now it did. What also didn't help was the sudden news that my best friends' parents had announced that they would be getting a divorce and would be moving away to a different part of town. With my best friend gone, I was left to search for a new group of friends to hang out with at school, which in turn, would bring me a whole new identity.

One thing I never enjoyed about school was having to ride on the school bus, so whenever I found the chance, I walked the extra 20 minutes home so I could have the opportunity to explore the world around me. I loved to hop fences that restricted any trespassers from their property, because I knew there was something fun and exciting that they didn't want to share with the outside world. Sometimes, this would be a plantation of orange trees that sat atop a hill nearby where my new friends and I would pick and throw rotten oranges at school buses parked just below. Other times, we would find ourselves on abandoned construction sites where we would load up our paintball guns and begin a game of capture the flag. Have no worries though, nobody got hurt by our foolish antics and we would all soon be caught and punished appropriately by the local authorities. I found myself in all sorts of trouble later that same year, and my parents had displayed quite some displeasure in my involvement with my newly troubling acquaintances. I was rebelling and hated the fact that because of no fault of my own, I felt like I was getting punished for having been born with a body unlike the rest of my friends and family.

Ironically though, it would be the local golf course, at which I would meet 2 of my new best friends Chris and Mike. The three of us would discover that we all had two things in common; the first being, we all lived right by Carmel Mountain Ranch golf course and the second, we were all taught at a very young age by our fathers how to play golf. I was still fully committed to playing flag football and wrestling, but on the weekends or when there was no practice being held, I would find myself sneaking onto the golf course with my new friends for a round. At first, I wasn't very good because I never really devoted any time to improving, due to the other sports taking up so much of my time. However, my competitive nature would eventually start to kick in and the more we played I began to despise losing to either Chris or Mike. Since we were only 14 years old and had no money of our own to speak of, the three of us came up with the only sensible solution for how we were going to be able to play one of the most expensive sports in the world. The first part of our plan was to "borrow" the universal key to all the golf carts at our local golf course and make 3 copies of it so we could all have one of our own. Chris had a friend who worked at the golf course at the time, so we relied on him to get the key and for me to pass it on to my other friend, whose dad worked as a locksmith. The second part of the plan involved Mike scoping out the golf shop's work schedule, so we knew who was on duty and when they were scheduled to work. The reason we needed to know this was because when the head professional was not down at the range teaching lessons and was in the Pro Shop checking in guests to play, we had no chance of being able to sneak on. We found this out the hard way a few months earlier, when all 3 of us were caught playing golf on the course without actually paying. We were young, so we thought we would just find a hole close to our house and just walk on out and start playing. In the beginning, this initial plan worked, and we would continued competition, I don't think I would have ever grown to compete and enjoy the game of golf the way I do today.

start on hole 11 and finish on hole 17. Unfortunately, on that particular day when the head professional was working, he had sent around a marshal to make sure everything around the course was running smoothly and there were no trespassers. So, it happened that Chris, Mike and I would find ourselves banished from the CMR grounds for life and our parents would be informed that if it ever happened again, they would have us arrested and charged for trespassing.

Now, maybe for any reasonable thinking teenage boys this would have deterred them from ever attempting to play golf at that specific course again, let alone trying to find another way on how to sneak back onto it without paying. However, we were no ordinary teenage boys, and I made a pledge to myself earlier that year that if I were healthy and not in the hospital, I would do whatever I wanted and not let anybody, or anything tell me otherwise. This way of thinking would come to restrain me in more ways than one later down the road, but I'll save that story for another time. Back to how my friends and I were able to find a way to practice and play golf for the next 2 years for free.

After weeks of planning, the opportunity finally came where Chris's friend had left for the weekend, and we were able to make 3 identical universal keys that would all be able to operate any golf cart at CMR golf course. With the keys in hand and a detailed report of who and when the staff would be working, the 3 of us were able to put our bags on any cart and drive on out to the course. Nowadays, this would never work because every cart has GPS tracking, and the golf shop would instantaneously know whenever one of their carts went missing. But, in the late 90's and early 2000's, GPS was nowhere to be found and we were left alone to play golf anytime our hearts desired. This simple scheme became our little secret and gave 3 working middle class kids a chance at becoming really good at the game of golf. I will admit that time in my life might not have been the best for my personal and moral development, but if it were not for Chris and Mike's

Chapter 19
A Dream Comes to an End

"I never lose. I either win or learn." – Nelson Mandela

Like most kids starting high school, I had big plans for what I wanted to do and ultimately how I wanted to be remembered. By the start of my freshman year, I had already trained all summer with the varsity wrestling program, as well as dialed in my golf game to where I was consistently beating most of the local competition around town. I knew the golf season didn't begin until the spring, so I stopped hanging around the golf course with Chris and Mike and really focused on training every day for the wrestling season to start. I was on track to making the varsity team my freshman year and I wanted nothing more than to be the youngest person in my family to get a letterman jacket. To our family, sports meant everything and was the true test of how you were measured compared to your peers. So, if I were to accomplish something that nobody in my family had ever done before in regard to athletics, I was going to do everything in my power to make that happen. One thing still persisted though and that was the fact neither my mom or most of my doctors really wanted me to continue wrestling, as they thought it was too strenuous on my body and could potentially be harmful to my physical well-being down the road. The one person I did have in my corner was my dad and as long as he had my back, I supposed what harm could there possibly be.

Two significant things happened that fall leading up to my first year competing for the Rancho Bernardo High School wrestling team, the first being my mom beginning to show faith in my decision to wrestle and the second, my dad coming to terms for the first time that his son was not as invincible as he had once believed him to be.

The first significant moment came when my dad and I were able to convince my mom for the first time in 4 years to come and watch me wrestle in the San Diego City Championships. This tournament was by invitation only and was considered one of the biggest events in the wrestling community all year. I probably will never know what ended up convincing my mom to come watch her little "miracle child" get tossed around a gym with only one kidney and 17 major surgeries tied to his name, but she showed up and I was not about to let her down. I was ranked the 2nd best wrestler in my division and cruised past the competition all the way to the finals. Everything was going as planned; I was wrestling great and for the first time I was showing not only my brother and sister what I could do but more importantly showing my mom that I was a lot stronger than she once perceived. Call it fate or just the world's way of putting things back into balance, but my next match would pair me up against last year's California state champion and one of the best all-around wrestlers I would ever go up against. Oblivious to this fact at the time, I stepped onto the mat and began to get taught a lesson by the much older and much more experienced wrestler that day. To my credit, I held my own all the way up until I was lifted into the air and had my face slammed towards the mat in the last couple minutes of the match. What happened next would go down in the Gandy family lore forever, as blood started to pour out of my nose all over my uniform and wrestling mat. The referee immediately suspended the match and walked over to the announcers table where he would go on to address the crowd of a few hundred people by saying, "Will the parents of Bandon Gandy please come down to the mat." My mom had just witnessed her worst nightmare take place right in front of her eyes and she looked over to my dad and said, "this is your fault." It was at this moment where I believe my dad shifted his mindset from believing that his son could really do anything he put his mind to and instead relented to the fact that the risk was not worth the reward. Nevertheless, at that time my dad walked down to where I was standing and looked me in the eye, with my broken nose and swollen puffy lip and asked how I was feeling. For my part, I was so hyped up on adrenaline, as well as the shock that this guy just manhandled me like a rag doll in front of all my friends and family, there was no way I was going to give up now. I will never forget what he told me then, "Son, I'm really glad you said that because your mom is up there in the stands terrified right now, so go out there and give her something to smile about." With the thumbs up from dad and the assurance from the team doctor that I was ok, I stepped back onto the mat and began to finish what I had started. In the end, I did eventually lose the match and finished in second place overall, but I held my head up high knowing that I was the only wrestler not to get pinned that day by the defending champ. I also gained a whole new level of respect from all my teammates and coaches for never giving up and playing through the pain even though my nose and lip were busted wide open.

    The second most significant thing that happened to me that year came later that night, when my dad and I sat in the living room, and he inquired about how long I expected to keep wrestling. My biggest supporter and constant optimist finally felt the need to express his concern for my future as he broke down the best- and worst-case scenarios in case I decided to keep going down this risky path. I was reminded that I could continue playing golf well into my old age, whereas in wrestling, the best I could hope for was to extend my career past college and try to make the Olympics. The thing was, I was way better at wrestling than at golf and I really felt like I could excel at both sports. Unfortunately, my body wouldn't allow me to do both and I either had to quit golf and start training my body for everything wrestling would demand from me or give up on my childhood dream and concentrate solely on becoming the best golfer I knew I could be. When I finally decided to call it quits for good after just 2 months into the wrestling season, I believed my whole family let out a long sigh of relief. They knew the physical stress that would be inflicted on me through lifting weights, running for miles, and putting my body through the constant pounding day in and day out would eventually do more harm than any good. I am pretty sure my mom never knew the real reason why I gave up the sport I dreamed of doing since I was a little kid, but she can thank my dad for taking the time to open up and share his wisdom, so I'd be able to finally learn, that becoming the next Tiger Woods could be just as cool as becoming the next Hulk Hogan.

by the time I reached the course. In a haste, I had Chris drive while I sat in the passenger seat and tried to get my shoes on.

What I didn't expect to happen next was, while attempting to tie my shoes, the golf cart suddenly made a sharp left-hand turn and projected me through the air onto the hard paved concrete. Crack! My right elbow snapped at the bone, and I immediately felt a thousand hot pins jabbed into the middle of my arm. I screamed and ran directly off the course, straight to my parent's house, where I filled the kitchen sink with ice cold water and submerged my right arm into it. My mom came running in and asked what had happened. Even through all of the pain I was currently feeling, I knew I couldn't tell her the truth about what had just taken place. In doing so, not only would I be admitting that I had my friend sneak me onto the local golf course I had been banned from playing, but I would also be throwing my friend Chris under the bus for being the driver that caused the accident to happen in the first place. So, I did what any reasonable teenager would have done in my place, I lied.

I came up with a story that my friends and I were playing golf, and I had hit a shot that I couldn't see land and while jumping in the air to see where it went, I fell down a slope and broke my arm. Surprisingly, she bought it and so did everybody else who I told the story to that spring. The only 2 people who knew the truth about how I really broke my arm were the two people who were there that day, and as long as I never told anybody, I knew for a fact Chris wasn't going to speak up. Luckily, the high school golf season had just come to an end and the only thing I had to miss was the parent-athlete golf outing at the end of the year. I didn't mind though because my dad and I had already played a lot of golf together and I still was able to attend the awards dinner later that same night.

What I really didn't like from having to wear a cast that went all the way up to my shoulder, was having to miss out on doing anything active for most of that upcoming summer. I essentially

Chapter 20
High School Confessions

"If you don't do wild things while you're young, you'll have nothing to smile about when you're old." – Krati Gupta

The year was 2001 and Tiger Woods was the most talked about celebrity in the world, just coming off winning all 4 major Championships for the first time since Bobby Jones in 1930. I couldn't believe it; a golfer was becoming the most popular athlete everyone wanted to be and it just so happened to coincide with my decision to dedicate myself to that very game. I traded in my wrestling shoes for golf cleats and reunited with some old friends who were still finding their way around our local golf course. By this time, Chris and Mike had already figured out a full proof way to grab a cart and play most of the holes at CMR golf course and that was by becoming employees of the course. With their connection at CMR and the high school golf season beginning to start, I didn't have to worry about finding a place to play because as long as you were good enough to make the team, you could golf for free. The only problem was, if you were not on the varsity team, you were only allowed to practice golf during the week and had to find your own place to play when it came time for the weekends. Being that I was 100% focused on wanting to play golf every minute of every day, I came to rely on my old friends to help book me those late Saturday and Sunday afternoon tee times.

It would be on one of those late afternoon tee times in particular that would change the course of how my high school experience would come to exist for the foreseeable future. Chris and I had just grabbed a cart and were driving to the tee box closest to my house. My mom had picked me up late from school that day, so I had been in a rush, and hadn't even put my golf shoes on yet broke my elbow clean down the middle, which required no surgery but on the other hand forced me to be without the use of my entire right arm for the next 3-4 months. As you could imagine, this felt like a death sentence and once again I found myself stuck inside for most of the day, having only the comforts of my tv and a couple of new video games to keep me company.

 The bright side to being injured and unable to play the sport I loved was it gave me more time to hang out with my younger sister and watch her excel at her own beloved sport. That summer, Tanya and I really began to hang out more than we had ever had before, and I had found myself attending almost all her water polo games because it was something that actually allowed me to get out of the house. Even though I wasn't able to compete or play in anything at the moment, it was incredible to watch my sister come to dominate a sport that she had just recently learned how to play.

 By the time that summer came to an end and Tanya was supposed to start her freshman year of high school, she had risen to become one of the top female recruits in the city of San Diego. With the anticipation of my sister joining me at the same school and finally being fully healed from my previous injury, the Gandy family was all set to start racking up W's (wins) and breaking records.

Chapter 21
Embracing Pain

"Without pain, without sacrifice, we would have nothing." – Fight Club

As expected or at least in regard to how our family thought, Tanya quickly became a household name within the high school water polo community. At only 14 years of age, she was setting season high scoring records that had stood for 5, 10 and sometimes even 20 years long. She had eclipsed all of the expectations her coaches and college scouts had placed on her the summer before and if it were not for a standout senior from the eventual CIF championship team, Tanya would have been named the first freshman Player of the Year in city history. At the same time, I was also hitting my stride as I had just won 2 local golf tournaments after firing the best rounds of golf I had ever shot before. I was locked in to being one of only 2 sophomores to start on the varsity team, but then came the injuries and a date with my old friend Mr. Pain.

The first part of my body to succumb to injury was my hamstring after pulling it while playing a game with my family called chicken in the pool. Quite simply put, it's a game where you climb on another person's shoulders while both of you try to push another team over into the water. Usually this is a harmless game for most, but I seemed to have been able to turn anything into a trip to the hospital that year. Three months before the golf season was to start, I was laid up during the holiday break, resting on a bean bag chair with ice packs wrapped around both my thighs trying to desperately recover in time before the season began.

It would take me 6 weeks before I was able to walk a full 18 holes again, only to be rushed back to the emergency room 2 weeks later with a bowel obstruction that would last for another 6 full days. This time around as I sat in my hospital bed waiting to feel better, something felt different, and I had a suspicion that this time around, something just wasn't right. It wasn't just the bowel obstruction the doctors were concerned about anymore; they were also concerned that I had been receiving an alarming amount of medication to fight several bladder and kidney infections I had been starting to experience more of these past 6 months. The reality was the doctors were warning me, as well as my parents, that I needed to drastically start drinking more water and going to the bathroom on a more consistent basis or they were afraid my urinary tract system would start to fail.

Even then I didn't really grasp the entirety of what the medical professionals were trying to tell me as I was more concerned with getting released from the hospital, so I could make the varsity golf team and start winning some major tournaments. As simple as it might sound, I had one goal and one goal only—recover from whatever physical ailment I was currently going through in order to return to kicking butt at the sport I believed I was born to play. So, this was exactly what I did, and just 2 weeks before the beginning of the season was scheduled to start, I went out and fired the best scores of any golfer during tryouts that entire year. It was finally done; I had earned my starting spot on one of the top golf programs in all of San Diego and I did it despite the fact my body was slowly deteriorating in front of my very eyes.

The straw that finally broke the camel's back in the late spring of my Sophomore year was when I pulled my right oblique muscle in the lower part of my back 2 days before the last tournament of the year. I had battled all season to finally get my game to a place where I felt I could compete against the best golfers in the entire city and was viewed as a contender to finish in the top 20 in the season's ending championship tournament. However, I would find myself yet again forced to play through injury that restricted my entire ability to swing a golf club down to only 70%. The tournament would come to highlight all the things that could have been, as I would end up finishing outside the top 20 and my hopes of having 2 All-American Gandys in the same household had vanquished into thin air.

After that, I would come to truly believe deep down in my soul that I deserved all of the pain that I was given, so the rest of my family never had to experience the type of suffering I would have to go through. As irrational of a thought this might seem, I had convinced myself that the reason I was the only person in my family to ever have to undergo a surgical procedure or spend weeks at a time in the hospital was because God had chosen me to endure all of their pain, so they would be able to pursue their dreams. To understand what I was going through at the time, I had just witnessed my sister become one of the best water polo players in the country, my brother was on scholarship at one of the most prestigious schools in the entire state, and both my parents were reaching the peak of their professional careers.

My doctors couldn't explain to me why these medical problems kept happening and if they were ever going to stop, and my parents didn't know why it seemed like every time it felt like I would take one step forward I would soon find myself taking 2 steps back. At this point in my life, I had no real relationship with any sort of higher being greater than myself, in which I believed could help bring clarity to a situation that I perceived to be unfixable. The only way I knew how to cope with the pain I was constantly feeling physically and now even more emotionally, was to rationalize in my head why I was burdened with this curse and how I was going to overcome it.

This was the beginning for me to formulate excuses on why I would continually get injured and how it was a good thing that I experienced pain because of all the benefits it would bring me and my family afterwards. An example of this would be every time I developed a small bowel obstruction at night and wondered why this kept happening to me, I would reverse my thought process and trick myself into believing this pain was for the greater good. Every bowel obstruction brought nights of not eating, throwing up and later diarrhea from all the laxatives I was given to flush out the food stuck inside my large intestines. This meant once the dust had settled and I recovered from all the traumatic physical stress my body had just gone through, I looked and felt a lot better than I did just a couple days before. I would tell myself I'm no longer bloated and instead seemed to appear more physically fit. I was training myself to embrace whatever pain was brought my way, even if it was ultimately unhealthy in the long run, because to me, this was the only explanation I could come up with on why bad things kept happening just to me. I changed from being solely an optimist and seeing the world as a place to learn and explore, to embracing a pessimistic view of looking at everything as something you had to fight and overcome. The veracity of my way of thinking would only come into question 6 months down the road, when I would happily find out that there was a lot more to living life, than just competing at golf and overcoming pain from time to time.

Chapter 22
A Whole New World

"Open your eyes, look within. Are you satisfied with the life you're living?" – Bob Marley

Up until this point in my life, my world basically consisted of playing golf, watching sports, hanging out with family, and visiting an array of medical professionals across the country. My view of the world was very short sighted, and I could see now how I was so easily fooled into thinking that the whole world revolved around me. Believe it or not, most teenagers around my age have fallen into this trap, and I was no exception. If my brother and sister were doing well in life, it was because of me having to sacrifice going through pain that they were able to do so. If my team lost, it was because I didn't play well enough or I was too sick or injured to even show up. I also believed that I wasn't going to allow anyone, or anything get in the way of me living my life to the fullest, even if that meant not listening to sound advice when it came to keeping myself healthy and safe.

My whole belief system on how the world worked was constructed solely within a small bubble in which I created and based on the little amount of life experience I had accumulated during my short time on earth. However, my narrow-minded attitude would begin to broaden as my parents gifted me with the one thing that could bring me a sense of pure independence and a source of infinite amount of adventure.

My first car was a black 2002 V8 Toyota Tundra pickup truck, that in my estimation was one of the single most important materialistic things I would ever come to own. The day I passed my driver's license test and was given the keys to my first set of wheels was the first day I began to see that the world was a much bigger place than just the small little town I came from.

However, my newfound freedom brought with it responsibility and real consequences if I couldn't live up to what was asked of you. I was no longer a kid who had the privilege to complain that life wasn't fair and if there was something that I didn't like I could just ignore it and go on doing my own thing. If I wanted autonomy, then I had to work for it and that meant I had to get a job, so I could pay the payments and gas it would cost to enjoy my new sense of independence. So, where else would be better than the place that I knew best, Carmel Mountain Ranch Country Club. That's right, my first job was as a dishwasher in the back kitchen of the restaurant that sat on the second floor of the 30,000 square foot clubhouse. Now, I know what you all are thinking, weren't you banned from ever stepping foot on that property a couple of years back and yes you would be right. However, that exile was brought on by previous ownership and since then, CMR was now run and operated by a whole new manager. In the wake of this new development, I was able to work within walking distance of my house, as well as get the full benefits of being able to play golf whenever I wanted without having to sneak my way on anymore. It was a perfect set up, I would work in the evenings and golf during the day when I didn't have school or was driving around in my new truck. The best part of my new job was that I was able to make enough money not only to cover the cost of my payments and gas, but I had enough money left over to spend on anything else I wanted to do.

 No shock to anyone, the addition of a new car and some extra money brought with it more recognition around campus, which led to more parties and weekend trips to the beach and movie theaters. I had my own ride and my own way of making money now; the only law I had to follow was a strict midnight curfew and I was basically free to do whatever I wanted. The confidence I gained from knowing that I owned my own car and I worked hard to pay for it meant everything to me and brought back a sense of pride in who I was and a change in what I thought life was all about. Now,

I would never begin to presume that all things just happen by chance, and you really don't have a say in what happens to you during your lifetime, but I will say that after I started working and driving around in my new ride, it just so happened that I would soon meet my first girlfriend.

It was halfway through my junior year when a friend invited me to a house party, and I would first be introduced to Adriana. She was wearing a short dress with white converse shoes, and I instantly thought she was wearing the coolest outfit I had ever seen. To this day, I still don't know what came over me to walk up to her and ask her if she wanted to come with me and my friend to go grab a bite to eat after the party, but I did, and she said yes. Like a true friend, my buddy came up with an excuse on why he couldn't join us at the local burger joint, and so it was that we had found ourselves alone to get to know each other a little bit better.

It turned out she really enjoyed laughing at my juvenile jokes and didn't mind in the slightest that I had a magnitude of different size scars running up and down my torso. It felt like fate had brought the two of us together and by the grace of the almighty, it seemed like my life had once again found some sort of meaning. In just a matter of months, I went from believing the world was punishing me so everyone else around could benefit from my misfortune, to having a new sense of purpose and a multitude of reasons to live a meaningful life.

Part Three:
The Long Years

"Ignorance is indeed bliss, but it is also dangerous and embarrassing" – Ted Nugent

Chapter 23
Seeing Through the Fog

Having been forced to grow accustomed to constantly being sick or injured, brought with it a high tolerance for physical discomfort and an unawareness of small bodily changes that otherwise, most people would instantly start to notice. I was well into my junior year and riding high on the fact that I just been nominated captain of the varsity golf team, celebrated my 1-year anniversary working at CMR, upgraded the truck with some new wheels and most importantly had not fallen sick or gotten injured since dating my new girlfriend. I had become truly happy and at peace knowing that if all I had to deal with was some annoying stomach pain for the rest of my life, I could learn to live with that one small inconvenience. Don't get me wrong, the seriousness to some of the pain I felt from those stomach issues really was scary and I wouldn't ever want to downplay how terrifying those experiences had turned out to be, but on the other hand, I had felt like at least I knew what to expect when those episodes started to come along.

When it came to dealing with bowel obstructions, abdominal hernias, and kidney infections you could say I was considered a pro in regard to how much pain I could endure from those three physical complications. Eventually, as I got older and the infections became more frequent in nature, it soon became a normal part of my life, and I didn't really see a problem with the amount of pain it caused me any longer.

What I didn't know and would later find out was hidden from me for over a year, was that my body was indeed in full kidney failure and was only operating at 20% kidney function. This would explain why I was routinely experiencing an increase in kidney and bladder injections, as well as being scheduled for more than the usual amount of doctor appointments the past several months. This would become all news to me a few years from now but for the moment, all I knew was that I was healthy enough to live the same life as everybody else and to be honest I really didn't want to know anything different. The only problem with sticking your head in the sand and hoping everything was going to be ok was that I had become naïve in thinking I was capable of overcoming any obstacle on my own and without the help of anyone around me.

When your body only has one kidney to begin with and that kidney suddenly starts to work at only 20% capacity, you will slowly begin to see some physical and mental deterioration. For me, it wouldn't be until I turned 17 years of age when I would first notice that I was becoming extremely tired throughout the day, as well as forgetting simple tasks that my teachers or coaches would ask from me just hours before. It's hard to explain, my mind felt normal or at least I thought it did, but when I relied on it to remember anything that I had read or done earlier in the day, I was left scrambling to recall any specific detail. It was like I knew I had studied for the exams I would take at school, but when it came time to actually take the tests, I had no recollection of anything I read the night before. I was also physically exhausted even if I had gotten a full night's worth of sleep and it was getting harder and harder to find the motivation to play the sports I used to love. I was in complete kidney failure and anybody who knew what to look for could see that it was beginning to affect the way I lived my life.

They're many reasons why my friends, schoolteachers and coaches never fully caught onto what seemed from an outside perspective to be such obvious warning signs. The first of them being, I was simply a teenage boy who was working into the late nights every weekend, playing competitive golf during the week, managing a full course load in school, and still finding a way to fill the rest of my free time with hanging out with my long-term girlfriend. It was because I had worn myself so thin with everything I had put on my plate, that nobody else around me ever stopped to wonder why I might have been extra fatigued or had trouble remembering simple tasks from time to time. This would start to change after I received my grades halfway through my senior year.

Usually, over the course of my academic life, I had routinely hovered around a 3.5 to 3.6 grade point average, but this time around, I brought home a staggering 1.6 GPA. In simple terms, that meant for the course of an entire semester I had failed 3 out of the 5 classes I attended. For me, as well as my family, this was unheard of and came as a complete shock to everyone who knew me on a personal level. Not only had I already been accepted into California State University San Marcos and been given a chance to play collegiate golf for the team in the next upcoming year, but everyone also knew that I never drank alcohol, took drugs, skipped school, or anything else that would have otherwise gotten in the way of performing at my very best. Something was wrong and everyone from my coaches to my teachers and counselors wanted to know why one of their best scholar athletes went from being on cruise control to all of sudden finding himself in jeopardy of not even graduating.

The thing was, my parents, as well as my doctors, had an inkling what was going on because back when I was in the hospital fighting a bowel obstruction the prior year, they had discovered that my one kidney was starting to collapse and believed I would require a kidney transplant within the next 4 to 6 years. Since 4 to 6 years seemed like a far time away and not wanting me to worry about the unfortunate prognosis until after I graduated from high school, no one wanted to break the news to me that my body was indeed betraying me, and instead, left everyone wondering what the hell was going on.

Now, if you have never had one of your organs slowly shut down, then you couldn't possibly comprehend the sort of constant haze your thoughts and memories feel like day in and day out. At the same time, my body was relentlessly drained of half its energy and there was not enough coffee or pre-workout mix in the world that could make me feel like my old self. It's like this, your kidneys act as filters that remove harmful wastes and extra fluid from your body, as well as acid that is produced by the cells and helps maintain a healthy balance of water, salts, and minerals that float into your bloodstream. However, when your kidneys, or kidney in my case, are not working at optimum levels, some toxins begin to slip through your natural line of defense and start to spread throughout your bloodstream, until they eventually come to rest in your brain.

Over time, the disease begins to accumulate to an unhealthy level where it becomes quite noticeable in how you look and feel throughout the day. Unfortunately, during my senior year in high school, my body was rapidly starting to deteriorate, where I was beginning to lose an excessive amount of weight and my eyes were starting to swell up where I found objects that were right in front of me blurry or sometimes even unrecognizable all together. At this point, I was basically living off fumes and it was just a matter of time before I would be forced on dialysis and put on the national kidney transplant list.

To my parents' credit, they gave me all the love and support I needed to push myself through that final year with all the extra tutors, study groups and personal time they showed me, just so I could experience all the pleasures that came with finally becoming a full-grown adult. Even through all the struggles, I was able to play out my final year as the captain of the men's varsity golf team, attend my senior prom and additionally, experience senior night and spring break vacation with all my friends and fellow classmates. I would turn 18 two weeks before I would walk across the stage and collect my high school diploma, where unbeknownst to me, my life would drastically take a change, but this time, there was a final certainty to the fact that it would never look the same again.

Chapter 24
Heartbreak

"When something bad happens, you have three choices. You can either let it define you, let it destroy you or you can let strengthen you." – Dr. Seuss

May 7, 2004 was an iconic day. I turned 18 years old, but that date would also go down as the day my mom and I simultaneously terrified one another to the point that neither of us would ever forget. It all started in the early morning of my 18th birthday when I had scheduled an appointment over a week back to get my first and only tattoo. I had acquired the idea after watching some of my favorite athletes showing off their tattoos on tv and thought it would be something cool that I could do to celebrate becoming an adult. I knew I didn't want anything big or something I would come to regret later in my life, so I decided to play it safe and go with 2 things which would never change, my family name and favorite number. After just a quick 25-minute session, I walked out of the tattoo parlor with "Gandy 55" imprinted over my left chest and with a new sense of pride that maybe now when I take my shirt off, people's eyes wouldn't automatically gravitate towards my scars, but instead be drawn to my new tattoo. This was something I wanted to do for myself and was the reason why I kept it a secret from everybody I knew, including obviously my parents.

One thing I learned from a very young age was when you have something difficult you have to do, then you might as well get it over with, so you can move on and get to the next adventure that awaits. In this case, my whole plan consisted of driving back home and immediately walking into the house with my shirt off to see if my parents would even notice the new artwork plastered on my upper torso. Spoiler alert, my mom knew instantly what I had done and without warning fell to the floor and started crying. My dad on the other hand, believed the tattoo was originally fake and tried to console my mom that his son would never get a real tattoo without at least telling him first.

Now, you can just imagine how I must have felt in this exact moment when not only did my mom despise the tattoo, but my dad didn't even believe I could make a life decision without him knowing beforehand. I expected my parents to not be thrilled with the idea of me getting a tattoo, but never in a million years did I expect the reaction from both of them to be so adamantly. I would soon come to find out in the next few minutes because my mom had become so utterly distraught over seeing just 7 characters pierced into my body in bold black ink that she would go on to blurt out, "You don't know what you have just done! You might have just killed yourself, Brandon! We wanted to wait until after you graduated but too late now, your body is in complete kidney failure and getting a tattoo can compromise you ever being accepted to receive a kidney transplant in the future!" These were the words that I remember my mom screaming on my 18th birthday, as the gravity to what she had just said hit me like a ton of bricks and quickly began to sink in.

She would eventually go on to explain that people with kidney disease are more vulnerable to contracting infections such as ink poisoning, HIV, Hep B and C, as well as have a much tougher time recovering from any infections because of their considerably lower immune system. I could recall just looking over to my dad for any sort of confirmation and feeling my stomach drop as all he could do was stare back at me with a sense of worry I had never seen in him before. I knew then my mom was not overreacting, but I was too shocked and to be honest, a little too scared to face what my parents have been waiting for over a year to tell me right in that moment. So, I told them I didn't believe them, and I denied that my body was in kidney failure because to me, that was easier than admitting I might have just ruined my entire life. This was a lie of course, it wasn't my fault I was in kidney failure, or I was constantly exhausted, or my eyes were always glossy and as much as I hated to admit it, I was starting to forget the scores I would shoot at yesterday's golf tournaments. None of that mattered though, all that mattered was that it was my birthday and it was not going to be ruined by the news of some medical problem that I would once again have to find a way to overcome. I told my parents I had plans to meet up with my girlfriend for lunch and they agreed they would wait until after my birthday, to sit down and talk about the next steps I would need to take moving forward.

    The next couple of weeks went by in a flash, as I went from one doctor's appointment to the next measuring and testing anything and everything that had to do with how my body was performing under such trying conditions. Luckily, the tattoo scare was just that, a scare and nothing more. Everything else though was just as terrifying, since my fears of really being as sick as my parents said I was, did come to fruition. My kidney function had dropped to just below 15% and the doctors projected that I would need a new kidney within the next 3-6 months if I were to stay away from being placed on a dialysis machine. To me this meant I still had a whole month before I was scheduled to graduate and even with all my medical problems looming over my head and well into my future, I still had some time to have a little fun and take advantage of my newfound independence.

    There were so many things that I still wanted to do before I started college or had a kidney transplant, like travel with my friends to Cancun, attend the year's biggest party on Senior night, become an All-American in the last golf tournament of my high school career and most importantly give my girlfriend a promise ring on the night we graduated. Alexandra and I had been dating for just over a year now and I wanted to make a promise to her that even though we were destined to go to separate schools, we could still stay together as a couple.

Obviously, the news of me having to get a kidney transplant sometime in the near future would have to be worked out and I knew it wouldn't be easy for anyone to have to go through, but I tried to not think of that and instead focused on how much fun we always had when we were together. Plus, she loved how my tattoo looked and for me, I guess I was in love with the fact that my medical complications never seemed to be a concern to her, which in turn, made it seem like they never existed whenever I was around her. This is why it was so unexpected when she invited me to the park and said she wanted to break up. That day my heart shattered into a thousand pieces. She wanted to end our relationship now, so we could both enjoy our summer vacation and not prolong a relationship that in her eyes was not going to last once college began. Unfortunately, this did nothing to help comfort me in the fact that the reality of what I was going to have to bear in the next several months would now have to be suffered alone. I understood the rationale behind her decision, but at that moment, I couldn't wrap my mind around how my life went from everything I ever wanted, to a sudden tragedy of epic proportion. I was hurt and confused all at the same time and this was just in regard to being dumped, let alone comprehending fully the extent of what being diagnosed with kidney disease meant and how it would affect the rest of my life moving forward. However, I was as stubborn as an 18-year-old boy could possibly be and I disregarded ever talking about what happened between Adriana and I from there on out. I pushed my physical concerns to the back of my mind because I knew I still had a prize that I had my eyes set on and my kidney, as well as my ex-girlfriend had nothing to do with achieving that one goal, or so I thought.

Chapter 25
The Clock was Ticking

"No matter what the problem, a miracle can solve it. Remember to ask for one." – Marianne Williamson

In between finishing school, daily blood draws, going to doctor appointments, and working the occasional night shift at CMR clubhouse, I was also practicing every waking hour on perfecting my golf swing for the California Interscholastic Federation (CIF) Regional golf tournament. I had just come off a 6th place finish in the Palomar League Championship and was starting to peak at the right time. My dream had always been to make the All-League team and to do that I had to finish in the top 20 overall at regionals. Regionals is the end of the year tournament where the best golfers from around the city come together and play in a 2-day tournament that ultimately decides which players will go on to play in the California State Championship. For all intents and purposes, this was the biggest event of the year and required my whole team and me to drive 2 hours North and stay overnight somewhere in East Southern California, known as Warner Springs. This in all likelihood would be my last such road trip, as I was told just days before that I was restricted from traveling anywhere outside the state of California just in case my kidney took a turn for the worse. With that information sitting in the back of my mind I was sure as heck going to make this last golf trip one to remember.

Our team decided to drive up one day before the event so we could check out the course we were about to play and have a little fun around the property before we would play in the biggest tournament of our youth. Here's where things began to go sideways, as after dinner some of my teammates and I strolled over to the recreation house where a bunch of the other teams were meeting up to play ping-pong and shoot some pool. Well, one thing led to another, and I got suckered into challenging a player from one of our top rival schools to a friendly wrestling match.

Now, before you laugh at 2 high school golfers wrestling each other in the middle of a 12 x 12 game room, I would like to clarify a few things that might shed some light into how this all came about. For starters, the guy I ended up wrestling with happened to be someone I actually wrestled with before, all the way back during my freshman year when we both wrestled for our respective schools. The second thing you need to know is that each of our teammates were bragging about how their school had the better wrestling team and they wanted to see 2 former wrestlers who actually were standing in the same room, go head-to-head. It was all just a matter of time before the 2 of us were coaxed into throwing down right then and there. For my part, I really was never against the idea of wrestling because I knew I had already beaten him once before and I didn't see why now I couldn't do it again. Years later and with a little more perspective, this moment in time would be one of many regrets during my childhood I wish I could have taken back. Anyway, that's neither here nor there and what happened next would play a significant role in why I would fall short in accomplishing my long-awaited dream of being recognized as one of the top golfers in all of San Diego. The reason why, is because even though I would end up wrestling this guy to the ground and ultimately showing everyone who the better wrestler was in that small moment, I forgot to take into consideration that I was in stage 4 kidney failure and my body was not in the right condition to take the physical toll a full-on wrestling match ultimately entailed. So, as I went to stand back up after the match was called to an end, I heard a pop in my lower extremities and immediately crumbled to the ground! Just like that, I tore my right meniscus 12 hours before I was set to tee off on the first day at CIF regionals.

Being the tough guy, I thought I was, and not wanting to show that anything serious had just happened, I stood back up and limped back to where my team and I were staying without a word. The next morning, I woke up to my kneecap ballooning up to the size of a large grapefruit and there was no hiding the fact that something was seriously wrong. The dilemma soon hit me, do I tell my coach what had happened, or do I try and tough it out so no one on my team would get in any sort of trouble? The answer seemed pretty obvious to me and so, I filled a plastic bag with ice, wrapped it around my knee and hobbled out to the course to warm up. It so happened that my dad took off work to come watch me play that weekend and as soon as he saw me, he knew I had done something horribly wrong.
    I've never been good at lying even when I was young, so as soon as I saw him, I told him what happened the night before and asked what he thought I should do. To my surprise, he didn't kill me right then and there, but instead, asked me how bad the pain was, and did I feel like I could continue to play for the next 6 hours. Considering it was just a matter of if I could manage through the pain after every shot or not, my answer was a defiant yes, and just like that, there was never a word spoken about how my knee was feeling for the rest of the day. Unfortunately, being able to play and being able to play at a very high level are 2 separate things and I learned that the hard way, as I would finish outside the top 50 and was forced to live with the understanding that I had just squandered my last chance at ever making the San Diego All-League golf team.
    Never in my life had I felt angrier with myself than I did on that ride back home after not only costing myself but my entire team a legitimate chance to compete for a regional title. On top of all that, my suspicions about my knee possibly needing reconstructive surgery were validated the next day, when an MRI showed that I had torn one third of my right meniscus completely down the middle.

With only a week to go before graduation, I had found myself, with no girlfriend, a knee that needed to be surgically repaired, a kidney that was prophesied to stop working within the next 6 months and the latest news that I would no longer be attending college in the fall because I would be too sick to attend class. My world seemed to be crumbling all around me and my friends were finding it harder and harder to find ways to cheer me up. Personally, I had lost hope of seeing any light at the end of the tunnel because of all the daunting statistics each new nephrologist my family and I would meet would continue to point out. At that time, there were currently 121,678 people waiting for lifesaving organ transplants in the U.S. Of those, 100,791 were waiting for a kidney transplant. We were also told, the median wait time for an individual's first kidney transplant was 3.6 years and could vary depending on health, compatibility, and availability of organs. The scariest numbers we would come to hear were that around 5,000 patients died each year while waiting for a kidney transplant. Roughly, another 4000 people would become too sick to even receive a kidney transplant. Quick math told me, around 13 people died each day just waiting for a life-saving transplant and add in the fact that I had already dealt with my fair share of complicated medical conditions, my chances of ever getting a kidney were looking slim to none.

    The only people who still showed any sort of hope for me making a miraculous recovery, were my family and the doctors at San Diego Sharp Hospital and Stanford University Medical Center. Together, they looked past the insurmountable odds stacked against me and pressed on with the belief that if anyone of my immediate family members were found to be a perfect match, then there was still hope. Sadly however, our family would run into all sorts of problems when it was found out that my 6'5, 315 lb. Dad had been ruled out as a potential kidney match. This was because of how much bigger his kidney was than mine, and it was believed that my body wouldn't be able to deal with the amount of stress his oversized kidney would ultimately place on my urinary tract system.

The next blow came when the doctors informed us that my younger sister, Tanya, who happened to be the #1 women's water polo recruit in the country at the time, was considered too young to be a donor and was no longer regarded as a viable candidate. But it wasn't until we learned that my older half-brother, Jacob, hadn't shared the same blood type as mine, that the true terror started to sink in and the ramifications of what would happen if my last hope of finding a match came up short. At that moment, our family was asking for a miracle and who would have ever guessed that miracle would come in the form of a 5 '1, 125 lb. 50-year-old woman.

The lab tests were read aloud, and it was confirmed that Linda A Gandy, my mom, had indeed matched perfectly in size, shape, blood type, health and every other possible category that was needed to become a living donor. Now, after being delivered this incredible news, all that was left to do was to find a transplant team and nephrology surgeon capable of performing such a highly complicated procedure where in fact they believed my body was healthy enough to survive a full-scale kidney transplant. But for now, the Gandy household had finally had their prayers answered and there was nothing that was going to stop us now that we could finally glimpse the light at the end of the tunnel.

Chapter 26
Limping Towards the Finish Line

"It does not matter how slowly you go as long as you do not stop."
– Confucius

High school graduation came and went and so with it the last of my adolescent perception of invincibility and the egocentric belief I could overcome anything. Before I was struck over the head with the news that I would soon need to go through a life-saving procedure, I once held true that no matter the illness or no matter the injury, my heart and mind was destined to overcome any and all forms of physical adversity. I honestly believed because of how much distress my body had already gone through, that simply willing myself back to health was all that it took for me to persevere, as long as I could mentally block out the pain causing my self-doubt.

Then came the moment when I became vividly aware of my own mortality and was forced to reckon with the possibility that this next hurdle put in front of me might actually be my last. From that first day when I was told I needed an immediate kidney transplant my life felt like I was living under a cloud of uncertainty and no one around me could provide the answers I needed to alleviate the anxiety I felt it was going to be like after I went through this life altering procedure. Yes, my family and I were told that my mom was a 50% match and was declared healthy enough to donate her kidney if she still deemed willing to do so. However, the odds of success and eventual long-term survival were still stacked high against me, and small trickles of doubt started to set in. What would happen if it didn't work? How hard will this surgery be on my mom's overall wellbeing? What are the side effects of being on medication for the rest of my life? And my real concern, will all of this sacrifice even be worth it? Inside my head, those were the thoughts that kept playing over and over during those first few months, all the way up until my mom broke the news that she had finally found a doctor who she believed had the experience and overall track record to make my unique surgical dilemma an overall success.

It was late June 2004 when my mom, dad and I would fly up to Palo Alto, California and meet the director of the pediatric nephrology transplant team, Dr. Oscar Salvatierra. At that time, Dr. Salvatierra was working at Stanford University' Lucile Packard Children's Hospital, which had been the only hospital in the world who performed non-steroid transplants. Since 1996, Dr. Salvatierra and his team have completed more than 4,000 kidney transplants with a perfect 100% success rate. He also questioned the need for corticosteroid medications for immune suppression. The drugs had been considered essential to prevent rejection of kidney transplants, but had serious side effects in children, causing possible growth suppression, high blood pressure, acne, vision problems and weight gain. In the early 2000s, Dr. Salvatierra was the pioneer in demonstrating that the steroid-free regimen not only prevented rejection but also did less damage to the transplanted kidneys than steroids. Nowadays, the steroid-free protocol has been adopted by most kidney transplant programs across the country, as well as around the world and was the main reason why my mom fought so hard to have him become my preferred surgeon for this existential surgery. It wasn't because we didn't like the doctors in San Diego or even that we knew they hadn't achieved as many successful pediatric transplant surgeries as Dr. Salvatierra, but it was because Stanford was offering a surgery that wouldn't require my already fragile body a life filled with possible side effects that an abundance of steroids would eventually bring with it.

What our family didn't know was that this personal decision on which doctor was going to end up operating on me was not left up to us but was instead decided by our insurance provider.

Unfortunately, it didn't matter that we believed Dr. Salvatierra would be a better fit for my long-term well-being because all that mattered was that our insurance would not approve us going to Stanford medical center and would rather prefer my mom and I to stay closer to home and have the surgery done in-network at San Diego Children's hospital. Well, you might have alrighty guessed by now how that might have gone over with my mom, who ended up taking it upon herself to rage a personal vendetta against the entire insurance industry after we received our first denial letter. This was why we decided to ignore what our insurance company had to say and moved on to the belief that I was going to receive my kidney sometime between late August and early October even if our family had to figure out how to finance it ourselves.

    So it was, the days began to fly by with doctor appointment after doctor appointment, sprinkled in with lab tests and biopsies of my kidney to break up the constant cycle of never-ending examinations. On top of all that, my mom was still fighting hard for an appeal to get us approved to have my kidney transplant performed up at Stanford University instead of down here at San Diego Children's hospital. In the meantime, however, we were given a target date of October 4th, 2004, for our transplant with Dr. Salvatierra, where my mom and I would fly up the week before and go through the final preparations before our big surgery. The only wrinkle now was the fact that I had to go into immediate knee surgery to fix the torn meniscus I had just injured one month prior. It was vital that I was fully healed before I went through my life-saving procedure in just 3 months and to ensure this happened, I was scheduled to go under the knife the very next day with the hope I didn't just put the whole transplant surgery in jeopardy. For the people counting at home, that would make surgery number 17 and the one operation that would force me onto crutches for the rest of the summer. The good news, my mom had become good friends with the San Diego Chargers orthopedic surgeon, Dr. David Chow and he agreed to operate on my knee as soon as possible. Everything went according to plan and after surgery I spent the rest of my time laying around the house watching tv and playing video games.

My mom and dad on the other hand didn't have it so easy, as my dad continued to have to work as he juggled with the challenges that came along with suddenly becoming a single parent to Tanya and Jacob. Mom and I were still around for the time being, but mom was hard at work finding us a place to live while we were expected to move up to Palo Alto once the surgery finally was given the green light. Not only was my mom battling for the right to just have the surgery approved by insurance, but she was also the liaison between the hospital and our family on how exactly she and I would make living 500 miles away from home an actual reality.

The thing was, Stanford University required all kidney transplant patients to stay isolated from the general public for at least 100 days and to be within driving distance of the hospital so they could come in and run daily tests on how the new kidney was functioning. As you can imagine, it was hard enough to get an average 18-year-old to agree to join their parents for dinner, let alone convince one to voluntarily quarantine with his mother for the next 4 months away from all of his closest friends and family. Somehow, my mom managed to keep everyone's spirits high even after 7 appeal letters to the insurance companies continued to come back denied. After expediting our case to the state courts and with only 2 weeks before our initial transplant date, we were given full approval to move forward with Dr. Salvaterra's original plan.

The day before the surgery, my mom would be admitted to Stanford Medical Center, while I had already been checked into Children's Hospital 5 days earlier for prep work. We were told when it came to the actual day of the transplant, the doctors planned to run more tests on both of us to ensure that everything was safe before they felt comfortable moving forward with the procedure. This was the moment where I remembered my mom telling me, "The scary thing is that the whole surgery could be aborted all the way up until the very end, even after we are both put under." That would continue to resonate with me all the way up until the late hours the night before our transplant because all I could think about was how even after everything we had gone through up until this point, I could still find myself waking up with the same 15 percent kidney function that I'd fallen asleep with.

I was assured for months now, that after the surgery I should wake up with three times the energy level and immediately notice a difference in having a fully functioning kidney. Except now, I had concerned myself with the thought that what if when I wake up, nothing had changed? What if I didn't feel any different at all and the surgery actually didn't ever work? What if I had just wasted the gift my mom had just given me, and all my family's sacrifice ended up failing because of me? For the first time in my life, I had started to doubt that everything was going to turn out just fine, and it would take a humbling reminder from someone I'd always looked up to in order to settle my nerves and bring back my unshakable confidence.

Chapter 27
A Gift That Can Never Be Repaid

"Without the organ donor, there is no story, no hope, no transplant. But when there is an organ donor, life springs from death, sorrow turns to hope, and a terrible loss becomes a gift." – UNOS

As I laid in my hospital bed staring up at the popcorn coated ceiling the night before I was due to receive a second chance at life, a million different thoughts passed through my mind. I was beginning to feel the pressure that goes along with knowing that everyone you have ever known is praying for your mom's kidney to safely be transplanted as your own and for both of you to magically wake up and begin to feel better. It was this kind of pressure where if anything went wrong and her kidney didn't actually end up taking, it would feel like I not only failed myself, but I let down everyone who ever cared for me. Rationally, I knew this would not be true but to me, in my own head I knew I would believe it to be so.

When someone you know, especially your own mother, wants to give you a second chance at life, it's scary. I didn't want to fail her or my family for that matter, by risking their own lives to try and save my broken one. Up until now, I never saw myself as a burden or as someone with chronic medical issues that would never know a life without the feeling of physical discomfort. Although now as I was just one-night sleep away from experiencing my 18th surgery, I was flirting with the idea that maybe I had been looking at my life all wrong and if I really thought about it, I was actually being selfish in the idea that I would even accept a kidney from my mom. It wasn't her fault I was sick all of the time and why did I think it was right to put her life at risk just for the small possibility that it would extend my own life for a few more years until my next medical disaster? At the same time, as I was wrestling with these demons inside my head, in walked the person who was due to donate her kidney to me the very next morning.

It was like my mom's motherly instincts kicked in and she knew I was in need of some sort of help that only she could provide. Somehow, she was able to recognize it wasn't that I was scared of the surgery itself because I had been through plenty of those before, but instead, there was something off about my demeanor that signaled to her I was not 100%. I quickly divulged all of the fears I had about not being able to live up to the expectations of what being blessed with a kidney transplant brings with it and how I didn't want her to come to regret making such a difficult sacrifice if things didn't turn out the way everyone had hoped. The moment after I had spoken my truth, my mom's next words changed the way I thought about the world for the rest of my life. That night, I grew up from a boy who perceived everything that happened to the people around him was solely based on the decisions he would come to make or didn't make throughout his life, into a new man who learned that the free will of the people he would come to know was what truly determined the outcome of every event.

My choice to let or not let my mom donate her kidney to me was not the decision that decided if I would come to disappoint my family or not but was my mom's own decision to trust the doctors around her and to have me as her son take the gift, she was willing to share and make the best of what I could do with it. It wasn't up to me to resolve whether or not she could possibly be making a mistake or not, it was my job to be appreciative of the opportunity I was about to be given and do everything in my power to make her unconditional sacrifice worthwhile. I recall my dad being right next to my mom during the whole entire conversation and reassuring the both of us that he couldn't be prouder of his wife and his son for what we were about to go through. He also joked about how he expected me to be ready to win the father/son golf tournament once I had healed back up and felt like I was ready to compete again. Without knowing it, my dad's sense of humor during that one moment inspired an idea of mine that would soon come to be synonymous with how I would go on to approach my recovery for the rest of my time at Stanford Medical Center.

The day had finally arrived where I was wheeled into the surgical room where my mom was lying in a gurney next to me all set to have her right kidney transplanted. Normally, the human body has two functioning kidneys that reside closer to the sides of your lower back, but for safety reasons during most kidney transplants, the doctors prefer to place the new kidney in the front of your abdomen, tucked away underneath your rib cage. This allows for more protection when you are up moving around and being physically active, as well as making it easier for the surgeon to access your old kidney without cutting through your much bigger back muscles.

Luckily for Dr. Salvatierra and his team, I had already had a road map laid out on my body from where exactly the doctors before had sliced into me. The whole surgery was scheduled to take up to 7 hours, with my mom being under anesthesia for only 3 of those. Most of the time, an average kidney transplant surgery only lasts around 5 hours at most, but because of my unique circumstances this surgery was planned to take a little longer. Everything seemed to be going well up until the 7-hour mark came along and my dad, brother and sister who were still sitting in the waiting room, had yet to hear any word on whether my mom, or I had gotten out of surgery. To my dad's credit, he was able to stay calm and not show any sense of worry in front of my other siblings.

After feeling like an eternity went by, the head nurse eventually brought him back to visit my mom, where he would soon become pleasantly surprised to see my mom sitting up with a mirror in one hand and a comb in her other, brushing her hair like she was expecting to go out to dinner that very night. It might have been the pain meds talking but just 7 hours out from donating her kidney to me, my mom was feeling great and was only experiencing a 2 out of 10 pain level post-surgery. Unfortunately, this would be the only good news my parents would come to hear for a while, as Dr. Salvatierra's second in command came into the room and explained to both my mom and dad that their son's surgery turned out to be even more complicated than they first assumed. Rather than being the 7-hour long operation they had first believed the transplant would need, now they estimated it would take an additional 3 to 4 hours before they would be able to finish. As far as news goes, this was not the news any parent wanted to hear about their child, who was alone and without their mom or dad to comfort them.

Quite the opposite actually, as my family were helplessly tucked away down the hall anxiously awaiting any hope that everything was going to turn out ok. Thankfully, my parents had been through these types of situations before and they knew as long as the doctors believed they had the situation at hand, there was no point in worrying about the things they couldn't control. All they could do now was to pray to God to perform one last miracle that brought their baby boy back to life again.

In the end, 12 hours would go by before my parents, as well as my brother and sister would find out that the surgery was finally over and Dr. Salvatierra would soon come out and speak with all of them about how everything went. Baggy-eyed and exhausted from tirelessly working to keep their son alive, Dr. Salvatierra would go on to explain that in all his 45 years of practicing medicine, there had never been a case as hard or with as much complexity as the one he had just performed on their son Brandon. The reasons he gave for his shocking statement was because of how much scar tissue had built up around their son's intestines, which made it virtually impossible to see where any of his vital organs were supposed to be. He went onto elaborate that it took over 7 hours just to make a clearing wide enough to transplant Linda's kidney into my own and if it were not for my overall physical fitness, he was not entirely sure that my body would have been able to withstand the prolonged amount of stress that was applied over such an extended period of time. He also spoke solemnly about how the next couple of days would be crucial to how or even whether my body would accept my mom's kidney or if my immune system would start to take over and destroy the foreign organ from the inside out. Before he could go on any further, my dad interrupted and blurted out "Is he at least going to be ok? Can we go and see him?"

To that, the doc shook his head and said "Brandon has been placed in a medically induced coma for the next 72 hours and will require being hooked up to a ventilator to help steady the amount of oxygen his body will need, so his new kidney will have the best chance at survival. As soon as your son's levels begin to stabilize, I would feel comfortable on trying to wake him back up."

For the next few seconds, the whole room fell quiet as the weight of what was just said processed through the minds of everyone in my family. As though he could foretell what my parents were about to say, Dr. Salvatierra quickly assured my family that he was encouraged by how the surgery went overall and still believed that after my body was given a few days to heal, I would wake up and go on to make a full recovery. As for my part in all of this, I was knocked out cold and wouldn't even be able to remember being rolled into the surgical room to start the procedure. What I did remember though, was that funny little idea I'd come up with the night before, for when I did eventually wake up from my stupor and fancied letting everyone in on the secret I had been waiting to convey, ever since my dad cracked that joke.

Chapter 28
Bad First Impression

"Every time you are able to find humor in some difficult situation, you win!" – *Avinash Wandre*

The sun was hot, and I could feel the heat radiating from the black top behind where I once went to school as a small boy. My friends Jamie and Jon were picking teams for a kickball game that was about to start and I was eagerly awaiting my name to be called so we could start the game. Something was wrong though because I couldn't hear anything the other kids were saying. I could see that they were shouting at me to do something, but it was like my ears were full of wax and I couldn't capture any of the words they were trying to communicate.

Then, just like that everything went black, and I found myself in the outfield, in my old 'little league' uniform during a game that I swore I had played in once before. I ran into the dugout and asked my coach "what's going on," to which he replied, "I don't know Gandy, I thought you would remember to always hit the cutoff man even if you thought you could throw the runner out at home." "No, I mean, haven't we already played this game before, I thought we had beat this team by 10 or 11?" As I waited for his reply, I noticed the whole baseball field started to cave in on itself and out spread a green fog that entrenched the black background of what my brain was having a hard time comprehending. Where was I? What just happened, and why am I standing alone looking over what looked to be a black sea full of kids dressed in green hospital gowns pushing their IV machines closer and closer to where I was standing? It felt like everyone was staring up at me, all waiting to hear what I was about to say, but I didn't know who they were and I definitely didn't know what they wanted me to say. I was confused and a little bit scared, but right before I took a step to go meet them, FLASH. My eyes blinked open, and I was back, staring up at that oh so familiar popcorn coated ceiling, as a rush of memory began to flood back into my head, and I was painfully reminded of the kidney transplant I had just risked my life to go through.

To my wonder, 5 sets of eyes were looking back down at me as two specialists, the doctor on call, the charge nurse and my dad were all standing over me in hopeful anticipation to see if I would be able to breathe on my own again. I was still hooked up to a respirator that required a tube as long as my forearm to be placed down my trachea so I could breathe easier as I was recovering from my 3-day induced coma. What everybody in the room didn't know was to what extent I was fully awake yet, which would play a pivotal role in what I was about to do next. After verifying with his colleagues that my vitals looked normal and I was starting to regain consciousness, the doctor on call decided to go ahead and remove the tube lodged down my throat. As far as uncomfortable goes, this moment absolutely makes my top 5 most awkward experiences I have ever experienced.

Picture how painful a 3-foot garden snake being pulled out of your mouth would feel and then add in the fact that it had been stuck in there for the past 72 hours. To my relief, the whole ordeal only lasted around 10 or 20 seconds, but as soon as the tube was out, and I could start breathing on my own again, that's when all hell broke loose. My body immediately went into convulsions and my eyes began to roll back into my head. The head nurse was the first one to react and instantly ran out of the room to go call for more backup. My dad on the other hand was frozen in shock as he was pushed to the side to make room for the other doctors around as they moved in closer to see if they could help alleviate any of my unstable trauma. Thankfully, my sister had already left the room and was sitting outside the door waiting to come back in because she didn't want to watch while the tube was being removed. The head doctor, who still had the ventilator tube in one hand and was trying to hold me down with his other, looked perplexed on how this might have happened and how he was going to get the situation back under control. All of this happened within 10 seconds, until the shaking abruptly came to a stop, and I winked up at the doctors looking down and croaked out "just kidding."

Now, between you and me, I had been planning to do this in front of my dad since the night before I went into surgery, but never in my wildest dreams did I believe for a second I would be able to remember to fake a seizure after just waking up from a 3-day induced coma, let alone do it in front of an entire medical team. Yet, I would also like to mention, I had been pumped with enough narcotics to put a baby elephant to sleep and as much as I would love to tell you that I remembered exactly what had happened next, I would hope you could understand why some of my memory from that day has slowly faded away. What I was told though, was that the assistant nurse was so mad that she was the first to scream out "YOU ASS" and proceeded to storm out of the room in complete disgust. My dad would later say the doctor whose job it was to pull the tube out of my throat would confess afterwards, "Your son might have pissed off the whole nursing staff with those shenanigans but personally I thought it was hilarious. I knew afterwards if he had the capability to crack a joke after waking up from a 3-day induced coma, he was going to be just fine."

The truth is, that no doctor in the world knows for sure if their patient who comes out of a coma is ever going to be 100% normal again, for the simple fact that no one knows for sure how much oxygen someone loses to their brain before the doctors can get them stabilized again. As for this incident, I had already been unconscious for over 72 hours, and it was starting to get to the point where some doctors were questioning whether or not the transplant had caused more harm than good. Although, I'll be the first to admit that faking a seizure probably wasn't the most kosher thing to do when you first wake up from a coma, but it sure as heck showed everybody who'd thought I might had lost a step while I was out, that I was back, and it was going to take a lot more than that to put me down for the count. Sadly however, it would take more than just a small sense of humor to help get me back on my feet as the next 4 months would test my will to survive and shake my confidence to the core with every painful day that passed by.

Chapter 29
Isolation

"It's your reaction to adversity, not adversity itself that determines how your life's story will develop." – Dieter F. Uchtdorf

I would spend the next 10 days in the intensive care unit (ICU) and another 3 weeks at Lucile Packard Children's Hospital being poked and prodded as I tried fruitlessly to recover as quickly as possible. In the meantime, my mom was released just 2 days after donating her kidney and looked like she was right back to being her old self. I hate to say this, but I loathed the fact that she was all smiles and pain free as I laid couped up in my medical bed fighting every day just to feel a tad bit less miserable than I had the day before.

Yes, I know I should have been thankful that she was healing so fast and no, I didn't really wish she had to go through the pain that I was currently experiencing, but damn, how unfair I thought it was that the person who was supposed to be gaining a kidney was having the more difficult time recovering than the person who just lost one of their own. Also, what didn't help the situation, was the fact that for the past half year I'd been told by everyone who's gone through this operation, that as soon as I woke up after receiving my second chance at life, I'd notice an instant rejuvenation on how much better I'd feel with the addition of a fully functioning kidney. Regrettably, I wish this sense of optimism had never been shared with me because as I lay in the hospital day after day, feeling worse and worse than I had ever felt before, all I could think was what was wrong with me? I should be feeling like the happiest person in the world, but all I felt in that moment was agony with a genuine sense of despair.

Each day would begin with me being woken up at the top of every hour so the nurses could measure how much fluid I was able to empty from my bladder and how high my blood pressure was reading at that specific time. The doctors who would come to work later that morning would then be able to review whether my kidney, as well as my heart had been working on overload throughout the night and if they had to adjust the amount of medication I was currently being given.

Every hour that went by would require a specially trained nurse to come in and withdraw what felt like a pint of blood from whatever vein didn't look to have been punctured too badly from the night before. Once I had fully conceded to the fact that I was done trying to get any proper amount of sleep, then came the morning medication delivery. This consisted of 22 differently sized pills that were somehow all necessary in order for the transplant to be a long-term success. This part I didn't mind as much because to me, this was the least invasive thing I had to do all day. By the end, I was actually starting to make small bets with my brother on how many capsules I could swallow in one go. Mixed in with all the antirejection, blood pressure, stomach ulcer, virus protection, anemia boosting drugs were a whole lot of pain medication to help keep my body and mind from going into a state of physical shock.

Sadly though, once the doctors tried to fix one problem with a certain medication, all of a sudden there'd pop up a whole new set of problems due to the side effects from the first. An example of this came when I was given an abundant amount of Vicodin to help dull the pain I was experiencing after the transplant, which would later lead to going to the bathroom utterly impossible because of the shutdown of my entire digestive system. The solution? Have me consume more medication, so I could ultimately go poop again.

The problem with that approach though was that the laxatives would end up causing me diarrhea, which had two negative effects that came along with it. The first being my body would rapidly start to get dehydrated and the second, all of the other medication I was taking would move too quickly throughout my body, which in turn wouldn't allow the appropriate amount of time to be fully absorbed. In the end, these were the types of minor problems the nephrology team at Stanford Medical Center were constantly trying to figure out and were the main reasons why it was mandatory I had my blood drawn and urine tested 24 hours a day. However, when it came to solving the main problem Dr. Salvatierra and his team were most concerned about, they were stumped on why the heck I was still pissing out blood clots the size of half dollar coins almost a full month out from surgery?

It was discovered that because of how much protein was being passed through my kidneys into my urine, my body was unable to break down all the excess bacteria, which effectively caused the blood clots to arise. Couple this with the fact that I had not gotten more than 60 minutes of uninterrupted sleep for the past four nights and had lost over 30 pounds of muscle since arriving in Northern California, you could just imagine how tired and defeated I must have felt when I was told the doctors were now considering extending my hospital stay for the entire 4 months. The original plan was to have my mom and I live isolated in an apartment down the street from the hospital once I was healthy enough to be on my own, but now, unless I could prove to the doctors that I could drink half a gallon of water a day without the assistance of an IV machine and be able to go to the bathroom without any trace of an excessive amount of blood in my urine, I would be required to spend the rest of my days trying to recover inside Children's hospital. Luckily for me, I had my family to help get me through those tough times and with determination and some supportive encouragement, I was able to finally make the breakthrough everyone had been so patiently waiting for. I was still very anemic and in all sorts of pain, but now, I was finally able to walk on my own and for the most part, be able to take care of myself without the aid of any life-saving apparatuses. This would be the first sign of good news on my long journey back from recovery, but now came a battle that no amount of time or words could have ever helped prepare me for.

I had finally been deemed healthy enough to be released from the care of Lucile Packard Children's hospital just to find myself locked away a mile down the street in a small 2-bedroom apartment with just my mom as company. My dad flew back to San Diego a few days earlier to go back to work, while my sister and brother left a week prior to attend their Senior years of high school and college. The initial fight to keep me alive was now over and it was time for everyone who was not immunocompromised to go back to their daily lives. For me, however, these next 100 days would ultimately determine if my body was strong enough to fight off infection once exposed to an outside environment, while at the same time, being medically diminished to the point it would not kill off my new kidney. It soon became a game of experimentation, where the doctors would try one set of new medications one day and then tinker with administering a new dosage the next. The reason for this is because every person's body is made up of a bunch of little white blood cells whose main job is to destroy any foreign bacteria or disease that might come to harm them.

Usually, most people would love a high white blood cell count because that meant their body could fight off a wide variety of viruses and infections and not have to worry about ever getting deathly sick. However, if you are a transplant recipient this works against you because the better your immune system, the more likely your body is to reject your new organ. Thus, transplant patients are given immune "compromising" medication to bring down their bodies overall ability to fight off common colds or illnesses. With that being said, it has come to be widely accepted in the first 3 to 4 months that a transplant recipients' immune system is considered to be so vulnerable, that even the slightest exposure to any virus could end up in the complete shutdown of their vital organs. To prevent this from happening, medical professionals seclude their patients from having any contact with the outside world for the first 100 days post-surgery, so their kidney has time to slowly acclimate itself with its new host body.

Long story short, this all meant I was now destined at the prime age of 18 to have no physical interaction with any of my friends or family, as well as losing my freedom to go to any restaurants, movies, or public gatherings of any kind. I had no school, no golf, no girlfriend, and no social media to keep me occupied throughout the day and all I could really do was sit alone and watch TV or play video games. Besides the times my mom would drive me to the hospital in the morning to visit the doctors and have my labs done, I had felt like the world was passing me by and there was nothing I could do about it.

The one thing that I will say about being forced to stay inside with just my thoughts to keep me company, is that I really did find out what I was really made of physically, emotionally, and spiritually. I'll be honest, those first couple of months took a real physical toll on me, where I had gone from weighing 160 pounds at the start of my transplant, all the way down to a scary looking 119 lbs. It also psychologically worsened my hope that things would ever start to feel better, and I could resume living my life like everyone else around me. I missed not being able to go outside and be with my friends or drive my car to the golf course and play 18 holes with my dad or teammates. It was exhausting knowing that every time I woke up, I would hope that this would be the day that I felt like my old self but could no longer walk across our small apartment without feeling like I was going to collapse to the floor. The only reprieve that I was able to find during those first 3 months of recovery was when I silently prayed to God every night before I went to bed to give me the strength to get through the hell I was currently living in, so I could rise again and fulfill the life I was meant to pursue. Well, that's not entirely true, as my mom would play a huge role as well in being able to bring a smile to my face by driving me around the bay area for hours at a time just so I could feel the wind rush through my hair, and I could see the outside world from the safety of our car.

I used to love it when she drove me to the redwoods so I could see the beauty of nature at its finest. I also enjoyed it when she drove me around to see special attractions like the Golden Gate bridge, as well as the million-dollar mansions around the neighborhood, where I would daydream about what it would be like to own something so big one day. It would be those long drives and rare surprise visits from my cousins and close family members that I would come to appreciate most during my time up in Palo Alto.

    I'll never forget when my Uncle Mitch and cousin Derek drove all the way up from San Diego to surprise me one day, just in the hopes that they would get a chance to see me from afar and remind me that everyone back home were still thinking of me. Even with all that, I was still having a hard time finding any prolonged happiness in regard to the situation I was currently in, but with some help from some new technology and with a little bit of luck, my outlook on life was about to change.

Chapter 30
When the World Blesses You with Hope

"Never go in search of love, go in search of life and life will find you the love you seek." – Atticus

I will never forget the day my mom and I were given the news that we were going home early, as it came as a complete shock that I had passed all the required tests 3 weeks before the 100-day marker. My kidney transplant was on October 4th, 2004, which would have meant that the earliest my family and I could have expected to return home was on January 12, 2005, exactly 100 days post-surgery. Somehow though, Dr. Salvatierra had enough belief in the fact that my new kidney was coming along at a faster rate than first expected, he was comfortable in releasing my care to the nephology team at Sharp Hospital in San Diego. However, he was still adamant about making me promise to stay in quarantine away from everyone else besides my closest family until I fully reached the original 100-day benchmark.

At that point though, all I heard was that I was finally going home and would soon be able to get back to living my life again. I had already felt like I had missed out on so much these past 6 months that all I could think of was everything I was going to do once I was released back into the world. Don't get me wrong I was still nowhere close to feeling like my old self and to be frank, I was still feeling pretty melancholy about not being able to bounce back like I had been accustomed to in the past. Looking back, it's hard to point to exactly why I was feeling so dejected with the progress I had been making, because in reality my body was actually recovering at a phenomenal pace. But if I had to guess, I think the accumulation of still feeling in pain and the never-ending uncertainty whether my new kidney would eventually give out, as well as the knowledge that now I was forever considered immunocompromised, all had a direct effect on why it still felt as though something was missing deep within me.

I needed my confidence back, my spark, the one aspect about me that said, "so what if you're not always going to be as healthy as everyone else because the days when you are, you'll be happier and more alive than anyone else anyways." I had lost that overwhelming conviction that I could conquer the world and I was terrified that just maybe it was never coming back.

It wouldn't be until the first time I walked on a college campus where I found myself indistinguishable from any of the other 20,000+ students, where I truly felt life had given me a new canvas to paint on. Nobody was staring at me like it was a miracle that I was even there, they didn't know I had just gone through a life-altering kidney transplant just 4 months earlier and they certainly couldn't tell that I had 18 major surgeries and was probably considered the most complicated health specimen on campus. None of that mattered to the students who attended California State University San Marcos, because to them I looked and acted like just another normal college freshman trying to find his way in this world. It felt like a blessing to have my autonomy back and I loved every single moment of it. I was no longer viewed as just the kid with all the surgeries or the student who needed all the special attention because of everything he's had to overcome throughout his life. Instead, I was finally free to forge my own path and create a new identity for myself.

My mom would later say "I remember the exact day when you made the turn. It was January 20th, 2005, your first day of college. You came home and it was like you were a different person. You told your father and me that you finally felt like you had your life back and to us, you seemed genuinely happy again. Ultimately, we had made the right decision in bringing you home early because it was about time you got a chance to experience the world outside just a bunch of laboratories and hospital rooms." That first semester back in school brought with it my joy for learning, playing intramural sports, and even traveling during spring break with my friends to Austin for my first trip in nearly two years. Yet, it would be an entrancing set of brown eyes with long dark black hair and a laugh that was so contagious you couldn't help but smile, that would undoubtedly have the most long-lasting impact on my journey back to full recovery.

However, before that happened and the school year was going to come to an end, I was to turn 19 years old and for this birthday, I wanted to celebrate with as many friends and family as I possibly could. Since I was in severe kidney failure and was not feeling well enough to throw a party for my 18th birthday the year before, I thought I would make it up by hosting a World Series of Poker No-Limit Holdem' tournament at my parent's house with all the chips, tables, dealers, and entertainment that you would come to expect to see on ESPN. At that time in my life, I had spent most of my free nights at my older cousin's bachelor pad, where we would eat some pizza and play some cards with whoever wanted a good game and a chance to win a little money. I was lucky, because I grew up with 4 male cousins who were all within 3 to 5 years of my age. Because of this, we had all become really close and after I returned home from being by myself for the past 4-6 months, they were right there to bring me back into their crew like nothing had ever changed. I had always been grateful for how Derek, Bryan, Mitch, and Tyler had taken care of me as though I was their little brother and now that I was healthy again, I wanted to celebrate with all 4 of them in the best way I knew how. However, what I didn't consider before I put this huge party together, was the fact that 2 weeks before, I would stumble upon a picture of a young woman who enticed me so much that I found it utterly unimaginable to throw a party and not have her there.

I'll be the first to admit, I was considered quite a beginner when it came to this new social media craze, as Facebook had just come out and Myspace was still the hottest thing since sliced bread. For the people who are too young to remember what

Myspace was, it pretty much was Facebook's more popular older brother, mainly because it didn't have the requirement that you had to attend a four-year university to be a part of their platform. Also, Myspace had a unique aspect to it where your profile would display your top 8 most important people in your life, basically your 8 best friends. Well, as it so happened, I was scrolling through one of my friend's homepages one day when I noticed a truly stunning picture of a girl who I couldn't ever recall meeting any time before. It was because of this rare oddity, where I thought I knew all of my friends' closest acquaintances, that I took it upon myself to send this newly unidentified and, might I add, a very mysterious young lady a personal message. "Hi, it looks like you're good friends with one of my good friends, so how come we're not friends?" To everyone's surprise, including the original architect who crafted such a revolutionary and thought-provoking question, the ravishingly gorgeous girl on the other side of the internet responded back with a simple, "I don't know?" And with that small gesture, flourished a never-ending conversation that lasted for the next several weeks, all the way up until it was ultimately decided that it was time for the two of us to finally meet in person.

Now, when it comes to how exactly my wife and I first got together, it really all depends on who you ask first. Even though this story has been highly debated for the past two decades, because I'm authoring this book, I will go ahead and tell you what I consider to be how Sharareh "Sherry" Mirzai and I first met.

It all started when I first invited Sherry to come to my birthday party, where I knew both of our friends would be attending. Somehow though, the dates got mixed up and instead of showing up to the party on Friday May 6th, Sherry showed up to my parents with balloons in hand the day after, which happened to be my actual birthday, May 7th. Shockingly, because Sherry only had a pager and no cell phone yet, she never knew that she had already missed my party and it was only me who would be answering the door with a baffled look on my face, that said what are you doing here? Immediately, my brain went into recovery mode, and I spluttered out "Hi, you're early, thanks for coming."

Thinking she must have accidentally forgotten somehow that I told her my party was on May 7th instead of May 6th and feeling quite confused, I quickly apologized for what had happened and said unfortunately my party was yesterday. Astonishingly, instead of being angry or upset that there had been a colossal mix up, her cheeks started to blush, and she softly mumbled to herself, "How embarrassing."

From then on, whenever I would do something that she would feel was not funny or kind of awkward, she'd simply say "How embarrassing." As for that night though, I would go onto beg my older brother and his girlfriend to come to dinner with Sherry and I, so Sherry wouldn't feel like I tricked her into showing up to my parent's house alone. I pleaded with them that if they agreed, I'd pay for their entire dinner. It worked and so it was, Sherry's and my first date had actually been a double date at TGI Fridays that was all paid for by my winnings from the night before. After a few more weeks of dates and 3 or 4 attempts at asking her to be my girlfriend, Sherry and I finally made it official and from then on had been inseparable until tragedy hit just a couple of months later.

Chapter 31
Blindsided

"Those who have had near-death experiences will tell you that realm is far more real than this world, more crisp, vibrant, alive."
– Dr. Eben Alexander

The world was finally mine and even though it took all the hard work and endless number of prayers to get me back to this point in my life, I had made it. The first semester of my college career had just wrapped up and I had been given a full bill of health from all my doctors. Physically, I was starting to get my strength back and was beginning to pack on the pounds that I had once lost so long ago. Good thing too, because swimsuit season was coming up fast and my friend Jon had already invited Sherry and me to Lake Mead for a summer vacation. It was the ideal getaway for young adults to ride around in a boat and soak up some rays for a whole weekend close to home.

Now, in my head this was a no brainer, Sherry and I had been dating for over a month, so I knew she was in, I had some money saved up from not having anywhere to spend it while being deathly sick for a half a year and the docs just said I was as healthy as an ox. Except, there was one little hurdle that I still had to jump through and that was convincing the donor of my kidney that it was ok that I travel out of state with a bunch of my teenage friends, so we could rent a boat and camp out on the side of a lake in 110-degree weather for an entire weekend. To nobody's surprise, my mom was not completely thrilled with the idea of putting my body in a state of dehydration over a long period of time, as well as potentially risking any harm to my newly acquired kidney by being towed behind a boat in a small innertube at high speed. However, she ultimately relented to the fact that I was now an adult, and it was up to me to be able to make the right decisions when it came to how I was going to live the rest of my life, for the better or worse.

Thankfully, this time around it all turned out well, and it soon would become one of the best experiences of my life. For one thing, Sherry and I were given a chance to get to know each other even better, as we were forced to see each other morning and night without the comforts of running water or electricity. If I could give any new couple some unsolicited advice, I would highly recommend traveling to a remote place in the middle of nowhere for at least 3 or 4 nights, so you can really see how your significant other reacts when they are placed outside their immediate comfort zone. As it so happened for Sherry and me, we were both pleasantly surprised when we found out that neither of us really minded not having the convenience of our everyday little pleasures, but instead were just grateful to be together in such a beautiful place with nothing to do but watch the sunset go down behind the snowcapped peaks of the Rocky Mountains.

Over that 4th of July weekend, we would both come to say those three words that were once thought to be forgotten to history, never to be spoken unless to our mothers or fathers but were now necessary to encompass the full emotion the both of us wanted to share about our feelings towards one another. How strange it was that fate once told me that everything I had ever known would be changed forever just a half a year earlier, but would come back again, to change everything once more with a simple "I love you." It would be those words that would stick with me for the rest of my life, as never before had I ever felt a personal responsibility for another person's life as I did for that young woman's heart on that one particular summer night.

See, the thing I learned about Sherry in that short period of time was that she was a fighter just like me. Her life was an uphill battle from the very beginning, but as the underdog she used her hardships not as a crutch, but a torch to light a path for her eventual success. Even though her trials and tribulations might not have come in the same physical distress as mine, that didn't mean that she didn't have to overcome anything less difficult in terms of her emotional and spiritual well-being. My eyes were widened to a type of pain and struggle that only comes from years of growing up without a mother. The unforgiving responsibility that came with taking care of her younger brother while her father, who came over to the U.S. as an Iranian refugee, worked two full time jobs, just so she could grow up in a community that provided her the best opportunity at receiving a higher level of education.

I was enlightened into the world of what a low income first generation female citizen who came from a single-family household had to go through daily just to survive from what her life demanded from her on a constant basis. I was entranced with every story she would recite during our long nights staying up well past midnight, reveling in the journey her dad took just to find his way over to America and raise such an intelligent, thoughtful, and highly driven individual. It had been captivating to hear her family's fortitude to push through every overwhelming setback, be it their fight for a better life, her father's sudden stroke brought on by the amount of stress he was carrying, or her early diagnosis of breast cancer at the young age of 16. Each saga left me asking, how? How did you manage to turn out the way you did, with a smile that could overshadow any darkness and an attitude to grab life by the horns even if those horns were attached to a 1,200-pound bull, whose sole purpose was to smash you into the ground over and over again? The funny thing was, I would soon find the answers faster than I thought, when 2 days after returning home from our 4th of July trip to the desert, my truck was struck on the driver side door by an oncoming car, leaving Sherry to test her resiliency once again.

It was around 9pm on July 6th, 2005, when I was driving over to Sherry's parents' house to surprise her with a packet of her favorite candy, Reese's pieces cups. Unfortunately, I never told her I was coming, nor did I tell my parents when I would be back home, so when my car accident happened nobody knew that something bad had just taken place.

To this day, everything leading up to that event has been erased from my mind and I personally think it was God's way of shutting out a memory that I had no desire to ever relive. However, what I do know from sworn testimony and the police reports is that as I was crossing the intersection a mid-size sedan who was timing a red light to change, hit my car going a speed fast enough to cause my Toyota Tundra to spin and flip 4 times in mid-air before landing on the hill across the street. The impact was so hard, that even though I was wearing my seatbelt, I was ejected outside the driver's side window and was found lying face down unconscious 50 yards away from where the collision first took place. Luckily, I was wearing a medical alert bracelet, so the paramedics had proper information regarding all my medical conditions and were able to transport me straight to Scripps Trauma Unit in La Jolla.

It would be later said to both my parents and me, if it were not for that medical bracelet, the paramedics would not have known the correct response to saving the life of a unique patient like me. In all likelihood, they could have either administered the wrong drugs or taken me to the nearest hospital, in which case, the doctors on staff wouldn't have had the proper resources to save my kidney and potentially my life. A fortunate stroke of serendipity had just happened as it was just 2 months earlier when I was back up at Stanford hospital for my 6-month biopsy where I met a young 10-year-old boy who I ended up making a deal of a lifetime with.

See, what you have to understand was that initially I never wanted to wear a bracelet around my risk and for the first 6 months after my surgery I refused to ever wear one. Then I met this family who was struggling to convince their 10-year-old son to have a biopsy procedure done and my mom knew I could help. So, she asked me if I would talk to him considering I was having the same procedure performed on me the same day. Ironically, he had the same fears as I once had, which made it a lot easier to connect with him on a personal level. We soon came to an agreement in which if he would go through with his biopsy, then I would agree to wear my medical alert bracelet. So, because of a chance interaction or was it divine intervention and a promise I made a few months back, I happened to be wearing the medical bracelet that particular night. On it, was the phone number to the medical records hotline that listed all the medications I was currently taking, as well as my complete medical history to whomever was in the crisis situation of trying to bring me back to life.

The 2 most important things those paramedics learned after making the call was that one, I had just recently had a kidney transplant and at no time should be given any kind of steroid medication. The second, I was to be taken to the nearest trauma unit in the city of San Diego that had a nephrologist specialist on call just in case my kidney had been damaged and needed immediate surgery. These precautions were put into place in case of an unfortunate accident where I would become unresponsive and could not communicate my health needs at that specific time. Miraculously however, I was able to open my eyes for a brief moment while inside the ambulance and I remember wiggling my toes and thinking to myself what was 5 x 5? When I came to the conclusion the answer was 25, I knew at least whatever had happened to my body, I would be able to eventually come back from. The reason for this was because I still had full brain function, as well as complete control of both my hands and feet. Unfortunately, this would be all that I would remember from that entire night as I would slip back into unconsciousness soon after, where for the second time in less than a year, I would experience a hint of what death had to offer, but this time I felt more alive than I had ever felt before.

It might be hard to imagine, and it might even be harder to explain when I say that I felt more alive the closer I got to death, but for me, it was like life had suddenly become more real and I was shown glimpses of what the true meaning of existence entails. The first thing I instantly noticed was that time itself had no meaning. While I was unconscious, I could have been in a place of delirium for an hour, or I could have been there for years. In that specific moment, it had felt like I had been wandering through a prism of my past and future with no start or finish in sight. In actuality, I had only been knocked out cold for 21 hours, but during that time I felt like I was no longer in the body once thought to be mine. Instead, I was living through the eyes of a physical being that I could no longer recognize as my own. This person had no scars and felt no pain, he had no medical complications or past personal trauma, he was older and more confident in the person he had become.

I remember walking by a table that seemed to stretch on forever in a great white building that you'd commonly see in ancient Greece. Along it had gold saucers that didn't bear any food or drink but instead showed events that were taking place amongst the world from its past, present, and future. I relived the events that took place during 9/11 where I bounced from the memory of sitting in my old Spanish class watching the tragedy unfold with all my other classmates, to ground zero where I had been running from a dark cloud of debris that would engulf my vision and bring me back to the table of continuation.

I would come to meet my future self in a house that wasn't mine but seemed to be familiar and it was there that I would realize that the life I currently was living wasn't mine to manipulate or try to change but was the blessing I was given by someone of greater power who needed me to tell a story that no one else could.

For my whole life I tried to act as if I was just like everyone else, I believed I was normal and wanted to hide the imperfections about who I really was. The state of mind I had traveled to once I had blacked out from my car accident was a sense of personal achievement and responsibility to all of the people who had sacrificed their time and prayers for my recovery. For which, I realized for the first time was the reason why I was never supposed to be normal in the first place, because being normal meant I would never be able to grow up to become the man who I had come to idolize and who has been standing right in front me this whole time.

This man was a representation of a future that I knew I could attain and all I had to do was accept the fact that even though I might have limitations and live with insecurities, ultimately, my lasting impact on this world would be defined by how I can help or even inspire the people around me by just being myself. But before I could turn my new comprehension of who I was to become, I had to come back to consciousness.

Chapter 32
Been Down this Road Before

"You gain strength, courage and confidence by every experience in which you really stop to look fear in the face." – Eleanor Roosevelt

To say that I have been through a severe amount of pain over my short lifetime would be an understatement, but never had I felt the kind of pain I experienced when I first woke up after my car accident when I was 19 years of age.

I ended up being diagnosed with a grade 3 head concussion, 4 fractured ribs, a broken left collarbone, a punctured lung, and worst of all a kidney that was bleeding from the inside. To put it mildly, I was lucky to be alive and I would need all the support I could get before I was to make the long recovery back to being my new self.

Mercifully, this time around I had a new partner by my side who refused to see the warning signs that a life with me might end with a story full of grief, but rather doubled down in her effort as a beacon of hope in which I could rally behind while I slowly healed back from despair. Every day she would sit by my side, while we watched movie after movie laughing at who could misquote the funniest lines the best. Unlike my time up in Northern California where I was recovering from a surgery isolated from everyone around me, I was inundated with all the love and support I could ever ask for. This is why I truly believe I was able to mend back to health quicker than ever and against all the odds that continued to be stacked against me.

The funny thing was, in the very beginning Sherry didn't have a clue to the extent of how devastating my crash actually was because the phone call she received was from my dad, who to his credit always saw the world with a glass half full mentality.

Sometime around midnight, Sherry was startled awake by a knock outside her window from one of her best friends saying, "Brandon has been in a car accident and Curt has been trying to get a hold of you." Still, at this time in Sherry's life she had not purchased a cell phone, so when my parents tried to notify her that I had been taken to the hospital, they could only reach her closest friend with the hope Danielle could somehow get in contact with her.

So, after being scared conscious, Sherry got on the phone with my dad and was told, "Don't be alarmed, but Brandon has been in a car accident, and he is here at Scripps Trauma Unit in La Jolla. He's doing fine, and you can come down to see him as soon as you want."

Now, in hindsight I'm actually happy my dad didn't go into the full extent of my gruesome situation because it might have sent Sherry into a panic and would have made her 30-minute drive in the middle of the night more dangerous. However, he could have warned the poor girl once she arrived at the hospital and before she walked into the ICU room for the very first time that what she was about to see might not look all that appealing.

Regrettably, none of this took place and Sherry was left to wander on in to see two doctors and a plastic surgeon huddled around her unconscious boyfriend debating whether they should repair his broken collarbone or try and reconstruct the left side of his face once the swelling subsided. Even though my dad might have technically been correct in saying his son was doing fine and he was eventually going to be ok, he neglected to mention that I had also been thrown from my truck and had half my face smashed across the asphalt no longer leaving any skin attached to the left side of my skull.

As described by Sherry months later, "you looked like a zombie straight out of a movie, where all I could see was pinkish muscle bubbling from the side of your cheek all the way down past your jawline."

It would take another miracle for me to recover from the physical deformations this accident inflicted, and it was then that the wolverine mantra was really born.

Ever since I can remember I always had a higher pain tolerance than most people I knew and could recover from all kinds of different ailments quicker as well. It wasn't until I reached adulthood when my family and friends really started to take notice of how my body would seem to be in an unbearable amount of pain one day and miraculously seem like nothing ever happened the very next. As for my injuries after the accident, the medical staff at Scripps La Jolla went onto perform magic as they were able to stop the bleeding from my newly transplanted kidney as well as stabilize my breathing so I could gather enough oxygen to my brain, so it would prevent any long-lasting complications down the road.

If it were not for their astute professionalism and skill my overall outcome would have looked and felt a lot different. With the life-threatening issues under control, it was now up to me and my unrelenting resolve to take the second, third or whatever number of chances at life God has given me and do something with it. In my head, I knew the challenges that were laid out in front of me and none of them looked impossible to overcome or outright unattainable. Did I happen to have to go through my 19th surgery to repair my shattered shoulder with a metal plate and 7 screws, as well as stay immobile for 2 months while my right lung and ribs fully healed? Yes! Oddly however, I saw all of this as a necessity as it forced me to stay home and take the proper amount of time to have my face and body recuperate what it had lost.

Somehow, I was able to walk away from that collision with an array of injuries the doctors and myself knew I would be able to come back from. Call it fate or luck, but I played a game of chicken with death itself and came back alive to tell the story. No longer was it a question whether I was going to fully recover but now it was a question of whether I was going to be ready to compete at the upcoming college golf tryouts later that fall.

Chapter 33
One Wonderful Weekend

"The world can be full of challenges, so do your best to overcome the hard times and when the good times come, embrace them with everything you have." – Brandon Gandy

The summer was coming to an end and that meant my chance at playing collegiate golf was fast approaching even if it meant I had to compete for a spot on the team just 2 months after the crash. I had already forfeited my chance on the team a few years back when I had to forgo my first semester of college to receive a kidney and was not about to let another year slip by without even attempting to see what I could do.

The good news was California State University San Marcos held a tryout at the end of each August for one student to have an opportunity to play his way onto the team. This was the chance I had been waiting for ever since I stepped back onto a golf course after my kidney transplant on October 4th, 2004. At that time, the left side of my face had 85% recovered but I still found it difficult to see through my left eye without having some sort of blurry background. I still had a newly constructed metal shoulder and the stamina of a 90-year-old man who just walked up a full flight of stairs. Nevertheless, I managed to try out for the team and after 3 days and 54 holes of golf I would miss making the team by 10 shots. I felt dejected because deep down inside I really believed I was good enough to make that team and if it were not for some timely bad luck a couple months earlier, I would be enjoying my spot amongst my teammates and on my way to living out my dream of being a collegiate athlete. But, like my mom had always said, "everything happens for a reason," and in this case she was completely right because 6 months after my 19th surgery, I went under the knife for the 20th and 21st time. I was to have the orthopedic surgeon take out the metal plate and screws from my left shoulder and repair a crack in my right elbow caused by a piece of broken glass that was dislodged from the front driver side window.

It took me another 6 months to heal but this time around, I had fully recovered and was ready to try once more at making the CSUSM golf team 2 weeks before my sophomore year began. Alas, it wasn't meant to be as I would fall short by only 4 shots on the final day of tryouts and the true desolation of my new reality began to set in. I was 20 years old and for the third straight year since graduating high school I had missed out on cashing in on my opportunity to live out my childhood dream. I was seriously starting to doubt if it had ever been an actual possibility that someone of my stature could compete at the highest level of competition or was I destined to continue to climb to the foot of every summit just to be dragged back down without ever reaching the top? I had known failure and I had grown accustomed to disappointment but at no time had I ever been a quitter, so when I was denied my chance at redemption, I took it upon myself to find another way to prove my worth as a viable candidate for the CSUSM golf team.

They say what doesn't kill you makes you stronger and I have more than my fair share of stitches to prove it. Up until this point in my life I had always played in between surgeries, which didn't allow me the same opportunity to hone my craft as well as my fellow competitors but did help me develop a patience that couldn't be broken when under pressure. This would come to serve me well as I continued to register for one amateur tournament after another hoping to break through and show the golf world I truly belonged.

All year long the best amateur golfers from around the United States played in weekly tournaments around their local areas on the Golf Channel Amateur Tour trying to gain enough points and status to automatically qualify for the National Championship in Palm Springs, California. Sadly, by the time I was healthy enough to compete in such events, most of the season had already concluded. However, I was able to sneak into 5 tournaments at the very end of the season, which had been the minimum requirement to gain entry into the tour championship.

Despite being winless and with no points accumulated all season, I truly believed I could still win. Which was a good thing, because barring anything else would disqualify me from playing in the National Championship. The thing was, California was the most competitive state in the whole country and whoever won the State Championship, no matter if they hadn't won anything all year, was guaranteed an automatic exemption into the National Amateur Tour Championship and a top 100 player ranking. The top 100 player ranking was what I had my eyes set on because if I could place myself somewhere among the best 100 amateur golfers in the country, I could use that status to gain access to a multitude of college golf programs. The opportunity was there, and the goal was set, now it was time to see if I was ready to step up and take my golf game to the next level.

Don't get me wrong, if there were any odds out on who had a chance at winning the California Golf Channel Amateur Tour Championship in 2006, I would have been 140/1. This was because I was essentially a no name competitor who was coming off a couple major injuries and wasn't even good enough to make his local college golf team. Yet, the one thing I did have going for me was that I had finally gotten healthy for the first time since my junior year in high school. I was also playing the underdog role where out of 144 golfers competing, I was one of the only golfers being overlooked. This ate at me and drove me to wake up early every morning before class to practice, so I was ready for when the time came, and I needed to be at my very best. That day would soon arrive in the first week of November when I would begin my quest at Sycuan Resort in Southern California for a 36-hole state championship.

The first day of the competition started off well as I finagled my way around the Willow course and finished firing an above average 2 over par, 74. Remarkably, this landed me in the top 20 as the course was playing extremely tough and players who teed off in the afternoon found it much harder to score with the 20 mph wind gusts. This was where I felt my luck had finally started to turn around, as I missed the high windstorms because of my early morning tee time and was rewarded with a pairing in the final 4 groups the next day. That night I tried to go to bed early because I wanted to be fresh for my final round but then came a familiar pain in my lower abdomen in which I knew immediately I wouldn't be getting any rest for the foreseeable future. My childhood stomach pains reared their ugly head right in the middle of the biggest tournament of my life and there was nothing I or anyone else could do about it. All night I stayed up throwing up into a trash can and curling up into a ball as I tried to vanquish the misery. All my efforts came to no avail, as the agony I was feeling was not to be relinquished and so it was I found myself stepping up to the first tee on the final round of the Tour Championship with an hour and a half of sleep and a dull aching pain in the pit of my stomach.

Conversely though, this was nothing new as I had gone my whole life playing through pain and this little stomachache was not going to have any effect on my ability to compete this particular afternoon. So, I started off with a bang, I birdied the first 5 out of 7 holes I played. Never in my life had I experienced the type of flow I was currently going through as it was like every shot I hit couldn't miss. I've heard it explained by other athletes as a type of zone a player goes to where they are on so much fire everything around comes to a standstill and it's just them playing a game they have practiced ever since they were kids. It was an 'out of body' experience for me because I wasn't expecting it and for it to occur during one of the most important rounds of my life was truly mystical. I remember thinking sometime between holes 8 and 9 that I was probably pretty close to being in the lead and if I can just hang on during that back nine, I might actually pull this thing off. My mom was there cheering me on as my dad was up in L.A. supporting my sister while she played in a water polo tournament for the UCLA Bruins. If there was one wish I could have today, it would be to have had my dad there to watch me play the final 9 holes of that pressure cooking round. Thankfully, my mom was there in full support and as I made the turn I was greeted with the knowledge that I had just taken over sole possession of the overall lead.

This was the moment I had been preparing for ever since I first played out this same scenario in my head as a young kid. It was like my dream was being played out in front of my eyes and I had a front row seat to the final act. As I drew closer to the 10th hole all I could picture was hoisting up the trophy with the commissioner of the tour shaking my hand in celebratory congratulations. Not exactly the image you wanted to have as I still had the back nine of golf to play with 143 golfers looking up at me searching for answers on how they were going to bring this young kid from Rancho Bernardo back down to earth. Just like that my magical run came to an end, as I would go on to bogey the next 2 holes and surrender my 2-shot lead with just 7 holes to play. I recall being very angry with myself, not on the outside for any of my competitors to see, but internally because I was frustrated with the attitude I was currently projecting onto myself. I had convinced myself as though I had already lost and there was nothing I could do about it. I had allowed the pressure of the situation to dictate the end result and I told myself that I was not about to cower to a measly game of golf that I was lucky enough to still be playing. This was my time and if I wanted to fulfill a promise I made to myself after I woke up from my second life- altering affair I needed to refocus and take back control of this contest.

Wishing it into existence was no longer an option, now it was solely on my newly repaired shoulders to get the job done and I could start by going on to birdy the 13th hole. With one perfectly timed swing, I was able to shape the ball from right to left where it landed on the front side of the right fringe and came to rest just 6 feet from the cup. I went on to make birdie and regain lone possession of first place over the next few holes to capture once again a 1 shot lead. All that was left was a daunting long par 5 where it would take all my fortitude to squash down my nerves and simply finish out the tournament with par.

    Somehow, I was able to find my way onto the green and with a 3-foot putt to win the tournament. It must have felt like an eternity for my mother who was anxiously waiting to see if I was going to be able to finish this thing off, so she could finally wrap me in her arms and tell me how proud she was of me. For me though, it was the quietest 2 minutes of my life as everything around me ceased to exist and the sounds of the commotion around me disappeared. All that I could focus on was the ball in front me and how I was going to get it to its final resting place just 3 feet away.

    With a slight touch from the face of my putter, the sweet sensation of sound flooded back into my ears with a clatter of ball meeting cup. I had done it; I was the new California Golf Channel Amateur Tour Champion and with it, the status of a top 100 amateur golfer. I had finally validated what my parents and I had always thought, and that was the fact that I could compete with the best golfers in the business, as long as I could stay healthy and keep away from any more hospital visits. I had just opened the door to a whole new set of possibilities, and I was eagerly awaiting to see where this next journey in life was going to take me.

Chapter 34
Valentine's Day Special

"It is with trifles, and when he is off guard, that a man best reveals his character" – Arthur Schopenhauer

Who knew one weekend of golf could change a person's fortune from being a mere spectator to a full-blown participant when it came to the game of success. In just a little under 72 hours, the news of my win had spread to the top ranks of every local college recruiter in Southern California. My name had vaulted all the way from obscurity to inconceivable significance and all of a sudden, I went from having no choices at hand, to a bucket full of golf programs hoping to add me to their rosters. The only disadvantage was by the time I won my first substantial tournament, the fall semester had already been coming to an end. This meant, I'd have to either transfer in the middle of the year to whichever university I chose to play for and sit out until I was eligible to compete, or join the CSUSM team, so I could immediately play in the upcoming spring season.

The answer was obvious, my dream of playing golf for a university was about to become a reality and I couldn't think of a better place to make it happen than right here in my hometown of San Diego, California.

The next two months felt like a whirlwind as I was officially offered a spot on the CSUSM golf team and everything that came along with being a student-athlete fell into place. The first of many things I had to get in order to be ready for our team's first contest was to pass a sports physical that said I was healthy enough to compete in any NAIA sanctioned event. Typically, when it came to most 19-20-year-old men being evaluated to compete in the game of golf, this step had just been about semantics. However, because I was no ordinary young college recruit this process had taken 3 weeks and 3 separate doctor approvals to finally get me eligible to compete at the collegiate level.

Once the athletic department had my official eligibility status verified, the fall semester had come to an end and all the students were sent home for winter break. That New Years I remember spending the whole night with Sherry at a party downtown, absolutely elated with the understanding I was about to live out my childhood dream in less than a short couple of weeks. We were celebrating the beginning of 2007 together and we both saw a bright future ahead of us. When the day finally arrived when I was to meet the team for the very first time, I was so nervous with anticipation I thought I was going to jump out of my skin. Like most first time recruits I was given a tour of the entire athletic training center, which included the gymnasium, locker room, recovery center, golf course, study hall, cafeteria, and my personal favorite player lounge. This is where all the athletes, like the basketball, soccer, baseball, and volleyball players all hung out when they were not practicing or sleeping back at the dorms. I would come to meet some of my lifelong best friends here and it all started when I was first introduced to the team inside CSUSM's yoga studio.

Being the new kid on the block and not having the benefit of experiencing the first day of practice with the rest of my teammates from the semester before, I was left to try and figure out how to transition from just being a student to becoming a student-athlete on my own. Fortunately, I had competed against 4 of the older players on the team while I was in high school, which gave me a little insight into each of their personalities and how I could come to fit in. One of those ways was taking the lead during our yoga sessions as nobody else on the team had as much experience with trying to enhance the strength and recovery of their bodies as much as me. I was accustomed to having hours of long treatment sessions from my days of being sick and injured, so when it came to 6 am training days, I had usually been the first one in and the last one to leave. I could tell my work ethic helped garner respect from both my coaches and teammates and eased any tension that came from being the newcomer on a veteran-led team. I had thought to myself; I had already overcome all the odds of just making the team but now that I was here, I might as well give it my best effort at trying to make the starting lineup.

Each college program has its own way of deciding which players were going to compete in the tournaments and who were the unlucky souls that had to stay at home. For the CSUSM golf program, the coaches would host a 1-day qualification before each event to see which 5 golfers were going to make the starting rotation. In my first attempt to crack the top 5, I beat out 2 seniors, 2 juniors and a sophomore to earn the right to travel with the team to play in the San Francisco University Invitational the following week. My family was so excited when I told them about the news over the phone, they insisted I make the 45-minute drive back home so we could all celebrate at our favorite hole-in-the-wall, Marieta's. My uncle "Big Mitch" even had a celebratory golf cake made up to commemorate my crowning achievement and everyone from my immediate family were there. The very next night happened to be Valentine's Day when Sherry and I had plans to go see the romantic comedy of the year, *P.S. I Love You*. Sherry had been looking forward to seeing this film in theaters all month and I figured if I was going to watch a chick-flick, then I might as well watch it on the most romantic day of the year. I had planned the whole night days before, where we would start off with dinner across the street at a local favorite of ours, Pat and Oscars. You haven't tasted a more delicious breadstick than what the big O can conjure up, especially if you pair it with their house chopped salad, you're guaranteed to nail any date night. After indulging ourselves with some fine Italian food, we made the quick walk over to grab a bag of popcorn and a box of Reese's pieces before the first premieres flickered on. Everything was going according to plan, up until I heard a deep rumbling sound coming from the inside of my stomach and I knew then, this night was about to take an unexpected turn for the worse.

It would later be said that no one could have ever predicted what was about to happen next, but one thing was for certain, I had never been more embarrassed or deathly sick than the night I almost saw the cult classic, *P.S. I Love You*. Not the aurora of Sherry's blossom flower perfume or my 20 years of stubborn defiance could halt the force of nature that overtook my body's will of self-preservation, as I succumbed to the war my large intestines were raging on my lower abdomen. Out came a distinct mix of last night's celebratory dinner and this evening's pasta sauce across the carpeted floors of Edwards Cinema.

In a desperate attempt to rectify the situation I apologized to my date as I tried to downplay the severity of how much pain I was currently in. To my good fortune, Sherry was not having any of it, as she grabbed me by the arm and insisted we'd go to the hospital. At first, I acted as though I had everything in complete control and there was no need to get any doctors involved, but as we reached the parking lot and I had vomited for the 3rd straight time since leaving our seats, I was resigned to the fact that there was something seriously wrong. Sherry's intuition once again proved to be correct as I was to be omitted into Sharp Hospital's emergency room where I was immediately rushed into surgery for the 22nd time.

It didn't matter that I was lined up to play in my first collegiate tournament the following week or even that I finally met the girl of my dreams, all that mattered, was once again through no fault of my own I found myself laying on a gurney, staring up at that oh so familiar popcorn coated ceiling, praying this wouldn't be the last thing I ever saw, again. I couldn't tell you how I managed to find someone who somehow didn't mind being in a relationship with someone who was constantly battling to stay alive, but I did. Not only did Sherry not mind, but she had also been an active participant in saving my life on a few separate occasions. In this case, if I had not made it to the hospital for another 8 hours, the inside of my large intestine would have burst, catastrophically diminishing any chance of my survival.

What was essentially told to my mom and dad once they had arrived at the ER, was that my large intestine had developed an excessive amount of scar tissue within my digestive track system, which caused an unbreakable blockage that only could be fixed by surgically removing a foot long of my internal organ. To none of our knowledge at the time, this specific operation was highly risky mostly because of the complexity of the operation itself, but also because the colorectal surgeon was dissecting on a person who was immunocompromised and had already been through as many life-or-death incidences as one person should ever have to experience.

The stress of the situation must have been unimaginable as my life laid in the hands of one man and his expertise in alleviating the pressure that had been slowly cultivating for the past two decades. Within that same moment it occurred to my dad that every night I had stayed up complaining about how much my stomach hurt, it had all been caused by the growing blockage within my intestines. The numerous surgeries I had undergone during my adolescence had come back to rear their ugly head and now it was up to the highly trained professionals at Sharp Memorial hospital to put on their capes and come to my rescue yet again.

Chapter 35
The Decision

"Always go with the choice that scares you the most, because that's the one that is going to help you grow." – Caroline Myss

Distraught with the awareness that my life was no longer in my control, I had closed my eyes with the solemnity that I had just lost everything good in my life to an invisible inevitability which had haunted me ever since I drew my first initial breath. I was destined to repeat the same pattern which had been plaguing me for my whole entire life and I couldn't see any way from getting out beneath the weight of self-destruction. The inside of a hospital building was becoming such a common occurrence, the people who cared for me the most stopped sending me get well cards to my home and instead, forwarded them on to my primary physicians.

Like a cruel joke created by the maker of this unforgiving world, I had survived my latest run in with death itself and had woken up to hear the summary of the past 12 hours. Not only were the events from the previous night's escapades described as being one the highest intensity and most volatile environments that this one doctor in particular had ever bear witness to, but he would also describe it as being the most magnificent piece of artistry in his 20+ year career. It had been obvious that the primary goal was to keep me alive and release the barricade that was preventing the food I was eating from making its way through my mangled up digestive system, but the way in which he was able to carefully maneuver around the unfamiliar lacerations from my previous encounters was what separated my case from all the rest.

He went on to say, he relied heavily on the assistance of his team to make the critical calls to my former surgeons, so he could get an exact picture of what he could and couldn't do to pull off such an unusually intricate procedure. As I laid there listening to him rattling off the laundry list of technical jargon that only a health professional with 8 years of medical school could possibly understand, I felt disengaged and completely numb to the reality of my new surroundings. Could that have been simply a result of just being given enough morphine to knock out a baby rhino and not the state of mind I was ordained to familiarize myself with after being punched in the stomach by Mike Tyson himself, maybe?

All I could say for sure was that in that moment I had been left alone to the misery of my own thoughts and fears, scrambling to find any escape from the prison of pain I had trapped myself in, as I searched for peace that seemingly never would come. It took another couple of days post-surgery for me to fully grasp the effects of what this physical setback had cost me in relation to my current academic and athletic undertakings. The most obvious and detrimental of them had to be the immediate forfeiture of my life's goal of playing in any NCAA Division 1 college golf tournament. Not to be overshadowed, was also the extended leave I was forced to take from my current enrollment at CSUSM, as it would be another 3 weeks before I would be released back home and under strict instructions to minimize any excessive movement that could potentially cause me more harm. I was once again delegated to house arrest, where I would be confined for the next 3 months and was forced to ruminate on what I was going to do next.

The force of nature that embodies the pattern of everything that happens in this world had not been content with just one imminent life or death scenario but was resolved to having the kind of sick humor only fate itself could invoke on one's imagination. With the skill of an expert craftsman and the ingenuity of a genius, the doctor who saved my life just a few weeks ago came to me with a recommendation in which he believed was a necessity if I wanted to end the unpredictable flare ups my body was repeatedly besieging on itself.

The choices were living with the uncertainty of not knowing if this would be my last medical phenomenon and dodging yet another date with the scapple or consciously choosing to go back under the knife and repairing the underlying nuisance to all my historical complications. It was the type of question in which the smartest people in the room willingly passed over the power to the young man who had to bear the consequences to whatever choice he ended up going with and to be fair, it was the right thing to do.

I knew all the scenarios that could possibly play out and the amount of risk that went into electing to have or not have the additional surgeries my doctors strongly encouraged me to undergo. The funny thing was, I had already been given this choice once before. A long time ago, when I chose to not go through with the experimental reshaping of both my already repaired clubfoot and the additional intestinal surgery necessary to ensure my long-term overall health. At that time, the thought was that I had been through enough pain, and any additional non-essential surgery was just too much to ask from an already broken-down adolescent.

In the end, both resolutions would have separate impacts on my life years down the road, as it would turn out that my feet would grow large enough to be able to sustain the heavy pressure I placed on them from an active lifestyle. On the contrary, allocating not to patch-up the slowly forming enigma that was known to be my internal organs had resulted in me sitting back in the medical office a decade later, pondering if I should go through with the same procedure. I was tired of the endless fight I was constantly partaking in that came with having 20+ surgeries, so I clutched onto the hope the specialists were selling and I agreed to put my body on the line for one more go around. However, I told my parents and Sherry that I would only do it if two stipulations were met. The first of them being, the world-renowned pediatric surgeon, Dr. Alberto Pena, who performed the surgeries that enhanced my way of living so many years ago, would be the doctor to operate on me. The second had to do with the fact that I was turning 21 in less than a month and before I chose to take a gamble on the expertise of my superior contemporaries, I wanted to make a few wagers of my own in Sin City aka Las Vegas.

Chapter 36
First Class Trip to 21

"On the roller coaster of life, your 21st birthday is like being at the top of the first giant hill with your hands in the air and no lap bar." – Greg Tamblyn

If I were destitute to being deprived of having any fun during the summer after which I had turned 21, I was at least going to do everything within my power to throw myself one hell of a going away party. Even though I was still recovering from the devastation of my unforeseen theater mishap, I was able to convince my doctors to postpone my 23rd and 24th intestinal reconstruction surgeries until after my 21st birthday.

Unfortunately, this meant I was pushing out my operation until early May, which I would soon come to learn was when Dr. Pena would be traveling around the world speaking at lectures on the great advances in modern medicine they have made within the past 20 years. I'd also come to realize my birthday landed on a Monday, which resulted in me delaying my trip to Vegas until the following weekend. Put these two things together and the window in which Dr. Pena was still able to perform my operation and I was to celebrate my 21st birthday in the city of lights was rapidly shrinking. But, when there's a will, there's always a way and for me, I was dead set on making sure my dreams became a reality even if it meant I personally had to force them into being. So, with a little finagling and a couple of compromises I was able to secure my Vegas vacation for the weekend after I turned 21 with the expectation being, I would make it to Cincinnati and be ready for my Monday morning appointment at 7am.

It was about time to abandon the safety of my parent's house where I had been held up ever since I had been released from the care of Sharp Memorial hospital nearly 3 months ago, but first I had to get my life in order and say my goodbyes to the people I cared for. Like my kidney transplant before, I would be flying hundreds of miles away with the hopes of coming back some time in the future with a story to tell and a gnarly scar to show off. But unlike my trip up to Stanford, my real concern was not whether the surgeries would ultimately be successful or not, but how my girlfriend of just under 2 years was going to handle the situation of her boyfriend being gone for an extended period of time.

Who could tell how someone in her position would respond to the fact that her boyfriend was proving to be made more out of a porcelain doll than an X-Men character who had the cool superpower of being able to heal from all the injuries he was repeatedly putting himself through? My trepidations were quickly put at ease when a couple weeks before we were set to leave on our trip, Sherry asked me if I had ever considered moving out of my parents' house and possibly living with her. Now, at that moment in time you have to understand I had never once contemplated meeting another human being that wanted to solely cohabitate with just me and was willing to grow to love all the baggage and challenges I was sure to bring along. This is why when we were sitting outside in the middle of the In N Out parking lot dreaming about what our future would look like if we were to ever live under the same roof, I made a vow to myself right then and there that I was going to marry this girl one day. I had lived with so much uncertainty in my life that when I knew I had a good thing going I never hesitated to let her know I was in it for the long haul. With my love life secured and a future to look forward to, all that was left to do was to have one last hurrah and prepare myself for what I hoped to be the final surgical battle I was destined to come across.

One thing I would certainly say is true when it comes to describing my family is they sure know how to throw a party. With the expectation this was to be my ultimate send-off, my parents, friends, and close relatives took it upon themselves to do everything humanly possible and under Nevada state law to make sure I was going to have the best birthday celebration ever. My mom called in all her favors from working in the entertainment industry for the past 20 years and she was able to secure tickets, dinner reservations, hotel stays and VIP access to some of the top restaurants, night clubs and attractions Las Vegas had to offer. Everyone I was close to had flown out for the special occasion and for the next 3 days I had never had more fun and felt more loved by the people who were there than I did during that unforgettable weekend. Sadly though, the party eventually had to come to an end where I was to fly out of Vegas to the city of Cincinnati and notch yet another surgery under my belt.

Unlike some of the previous surgeries I had gone through, I had no doubts about whether I was going to come out of this one a better version of my former self, because this time around I had a new sense of confidence in who I was and what I was planning to do once I was determined to make my highly anticipated comeback. On the day of the operation, I remember smiling and telling jokes with everyone around as though this was just another simple root canal and I'd soon be up and out of there in no time. If only I was so lucky, 8 and half hours and two separate incisions later I was out of the OR and back in my hospital room reeling from the sheer magnitude of what had just occurred. I can honestly say now, having your belly opened up so a doctor could poke around and rearrange all of your inner intestines with a pair of scissors and an Exacto knife is not as simple as just another root canal.

Maybe it was a false sense of reality or my preconceived notion that somehow this one time everyone's expectations for how bad it was actually going to be had been grossly overstated, but to my displeasure I was not expecting the level of pain that coincided with what had just taken place. I was beaten up and it felt like someone had just taken a jackhammer to the middle of my stomach and I was just now noticing the pain for the very first time. This would last for an additional 2 weeks as I would be monitored every other hour by the medical staff on call, just to make sure my body was recovering at the speed that they had foreseen and wouldn't suddenly fall into a state of shock.

I had passed the test and the miracle everyone had been praying for had suddenly been answered with an overwhelming amount of success. For the next 15 years after Dr. Pena's extraordinary gift, I would never experience another intestinal bowel obstruction ever again. I could never repay or thank Dr. Pena and all the doctors and nurses enough for taking away a pain that I'd been living with for such a long period of time. With some Wolverine rejuvenation I would now be able to heal up just in time for the upcoming fall tryouts. I still had some unfinished business that needed to be made right and hopefully this time around the 4th attempt at becoming a collegiate athlete was exactly what the doctor had ordered.

Chapter 37
Triumphant

"Success consists of going from failure to failure without loss of enthusiasm." – Winston Churchill

Once I was able to get back home from my month long stay in the great state of Ohio, I decided to use the rest of the next 100 days to get in the best shape of my life while dialing in my golf game, so I was ready for when it came time to win back my spot on the CSUSM team. In between taking daily medications, weekly blood draws, and the occasional trips back up to the bay area for a few biopsy procedures, I had spent the rest of the summer 100% focused on not straying away from my rehab schedule.

By the time August rolled around I had rediscovered the confidence I had once lost and became more determined than ever to prove to myself I was still capable of achieving the goals I had set out to accomplish so long ago. I knew it wasn't going to be easy as I had already missed making this same team twice before, but with the tryouts being held in my own backyard, I had a sneaky suspicion things would turn out a little different this time around. Even though it was a real bummer that I had to forgo my place on the team due to injury, I grew to become content with the fact that at least I was given an opportunity to earn my way back onto the team the following year. I was also pleased to hear that instead of just one opening being extended out to everyone who tried out, a total of 2 walk-ons would be given a bid to play in the upcoming season.

This new piece of information tremendously helped ease the pressure I felt in having to be perfect on the day of tryouts and what I believed allowed me to loosen up and swing freely for the next couple of days. With 20 contenders all vying for only 2 spots, the competition was at an all-time high and it was going to take a solid performance on my part if I was going to have any shot at finishing in the top 2. Nevertheless, I knew San Luis Rey Downs Country Club like the back of my hand and at no other point up until then had I ever felt like I was going to do something as special, as what I was about to do over the next 3 days.

It all started with me firing a 74 on day one, a 75 on day two and another 74 on day three where by the time I knew it, or another freak accident could take me out of competition, I had found my way back onto the CSUSM golf team. This time however, there would be no big party or family get together as I was not going to let myself celebrate anything until I had achieved my final objective. That time would soon come as the very next week the whole team would find out every starting position was up for grabs and whoever shot the 5 lowest scores over the next 2 days would automatically claim their plane ticket to the first tournament of the year.

I liked my odds once the coach announced how he was going to select the starting 5 because I knew unless I absolutely blew it, I could beat out 4 of the 9 players left on the team. It wasn't because I had been much better than the rest of my teammates but because I knew there had been a high amount of turnover from the previous season, which left our 2007-2008 team with little experience and only 1 remaining senior. The lack of familiarity and numerous fresh additions meant that our team was pretty raw and not even the coaches on hand could tell for sure how high our potential could climb. One thing was for sure, it was going to be hard for any team, be them full of Seniors or not, to emulate the kind of success of last year's squad. After being forced from competing in the 2006-2007 season because of injury, that very same team led by 4 Seniors went onto win the NAIA regionals tournament and also come in 6th place at Nationals, the highest ever finish for any CSUSM golf team still today.

I digress though because that was then, and this was now, and the main focus was to make my dreams come true by creating memories that would last a lifetime. So, when the sun rose from the East over the tall Palomar mountains and I could smell the freshly cut grass from the first early morning mow, I hit the ground running and never looked back. I took advantage of the opportunity given to me with pure determination to never give up on chasing what I really wanted out of life and was rewarded with capturing the prize that had been alluding me for so many years. After winning my starting spot on the roster all that there was left to do was to patiently wait for the first tournament to begin, so I could finally lay to rest the notion that I was never going to play in a collegiate event.

The Santa Clara Invitational was known amongst many to be one of colleges biggest West Coast tournaments of the year, where some of the top teams from around the country came to play because of the high level of competition they were guaranteed to face once they got there. Being a rookie and not realizing the amount of pressure that came with being a low-level participant in such a highly competitive field as what the Santa Clara Invitational brought with it, I approached the event with the same amount of swagger and self confidence that I'd had when I was playing just another round of golf with my pops on a late Saturday afternoon. If I had known future PGA professionals like Ricky Fowler, Jamie Lovemark and Blake Trimble were in the field I might have crumbled amongst the sheer weight of their combined celebrity personas.

Thankfully, my ignorance of the situation had played to my advantage as the only thing that was giving me any sort of butterflies before the round was how this was going to be the first time playing competitive golf in front of my parents, since I went through my kidney transplant 3 years ago. It was a moment I would never forget, as both my dad who first put a club in my hand and my mom who selflessly offered her kidney to save my life got to witness their son go toe to toe with some of the best golfers the game had to offer. Ironically, the scale in which CSUSM was looked upon as the heavy underdog because of its NAIA status compared to its much more esteemed NCAA division 1 counterpart, had little effect on the ultimate result of where our team would end up after 3 rounds of competition.

When all was said and done, we would come in 7th amongst 26 division 1 and NAIA teams, with me leading the way with a top 20 finish. Later that year, I would come to see myself place as high as 3rd but would always look back at my first college performance as one of my all-time favorite memories. My junior season as a member of the CSUSM golf team came with many highs and very few lows, one of those being nominated as the team captain by my fellow teammates. Considering it was my first time being nominated and I was well admired by my coaches and colleagues, I had been chosen to lead our team into battle week in and week out for the next two years.

If somebody would have said after I was first told I was going to have to forgo my first semester of college because I was in chronic kidney failure and needed an immediate kidney transplant, that 3 years later not only would I be starting for one of the best college golf programs in Southern California, but I was also nominated as their team captain, I would have never believed them. Thankfully, I remember hearing a phrase from a famous movie scene, "life is like a box of chocolates, you never know whatcha gonna get."

Getting a chance to be a part of such an extraordinary great group of guys during my time playing at California State University San Marcos is something that I hold close to my heart and has produced some of the best friendships that I continue to have to this very day. One of those friendships is with a guy I consider to be one of my closest friends, Curtis Gruidl, who I first met the following year during my Senior season. We immediately hit it off and if it wasn't for our time playing together on the same team in 2008-2009, I would have missed out on getting to know one the most interesting and thoughtful individuals I have ever met.

Throughout my 6 years in college, yes, I said 6, I had come to compete for a NAIA regional championship, meet the love of my life, my best friend, obtain a corporate finance degree, and still find time to take on 2 internship programs at Northwestern Mutual and Cobra Puma Golf. Which I can say with confidence both came to be very helpful in allowing me to gain the experience necessary for a successful start to my life after college. However, it would also be the passing of my players ability test (PAT) which allowed me to turn professional in the game of golf, that really brought me to a fork in the road when I first began my transition into the real world.

My time as a student/athlete at CSUSM saw me grow from a young naïve teenager to a well diverse and battle tested man. I came to embrace all my limitations and was able to draw back on my past endeavors to overcome every challenge this last half decade brought with it. Up next was adulthood and as much as I thought I was ready for all the new responsibilities and obligations that came with it, I was not nearly as prepared for what the next chapter in my life had in store for me.

Pictures
Adulthood

"If you can't fly, then run. If you can't run, then walk. If you can't walk, then crawl. But whatever you do, you have to keep moving."
– Martin Luther King Jr.

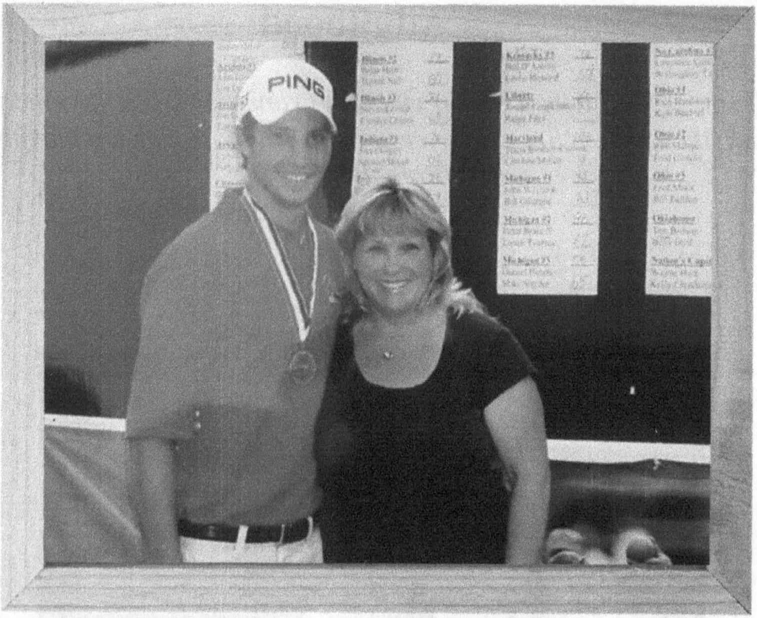
PING

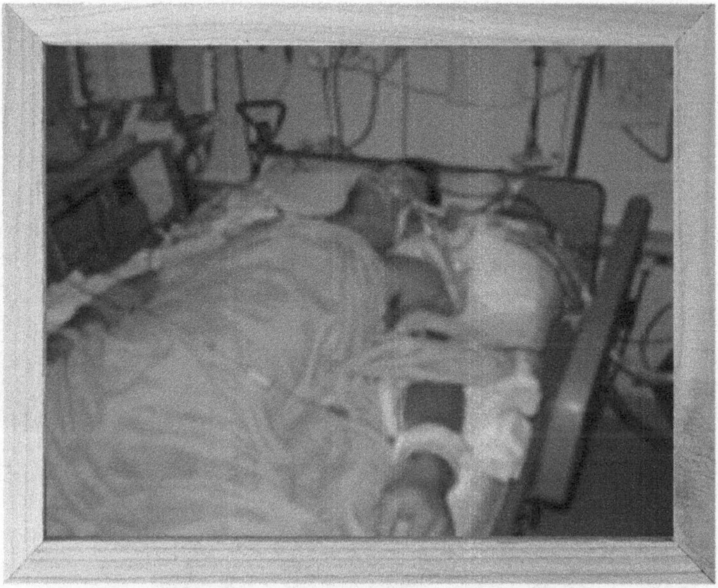

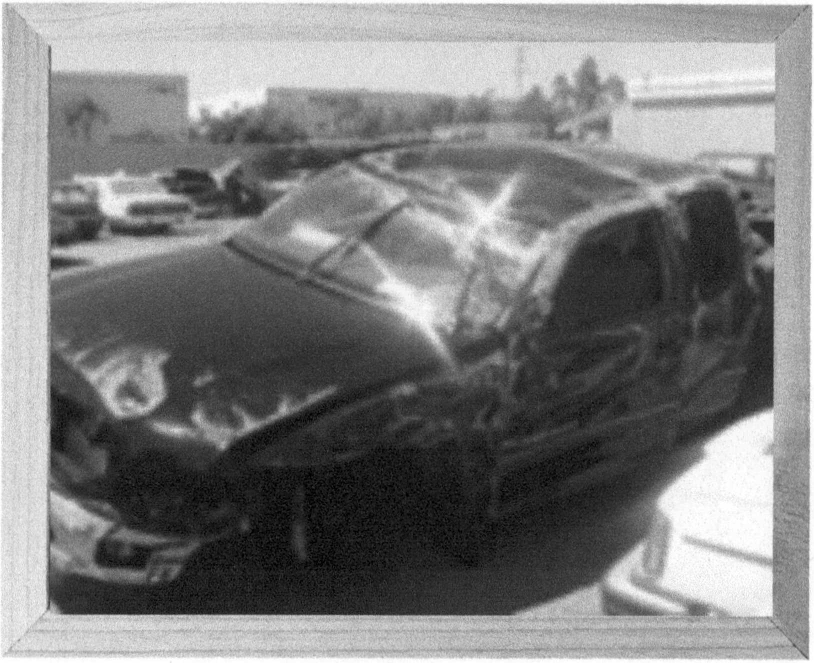

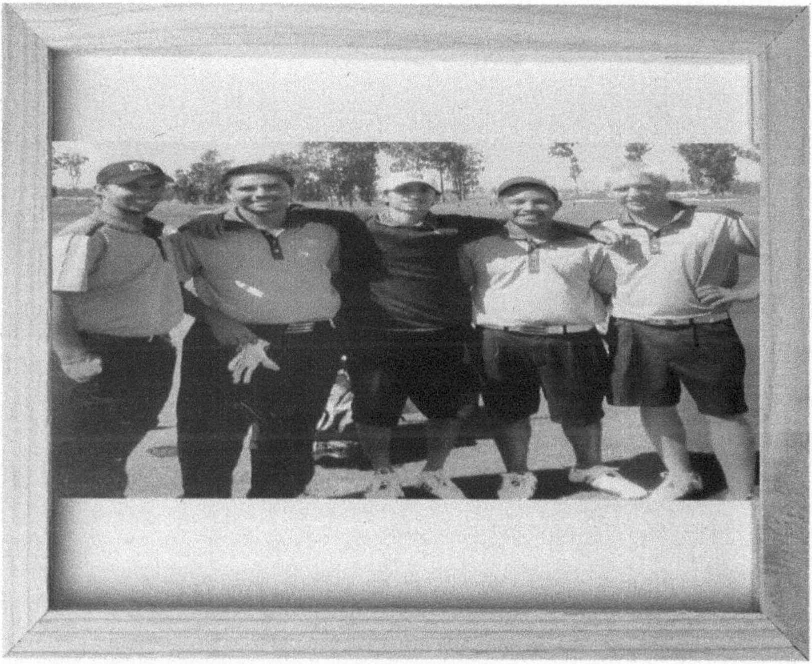

Part Four:
Lost and Found

"Maturity is when your world opens up and you realize that you are not the center of it." – M.J. Croan

Chapter 38
Is this Real Life?

The summer of 2011 saw me turn 25 years of age and with it a change in lifestyle that could only be described as a complete whirlwind. I had escaped the irrevocable challenge my body had rendered on me since my last meeting with death 4 years ago and with the presence of my eternal guardian angel by my side, I was finally able to enjoy the fruits of my labor. The power of perseverance stole me from an endless cycle of solitude and incorporated me with a regime filled with meaningful purpose. I was now a graduate of California State University of San Marcos and holding a diploma that declared I had been considered an expert in the field of Corporate Finance.

I was now looked upon as someone who was fully prepared to embark on his life's journey into the workforce even if deep down inside, I still had no idea who I was or what I even wanted to do. However, what I did know was the small 2-bedroom condo in which I had cunningly purchased 2 years prior with the help of a few roommates and the luck of an economic crash that hasn't been seen since the great depression was about to welcome my newly engaged fiancé into the picture. My prolonged stay as a bachelor was about to come to an end, and it was time for me to embrace adulthood and all the new responsibilities that came with it. One task in particular was building up enough courage to ask Sherry's father for her hand in marriage with the complete knowledge that he had no clue who I was and that I had been dating her for the past 5 years.

This anomaly was not solely the fault of her father wanting Sherry and me to suffer in exile for the rest of eternity but because of the simple fact of not knowing how to integrate 2000 years of middle eastern culture with modern day American societal norms. See, Sherry was a first-generation Iranian American citizen who wasn't raised with the Western philosophy where it had been more common to date a person you planned on marrying and introducing them to their family well beforehand. Quite the contrary, as I would soon come to find out as it was more mutually acceptable in the eyes of middle eastern civilization that if one desired to marry a daughter of someone within their community, it was first to be decided by the father of the bride and then negotiated amongst the two families thereafter.

Resistant to this approach to love and matrimony I found myself hesitant to dive into my future wife's ethos as it was different from my own, which could only mean it was wrong and shouldn't be accepted as truth. Yet, my upbringing demanded from me that I received her father's blessing and so after nearly a half decade of avoiding the big elephant in the room, I was to swallow my pride and make a conscious effort to show this man who I had never met before, how much I truly loved his daughter. There was only one problem, I didn't really know how to get in contact with him and I was quickly running out of time.

I had strategically set everything up months beforehand in the hopes of asking Sherry for her hand in marriage, as I bought the ring, scheduled our trip to Las Vegas and even orchestrated a hot air balloon ride on the day of our 5-year dating anniversary. The one thing that I kept putting off until later be it because I was waiting for my maturity to kick in or I was just simply petrified on the possibility of hearing the word no, was introducing myself to the man that the love my life held in such high regard, Babajan "Bobby" Mirzai. I had procrastinated this act of respect up until the final week before I was supposed to fly out to Vegas and had left myself very little options on how I was going to execute my plan. So, the best I had come up with was to show up at Bobby's place of work, which I knew because I had overheard Sherry talking about it a couple of times before, and kindly ask him if he would like to have lunch with me so we could get to know each other a little bit better.

    You're probably wondering why I didn't just wait until he got off work and went to his house to have such a personal conversation with the man, and to that I would say, good question. My immediate thought was I didn't want anyone else to be home when I spoke with him and thought I'd have a better chance at just having a one-on-one conversation if I was able to catch him on his lunch break. Needless to say, no plan was going to be ideal so I went with the one that I thought would be best if things went downhill and I had to get out of there quickly. This is how I had found myself standing outside in the parking lot of Scripps Memorial Hospital asking a man who I had just recently met if it was ok if I could marry his daughter.

    Sweating bullets and anxiously awaiting any kind of acknowledgement that he had actually heard what I had just muttered, I sheepishly smiled and braced myself for what was about to come. "Come here Brandon, Let's take a walk." Just like that, Bobby had his arm around my shoulders, and we were walking in a circle around the hospital for what felt like an eternity.

    "SOOO Brandon, what did Sharareh say?"

    "Oh, no Mr. Mirzai, I haven't actually asked Sherry yet, I wanted to ask you first."

"Hmmm, well thank you for coming all the way down here to talk to me, but I'm not completely sure yet. I will talk with Sherry and Afsaneh (her stepmother) and we can have you and your family over for dinner sometime soon."

Too stunned to fully understand what had just happened, I nodded my head and said, "That would be great sir, thank you for speaking with me and inviting me over to your house. I'm really looking forward to it."

Then, before I even knew it, we were walking our separate ways and it dawned on me I had just been politely turned away. Was that a no or some different kind of way of saying yes? Is he really going to talk with Sherry and possibly let her in on the secret I have been planning to unveil for the past 4 months? After just 10 minutes with the father of the woman who I wanted to spend the rest of my life with, I was left with more questions than answers.

For the next 3 days as Sherry and I were celebrating our 5-year dating anniversary in Las Vegas I was nervously thinking was today going to be the day when Bobby called Sherry and filled her in on the upcoming proposal? But nothing ever came and just like I had envisioned the whole day going in my head 1000 times before, I dropped down to one knee, 10,000 feet in the air and asked the most beautiful person in the world if she'd marry me.

Now, here is where I would like to stop and preface, through many joyful tears and a smile that could stop a man dead in his tracks, Sherry did nod her head with a yes, however, the first words that actually came out of her mouth were, "What did my dad say?"

To this, I simply replied, "He said he'd talk to you."

Like I said nothing at all, she let her worries and curiosity go right out the window, or in this case the hot air balloon and embraced me with a hug as she let herself be swept away in the moment. I will say this though, as soon as we touched down on solid ground, the first-person Sherry wanted to call to share the exciting news with her father.

"Dad, I'm engaged! We are so excited, but can you please tell me why you didn't just say yes, Brandon, you can marry my daughter?"

To his credit and to my lack of cultural sensitivity, he explained that he didn't feel like it was his place to say yes or no to who Sherry could or couldn't marry. As he went on to elaborate, it had become quite obvious that his intentions were sincere as he was not trying to be the gatekeeper to his daughter's heart but instead trust that whatever decision Sherry made was going to work out for the best. Which is why, I instantly grew to have the utmost respect for him and craved to learn more about the type of man he had become.

From that moment on it was like I had been a part of their family for years and for the next 14 months leading up to the wedding I had been inundated with Persian culture and their family history. Sherry and I would go on to tie the knot the following year on August 6th, 2011, and would begin living together as a family with our new dog, Hooch. The world I thought I knew was starting to change and it was quite apparent after my time spent with the Mirzais there was still a lot this 25-year-old needed to learn about being a husband and caring for the people I loved most. I would soon come to find this out as now, I was not only responsible for myself but for the safety and well-being of my entire family, which meant it was time for me to step up and find a way to financially provide for them.

Chapter 39
Welcome to Corporate America

"More than we sleep, play, or make love, we work. Yet despite – or perhaps because of – this dominant daily grind, much of our literature is biased toward other pursuits." – Paul Di Filippo

Cast away from the terrors of the unknown and incomprehensible bitterness I held towards my own physical makeup, I was now obligated to prove that not only could I succeed on my own but thrive as a relatively healthy individual. Minus the inconvenience of the extraction of my wisdom teeth during the winter after I had just gotten married, I had no new visits to the surgery room and by all standards was fit as a whistle. This allowed no room for any more excuses about why I couldn't achieve everything and anything I wanted and placed a separate kind of pressure on the back of my shoulders, which I had never experienced before.

My whole life I had been given a reason or justification for why I couldn't amount to my full potential and now I had no explanation for the cost of failure and in some way that scared me even more. I was fresh out of college, married and with a mortgage to pay, so it was up to me to make this life that I had set up for myself last. Sherry now was reliant on me to make sure we had food to eat and a place to sleep at night while she tirelessly strived to gain her PHD in Clinical Psychology. The long game was clear, and the future was bright but as for the present we were left to make the best of what we had and not obsess over what we didn't have. With that in mind, my decision between pursuing a livelihood in the game of golf and jumping straight into the more lucrative financial world was made for me and it wasn't long before I saw myself hired on as a junior staff accountant.

In spite of my youth and my new company's exasperating parsimony I excelled in my new position and within a year had been promoted to Fixed Asset Manager. My boldness to contradict the norms of most novices who start out in the world of business persuaded upper management to take me under their wings and show me the tricks of the trade which otherwise was only known to tenure employees. Every day felt like I was climbing the ladder of success and every day I felt like my soul was withering away from the inside out. It wasn't because the job was bad or that I wasn't any good at it because in truth, the position was highly sought after, and I had become a tactician at acquiring money on the regular.

What the problem was and why I felt suffocated every morning once I stepped into the office and sat down in my melancholy cubicle was the familiarity. I associated the small space I was currently in to the repressed environment I had been desperately trying to avoid my whole life. The nostalgia of being confined to the inside of four walls with the formalities of the everyday nuances that made up my daily agenda tormented me to the point where I morphed into a radically argumentative and condescending persona of my former self. I understood the prosperity I had been fortunate enough to attain, but I couldn't psychologically differentiate the irresistible resemblance my current path of isolation was to the period in which I felt like I was wallowing away in obscurity.

Sherry was working diligently as a postgraduate student at Alliant University and had little time if any to focus on entertaining her grown ass husband every time he felt just a tiny bit bored. I no longer had the athletic regimen and personal connections to my teammates that helped fill an identity I'd been yearning for, ever since I finally escaped my miracle child label. Don't get me wrong, I was willing to sacrifice myself for the sake of patience but internally I felt lost because I made the more prudent choice which in turn challenged my resentfulness towards that decision just a couple years later.

The circumstances in which I had put myself in were startling, as I had never at any point in my life been healthier than I was after my 26th birthday, but on the flip side I had never felt as confused and uncertain of where I saw my life going than right then and there. I was working towards a career in the finance sector, and it had become quite obvious I didn't see my legacy being defined for the next 30-40 years as a man in just a suit and tie. If I wanted out, I was going to have to manifest my own destiny with something out of the ordinary and more to my liking.

So I devised a plan, or an agreement some would say, with myself, that once Sherry had finished graduate school and acquired her licensure to practice in the state of California, I would abandon the countless number of hours staring at a screen and chase whatever dream I believed was solely intended for me. Needless to say, this was all pie in the sky as Sherry was still at least 2 years out from finishing her dissertation and had at least another 2 years of internships before she would be even eligible to sit for her board exams. Inevitably this meant I was to find a way to overcome my absurdity of being misunderstood and preserve the merriment I had once relied on during the darkest of times. In accordance with my true nature, I gravitated towards the one thing I knew had always brought me comfort in the past, sports!

It wasn't my health or doctors keeping me away from the gridiron or basketball courts, it was my determination to be the best at the one sport I grew to love most, golf. But, now that I was no longer competing for a team that relied on me to be at my very best, I was free to explore all of the possibilities in which my body and mind wanted to be challenged. With Sherry occupied with her studies and the lack of fulfillment I was missing from my daily routine, I entranced myself into the world of adult recreational sports leagues. I searched for the type of glory I was deprived of in my youth, and it felt good to finally invade the athletic realm of contact sports, but there was a price to be paid for the recklessness of my misadventures and it was about to come in the form of excruciating pain.

Chapter 40
Heedless Fun

"As long as you're chasing the "ghosts" of your past you can never fully embrace your future." – Oprah Winfrey

Stuck in my mid 20's and searching for any reason to grasp onto a new identity that could gratify my hunger to experience the thrill of competition, I hurled myself back into the past where I was hoping to uncover a long-lost talent nobody knew was there. In some way I found solace in being a part of a team environment where I could relive the moments that alluded me from my adolescence and attracted my pernicious vice to cross the lines of self-preservation and tempt fate with my uncanny brashness.

I felt obliged to not only conquer my mother's fear of the sport they called football but incorporate a multitude of all kinds of physical activities including, volleyball, soccer, basketball, softball and even kickball. I was rebelling against the implacable watch and judgement that I felt stealthily followed me, as a precaution for my ineptitude to be able to look after my own self. So, when I was given the chance, I took it upon myself to keep my mind and physique from resting in order to escape my fears of everlasting complacency and my body's imminent unknown.

I started out mild as I made a quick addition to an already formed co-ed soccer team that soon morphed into an all-men's division 1 weekly scrap. I loved how the excitement and comradery amongst my teammates molded my desire to compete at the highest level of recreational competition and not the critical eyes or scolding from my family were enough to pull me away from my newfound passion of after work sports leagues. In fact, 2 nights a week of playing indoor soccer was not enough to quench my thirst for adrenaline as I went onto form a Thursday night division 1 flag football team, as well as a Tuesday night basketball team. This pattern of nightly events would continue on for another year and half until finally my luck had run its course and the foreseeable aftermath of nearly two years of high intense action claimed its next victim.

It would all happen during a frivolous exhibition during a lunch break pick-up game with my co-workers at our local gym, LA Fitness. After hours of sitting in my office chair hypnotically sifting through stacks of financials, I threw on my basketball shoes as the big hand touched 12 and raced over to the courts to get in my daily fix. Unfortunately, be it old father time or my foolhardy self-assurance that my body was invincible to common injuries of mere mortals, I was kindly humbled when I twisted to go make a pass and heard a loud pop as my left knee buckled from underneath me. Humiliated that I had fallen down in the middle of the court, and slightly apprehensive that I might have actually caused serious harm to my lower ligaments, I picked myself back up and hastily hopped over to the sidelines. As I sat on the bench processing what I had just done, I slowly gazed down to see a pinkish-bluish ball of flesh about the size of a small cantaloupe where my knee used to be. It was then when I realized I had just torn my left meniscus because the pain I was feeling was an exact replica of what I had experienced way back when I first wrestled that young teenager from Poway during the regional finals my Senior year.

As memory serves me well, my intuition of what I had done was ultimately validated when my long-time orthopedic surgeon Dr. Chow walked into the examination room with the results from my MRI scan and confirmed what everybody had already known, a complete tear of my left medial meniscus. The news of my injury left me trembling with angst because I knew the type of surgical procedure that came with a diagnosis of this kind and just like that, I had thrown away my freedom for the isolation of physical rehabilitation. Unlike all the times before, I had brought this sequestration on myself, and I had nobody to blame but my ego and unremitting pride. Worst of all, I had to tell my wife who was working hard to finish up her post-doctorate degree that her husband for the 6th time since dating him was to require surgery once again and be immobile for the next 3 months. I had bit through my lip during a flag football game one time which required 16 stitches and been taken to the ER after fracturing my ankle during a soccer game, but none of those compared to what I was going to experience on the operating table for the 25th time and Sherry knew it.

    I could tell by the look in her eyes once I disclosed the severity of my injury, I had let her down, not because she had already resigned to the fact when she married me that more than likely I was going to have my fair share of medical complications in the future, but simply for the carelessness I went about not trying to avoid any unnecessary harm to my already fragile frame. Her once charitable and humanitarian efforts to cheer me up while I struggled through the endless cycle of rest and recuperation were no longer there and instead were replaced with acrimony and frustration for a man she believed could do so much more with his life if he was just able to get out of his own way.

    The truth was I had fallen back into a state of dejection, but it wasn't because I understood where my wife was coming from because to me she already knew who she wanted to be and had been excelling at making those dreams a reality ever since she first declared psychology as her major. No, what brought me misery was that I was now grounded to stay locked away with only the infinite thoughts of what I was missing out on because of an unfortunate accident produced by the roll of the dice from lady luck herself. Thankfully, I didn't have to wait long to get my surgery on the books and after a quick 90-minute preordained slumber, the surgery was deemed a full success.

    Everything went according to plan for a change, which meant instead of discovering additional damage while opening me up, Dr. Chow confirmed his initial prognosis and went on stitching me back together. For the next 10-12 weeks I was to be confined to the comfort of my couch with the only exception being to use my crutches to get around the house and Sherry driving me to and from work. Sometime in the middle of my recovery I received a phone call from the commissioner of the Poway Sportsplex, who knew I was the captain of last year's men's softball division 1 champions and wanted to confirm I was coming back. He informed me that the rumor which had been floating around for the past couple of years that the San Diego Chargers were putting together a softball team was true, and he wanted us to be their first opponent. As much as I was chomping at the bit to get back on the field and play again, I was starting to contemplate whether what I was doing to my body was worth the risk. But once I had been told I had a chance to put my talent up against some of the best athletes in the world I was once again rejuvenated to make my highly anticipated return.

So, I focused all my efforts into rehabbing my knee for the start of the following season and set my goal to come back on February 14, 2014. Obviously, I hadn't learned my lesson quite yet because if I had been thinking at all I wouldn't have decided to rush back to play in a meaningless softball game on the exact day I had once gone through a lifesaving procedure. Not because of any superstition but because of the fact it wasn't worth jeopardizing my personal long-term health and my family's livelihood with the possibility of reinjuring my partially repaired knee and forcing my wife to relive the torture of her significant other sullenly lying around the house useless and miserably depressed. Nonetheless, I played naïve and threw all caution to the wind as I showed up to Opening Night of the softball season and shook hands with 8-time pro bowler and San Diego Chargers legend, Philip Rivers.

Chapter 41
Too Late

"Sometimes you need to know to quit while you're ahead or at least before things get much worse!" – Amy Poehler

One relatively warm winter's evening, a group of friends played out their childhood dreams when they faced off against their hometown heroes in a small game of slow pitch softball. No, this wasn't a movie you once saw or even a book you might have read, this was actually the scenario my buddies and I found ourselves in when we showed up to play in our weekly after work softball league.

Somehow, with the ingenuity of modern medicine and the blessing of natural genetics whose regenerative blood cells were abnormally supersonic, I had healed up just in time to captain my championship team of beer drinking, softball smashing, All-Stars on the night we were blessed to play on the same field with 15 national football association players. At this point in my recreational athletic career, I had toned down the nightly competitions and zeroed in on just making myself available once a week to toss the ball around with my pops and old-time friends. I no longer concerned myself with the torturous schedule of juggling 4 to sometimes 5 separate sports leagues with no time for rest and a definite possibility of further injury. This is how I was able to convince myself and the worrying parties around me that even though I was only 12 weeks removed from having a full repair of my left medial meniscus, I had learned from my previous mistakes and was only playing for fun instead of outright glorious victory.

With that mindset, I truly believed I was being sincere, as I knew in my head, I had to ratchet it down a few hundred decimals or I was going to seriously do something that even I wouldn't be able to come back from. Unfortunately, that all changed the first time I shook hands with the $100 million quarterback of the San

Diego Chargers, and he said to me "Just to let you know, we're out here to win it all and that's why we wanted to start with the best." With just a few words and a chuckle of condescending superiority, all my reservations were tossed out the window and I was resolute in showing these celebrities they had just walked into my house now.

   Drastically, I had transformed from just being content in sharing the same field with so many greats to doing everything in my power to overcome our perceived underdog role and come out on top. Understandably, the team made up of all professional athletes with a combined salary of $200 million were overwhelmingly the visible odds-on favorites compared to us out of shape, disproportionate average looking joe schmoes. However, on this occasion the super team hadn't quite yet comprehended all the rules that came along with playing in a recreational softball league, which in turn helped level the playing field and make up for our lack of physical prowess. Their power inherited from generations of big genes were limited to just 1 home run per inning which really disoriented the psyche of super stars like Eric Weddle, Phillip Rivers, Nick Hardwick, and Danny Woodhead. Though this in no way took away from any of their jaw dropping natural ability to run fast and highlight their God given talent to make remarkable play after remarkable play. It did, however, affect their initial insinuation that these games were going to be a cakewalk and teams like ours were just going to roll over when we first stepped onto the field. This is why I suppose we were able to pull out a 10-8 victory over them in the first game of the season and it looked like their whole team was having a hard time reconciling with the fact that they had just lost to a bunch of corporate suits and construction workers.

   Exhausted and throbbing with soreness after giving it my all, I sat down next to my teammates and enjoyed a well-deserved cold one. Sometime shortly after I polished off my drink, I received a slap on the back from none other than starting safety and 2 time

All Pro Eric Weddle, who said, "Good game tonight and can't wait to see you guys in the finals." I smiled and replied, "Looking forward to it and by any chance can I get a picture with you?" I wasn't too prideful to miss a chance to steal a photo op with one of my favorite football players to watch on TV, as I had to have evidence this wasn't all just a dream. Like a class act he said yes and assured me once again his team would be better prepared for the next time, they saw us. In my head, I was just happy I had made it through the whole game without reaggravating my surgically repaired knee and was able to walk away with a story to tell my grandchildren when I got older. I knew I had been fortunate to not have gotten hurt and the longer I played with fire, sooner or later I was bound to get burned.

My body was slowly healing back up and for the rest of the season I decided to play very sparingly where I never saw myself give more than a 60%-70% effort. Sherry was still meticulously chiseling her way through school as I was still doing the daily grind at work, but once a week I had something I really looked forward to and kept me intrigued enough to stay disciplined for the rest of my rehab. Absurdly, everything our team and their team wished for came to fruition as we were both able to reach it to the championship game, where the stage was set for something monumental to go down. Two days prior, I received a phone call from a reporter with the Wall Street Journal who somehow heard about the huge event through a fellow colleague who happened to have had a son who played in the same league. One thing led to another, and he ended up reaching out to ask if he could interview me for a story. He was going to write about our experience playing competitive softball with the San Diego Chargers. If that wasn't enough pressure, every friend, family member and additional 400+ fans who were in the stands the night our ragtag team of misfits went toe to toe with Philip Rivers and company.

It all started with a bang when Chargers Center, Nick Hardwick, hit a bomb that cleared the fences where it must have landed 500 feet away on the roof of the office buildings behind the parking lot. The crowd was deafening as they cheered for every extraordinary play the star-studded squad was able to make and it was turning out to be a real barn burner. Even my apprehensive wife and mother were in the stands rooting for my dad and me to do the impossible even if it meant for this one night only, turning their cheek to the possible risks that comes with giving 110%. Eventually, after both teams were able to manufacture a combined 36 runs and the score was tied 18-18 in the last inning of the game, it had come down to me with a once in a lifetime opportunity to win the game with one swing of the bat. I stepped up to the plate with the bases loaded, 2 outs and a team of giants standing across from me waiting to see if I was going to crack under the pressure.

    The ball was tossed, I squeezed the bat, and, in an instant, I had projected myself into folklore. I had ripped a ball in between the diving gloves of quarterbacks Brad Sorenson and Phillip Rivers allowing for the go ahead run to score and putting the final nail into the coffin of any Chargers hopes at sweet redemption. Like a story straight out of Hollywood, the whole team rushed over and hoisted me up onto their shoulders as they paraded me around to the endless cheers from the crowd. Once it was all over our whole team was able to get a group picture with the entire Valley Farm Market squad, where it still hangs in my house today. The pouring of emotions and intense satisfaction I received from that one moment is what provoked me into later making one of the most regrettable and life-threatening decisions of my life.

    Remember when I said way back in my adolescent years that my attitude towards life and not letting anybody prevent me from doing what I wanted to do was going to come back to haunt me? We'll this is when it happened, right after my legendary walk off I was handed an invitation to come play for a basketball team who played in the same league as NFL Hall of Famer Antonio Gates and future NBA prospects Jamal Franklin and Chase Tapley. In hindsight, I should have immediately said no and walked off into the sunset after accomplishing something I'd only ever had read about in story books or seen on the big screen. Except the temptation of being able to say I was able to compete against not only one professional team but two professional teams in an entirely separate sport was too enticing for me to say no.

So, there I was once again putting my body on the line to chase an illusion of what I thought it meant to be alive and then SMACK! An elbow smashed right into the side of my nose and instantaneously my vision went yellow and black. As I fell to the floor, I remembered thinking where the hell did that come from and as I went to pick myself back up the whole room started to spin, where then I proceeded to collapse back to the ground. To make matters worse, Sherry was in the stands and had to witness her husband get knocked out unconscious and escorted to the nearest hospital. It was there where I would regain full consciousness just to learn that I had been diagnosed with a grade 3 concussion, a broken nose, and a fractured right orbital. Needless to say, I was beaten up and there was no just walking this one off. I was to have immediate reconstructive plastic surgery and no physical contact from playing sports for at least 6 to 8 months. All in all, I had really screwed up this time with yet again having to go in for my 26th surgery and delivering a scare that neither my wife nor plastic surgeon would soon forget.

Chapter 42
Is Anybody There?

"Faith is unseen but felt, faith is strength when we feel we have none, faith is hope when all seems lost." – Catherine Pulsifer

The night before my 26th major surgery I couldn't sleep and stayed up thinking to myself how the heck did I put myself in this position all over again? It felt like just yesterday that I was on a gurney looking up at the bright light shining above me waiting for the mask to be placed over my face so I could be put to sleep. I promised myself and the people who cared for me that I was going to take more responsibility for my overall well-being, so I would ensure I made it to my 30th birthday.

In all honesty though, I had always had a premonition that I was never going to live past the age of 28 years old ever since I first cheated death by surviving my life altering car accident almost 10 years ago. For some reason, after that event I would continually have nightmares of my own demise and it would play out always in the same way, on an operating table grasping for hope that once again the magic of the doctors on call could save my life for the umpteenth time. I never told anyone these intuitions besides my wife after we were married, when she had asked me if I had ever wanted to have kids.

At first, I would always try and skirt around the question by saying of course I do but always prefaced much later down the road. As time went by, however, Sherry wanted more genuine and in-depth answers to a future she was expecting to start planning for. This is when I first conveyed to her my reservations for thinking too far in the future because quite frankly, I wasn't convinced that my body would allow me to live for that long. Be it my ignorance to the type of perseverance my own body had or the simple fact that I honestly was scared that I had already used up all

8 of my 9 lives and the next misstep was more than likely going to be my last.

Thoughts and words like these were uncommon to hear from my normal upbeat and usually optimistic vocabulary and is probably why it shook Sherry to the core when I first confessed them to her. She believed I had just told her I knew something was going to happen to me soon and she might as well prepare herself for the absolute worst. I didn't mean it to come across like that at all, because in actuality, it was probably more of an excuse than anything to keep testing the limits of how far I can push my body without being hindered with the concerns for my future self. I let the delusions of my past dictate the actions of my present and now as it was getting closer to the end, I was being confronted with the truth that I was going to have to live with the reality of the choices I had made for my older self. One of those choices was staring back at me in the mirror the morning of my upcoming surgery to reconstruct the right side of my face after being absolutely disfigured from a senseless game of pick-up basketball. My nightmares had turned into my new reality and as I was being wheeled into the operating room, my last thought was, why does this time feel so different from all the rest?

Customarily, orbital floor fracture repair is a routine medical procedure that does require the patient to go under general anesthesia, but the patient is only expected to be in and out of surgery for no more than an hour or two. It's actually the 3rd most common facial fracture that plastic surgeons see when working with patients who come in for reconstructive repair. Nonetheless, I had been through 25 of these types of medical procedures before and never had I remembered thinking to myself something just didn't feel right about the situation I was currently in. As I was racing through my mind to decipher why I was feeling this way the sharp smell of permanent marker filled my nose and without notice I had been sent away to 'Never Never Land'. While I was asleep, Sherry and my mom were outside in the waiting room waiting for me to come out of surgery so they could drive me back to the house for some rest and recovery. In total, they were told the whole experience would take no longer than an hour and a half and they should expect to be able to come back and see how I was doing in just under 45 minutes. During this time, something happened that I had never experienced in my life before and that was a vivid recollection of what I perceived to be what the afterlife would be like.

Now, I have never been the religious type and really for the most part never fully believed in the whole idea of a higher power. Partly, because I could never wrap my head around the fact that I was told that I was supposed to feel lucky that God had decided to save my life on so many separate occasions and it was a blessing that I had been able to persevere through the types of serious complications I had habitually undergone. My attitude was if I was so lucky, why did I have to go through any of those difficulties in the first place? It was a self-indulgent thought but at the time it's how I felt, so when I was put under during that 26th operation and I had for the most part encountered what I believed to be just made up, it was quite profound. Obviously, based on my skewed perspective of what I imagined God and the afterlife to look like, I was captivated to learn more about where I was and what I was doing there. It was odd because I had never thought or expected I would get a chance to actually speak with the proclaimed creator of the entire universe but there I was in a vast expanse of never-ending color chatting with God himself about my observations on how my life was currently going. What I didn't know was at the exact same time I was having my divine intervention, back in the real-world things had taken a turn for the worse and my life was in serious danger of suddenly coming to an abrupt end.

Apparently, the simple surgical procedure that was so routine the doctor didn't even feel it was necessary for my wife to go grab a bite to eat before it was time for her husband to be sent back home, had already elapsed the 3-hour mark and the code for all personnel to report back to the surgical room was being played over the loudspeaker. At this time, the experience didn't do my mom any favors as she knew instantly something had gone wrong and she thought to herself, "here we go again." Fortunately, my wife, who had a lot less exposure to all the medical jargon that was being tossed around was oblivious to the fact every doctor on staff was in a mad rush to help stop the internal bleeding I was currently suffocating from. Sometime throughout the procedure my nose cavity had been nicked, which caused an outpouring of thinly red blood to protrude out my nose and down my esophagus.

This was compounded by the fact I was currently taking immunocompromising drugs, as well as blood pressure medicine which thinned out my blood making it doubly hard to stop. Unbeknownst to me, I was quickly falling into the category of either bleeding out or suffocating on my own blood if the medical staff on site were not able to bring the bleeding to a complete halt.

Back in my little utopia unaware of what was going on in the mortal world, I was being exposed to colors and lights that I had never registered before. It was like I was being shown the possibility of what the universe had to offer if I just allowed myself to step back and look around. Sadly, besides the visual spectacle that was shown to me, I don't remember much else of what was said or experienced during my out of body experience. What I do recall taking away was a better understanding of why I endured all that I had to earlier in my life, so I would be better prepared for what was going to be asked of me later down the road. All that would have to wait though because right now I was currently coming back to life and it felt like someone had just taken a jackhammer to the inside of my throat, as well as the entire right side of my mangled looking face.

Miraculously, the doctors were able to stop the bleeding but not without doing some painful damage that I was not at all prepared to experience once I opened my eyes for the very first time.

It was later described to me by both my wife and mom that after the head surgeon was able to bring down my blood pressure and restabilize my heart rate to a more acceptable level, he walked into the waiting room sheet white and visibly shaken with what had just taken place. He humbly admitted that he was not prepared for such a routine surgical procedure to turn sideways so quick and at one point during the operation he became seriously petrified that he might have lost me with the amount of blood that had made its way down into my lungs.

As scary as it was to hear my life had almost come to an end, I was more curious on why I actually didn't die and for what reason was I brought back to this world? All my intuitions leading up to my 28th birthday were pointing towards this being my last, but I was still alive, which led me to believe I still had a lot more to give with the rest of the time I still had on this earth. Now, what that was exactly I wasn't quite sure yet, but one thing I knew was that I had faith in the fact that for some reason somebody up above believed I still had something to offer this world and it was about time I took it upon myself to make the drastic change necessary to see what that could possibly be.

Chapter 43
Living with your Psychologist

"Out of your vulnerabilities will come your strength." – Sigmund Freud

When you come within mere seconds of having your whole life taken away and there was no warning beforehand to let you know it would be happening, something deep inside of you starts to change. No longer are you so concerned with how much you can get out of life but rather, who you want to spend that time you do have with most. For me, it only took 28 years and 26 surgeries to get to that point in my life. Not only was I just grateful to have survived the mishap with almost bleeding out all over my plastic surgeon's operating table but was now enlightened with the understanding I had been given another chance to make the best of the opportunity I had been afforded.

First though, I had a long painful recovery from the brutal surgery I had just gone through, which gave me and my significant other plenty of time to contemplate what was going to be our next step moving forward. One thing we could both agree on was that my playing contact sport days were over, and I had officially announced my retirement. This news didn't just fall hard on me, but it really devastated my core group of friends who always depended on their captain to organize the sporting events and create the teams they loved to play on. It was time to move on though, and as much as it's always hard to say goodbye, I knew I was making the best decision for my future because I was actually eager to see what I was going to do next.

Speaking of what was next, I hadn't the slightest inkling about what that was going to be or what it was even going to look like, but for the first time in a long time I had restored my faith in the belief that I was going to be able to figure it out. One reason why I was so confident in this new clairvoyance was the simple truth that I had a partner beside me who was tirelessly and enthusiastically pushing me to better myself not only in my professional career but more importantly as a person.

Sherry has worn many hats over our long time together; wife, friend, critic, motivational speaker, philosopher and sometimes even psychologist. The fragility of the human brain is still a mystery to many, but for her, she has been able to crack the code of my own psyche and discover what has been corrupting the devious thoughts that have been feeding on my anxieties and manipulating any conventional way of thinking. With her never-ending love and compassion to help me grow and sharpen my rarefied ability to take the risks most people would tend to back away from, my fears of letting her down and disappointing everyone around me evaporated and I started to free my mind to the possibility of a new beginning.

A couple of things were working in my favor, as I was healing at a much faster pace than what was initially expected and Sherry had finally finished her dissertation, as well as graduated from her postdoctoral program. She was finally able to pursue the last step in achieving her goal of becoming a clinical psychologist and that was to pass the final 2 board exams the state of California required from all their aspiring licensed psychologists.

In the meantime, however, she was now able to start making a little bit more money at her last internship site which really helped boost our annual savings projections. Add in the fact that I received my second raise in less than a year and we were financially starting to see ourselves in the best shape we had ever been. The only thing that was missing now, was my passion for the work I was doing, but I was in a much better place than I once saw myself and I knew if I kept my head up high and the door open for new possibilities, something was bound to come along that sparked my interest. Then, without warning, two things would happen within weeks of each other that would set my life's course in an entirely different direction than the current trajectory.

Paradoxically, it would be a revisit of an old life that would help lay the foundation for a bizarre twist of serendipity, which would lead to an opportunity I would later refuse to let pass by. It all transpired one afternoon at work while I was sitting at my desk counting down the minutes until it was time to finally dig into my wife's homemade egg salad sandwich with Hawaiian BBQ chips sprinkled on top, when I received a call from a friend who I hadn't spoken with in nearly 2 years.

"Hey Brandon, this is Scott, do you still know a bunch of guys who play flag football? My company is doing a photoshoot for a new product line and needs a bunch of athletic looking dudes to come out and play catch while our team took numerous pictures of them. If you say yes, you and your friends will get free lunch and some cool company swag."

Now, normally I would be all over this as it was a golden opportunity for me to skip work, hang out with my buddies and get some cool gear, but now that I was technically out of the game, I had to ask a few imperative questions before I totally signed off on this whole idea.

"Hey Scott, thanks for calling. I don't play football anymore, but I still know a bunch of guys that do. Are you wanting them to play a real game and your team is going to film all of it?" "Nooooo, nothing like that, we just need you guys to act like you're playing football, and our digital team can do the rest. I mean heck, we don't want anybody getting hurt and our company is on the hook for it, ha-ha."

Then it dawned on me, there was no potential for serious injury if we were all just acting, so I thought what the hell, gather up the boys and let's do this thing.

"Alright Scott, shoot me over the address as well as the date and time to be there and I'll make sure to bring 20 or so of my best guys."

After sending off one simple group text message, I quickly recruited my team of players to show up and ball out 3 weeks before we were all to become part-time actors.

At the same time this was all happening, Sherry had received an invitation of her own, to attend a wedding all the way across the country in Annapolis, Maryland for a high school friend getting married just a month after my scheduled photoshoot with Scott's company. The timing couldn't have been more perfect, as we hadn't gone on a proper vacation in over two years due to my unfortunate health miscues, but since the both of us had built up enough vacation time over those years to enjoy a couple weeks away from the office, we couldn't have sent our RSVP letters back fast enough with the unequivocal answer, YES! So it was, Sherry and I found ourselves planning an entire summer's worth of traveling into a short 3 weeks. We were scheduled to visit Boston, Philadelphia, D.C., Virginia, Baltimore, and of course Annapolis, Maryland. We were determined to pack in all the sightseeing we could and barely left enough room to attend a wedding where I knew I would not know anyone except the bride. None of that mattered though because Sherry wanted to be there for her friend, and I wanted an excuse to go see Fenway Park and the Lincoln Memorial.

It so happened, Chelsy was so excited that Sherry and I were attending her wedding, she ended up telling her soon to be husband that I loved to play golf and he should introduce me to his boss's partner who just recently started working in the golf industry. One thing led to another and during the morning of the wedding while Sherry was getting her hair and makeup done, I was scheduled to play golf with a guy I had never met before at his home course in the middle of nowhere. Honestly, I didn't think anything of it because Chelsy was right about one thing, I loved to play golf and it sure as heck beat sitting in the hotel by myself watching SportsCenter and eating room service all day. So, I jumped into a taxi and made the long drive out to Beallsville, Maryland to meet the man, the myth and the legend, Jeff Renzulli. Now, I didn't know anything about who Jeff was or what he did besides the fact that he loved to golf and supposedly was the nicest guy you'll ever meet. After meeting him just once, if those weren't the truest words ever to be spoken then I haven't heard them. The reason I say this is because for the next 6 hours Jeff showed me around his club and treated me like a friend that he had known his whole life.

He asked me everything he could about who I was and what I liked to do and after the round he requested I stay for lunch and enjoy a drink with him. I was so taken back by all the hospitality that I remember going back to the hotel room later that day and telling Sherry I hope we sit at the same table with this guy Jeff, because you'll be blown away by how awesome he really is! As luck would have it, we would find ourselves being sat at the same table with Jeff, where we all secretly joked, we were the people the bride and groom had nowhere else to put. This is where I first learned he had just taken over control of a small traveling golf society with a mission to visit some of the nicest golf courses in the world while at the same time meeting some of the nicest people along the way.

Before he was about to call it a night, he said his company was hosting an event out in Las Vegas at the end of the year and I should consider coming out and seeing if I'd like to join the group. I took it as a nice gesture somebody made when they're trying to leave but never really expecting anything to come out of it and proceeded to enjoy the rest of my time with Sherry on our wonderful vacation to the East Coast.

Four months later, while I was at work sitting at my desk counting down the minutes until it was time to finally dig into my wife's homemade chicken Caesar wrap with crushed Fritos instead of croutons inside, I received a call from Scott, who frantically told me, "Bro, out of all the guys who were photographed for the cover of our new flag football product your picture was the one that got chosen and now will be distributed to every sporting goods store around the world." A bit perplexed I asked, "Are you sure?" "Yes man, the news just came down today and I wanted to let you know before somebody you knew walked into a Dick's Sporting Goods store and called you to say that they saw your picture all over the football section of the store." That was the moment I leaned back into my chair, stared up at the ceiling and daydreamed for the next 30 minutes of what life would be like if I somehow became a Hollywood star. Then I came back down to planet earth and called my wife to tell her the unbelievable news. Without fully rolling over with laughter but enough where it took her a moment to catch her breath and properly congratulate her husband on this wonderful accomplishment, she managed to chuckle out a "I'm so proud of you, Honey," while unsuccessfully holding back an unapologetic smirk. Three days later, those chuckles turned into gasps as I received yet another phone call at work but this time from a modeling and acting talent agency named Shamon Freitas and Company, who was calling to see if I already had any sort of representation and if not, would I be interested in signing with them. I ensured the nice lady over the phone that she must have been mistaken because at no time in my life, had I ever gone through any professional training of any kind to be asked to become a model or actor?

To which she kindly replied, "We heard about your marketing ad from a friend of yours and wanted to see if you'd like to pursue this kind of career any further?"

Too stunned to respond fully I blurted out, "Thank you for your call and I will have to think about it, can I call you back later?" Graciously, I was told I could have 2 weeks to think it over and if I decided the answer was yes, to come down to their office and we could talk more about the contract I was being offered. If things were not strange enough, that same weekend I was scheduled to fly out to Vegas to attend a 3-day golf event with none other than Jeff Renzulli and his newly founded golf society, The Friars Golf Club. It turned out Jeff's idea of bringing good people together to play great courses around the world was something golfers really were starting to like and wanted more of. It also turned out, Jeff wanted to softly pitch me on the idea of coming to work part time for him as the Friars' Membership Director, where I would help organize and run golf outings. In a matter of 2 weeks, my life as a senior buyer for an electronics company had been seriously put into question, as I was now handed not 1 but 2 golden opportunities to step outside my comfort zone and chase a dream I never even thought or for that matter knew was possible.

Inspired by the success my wife had achieved by passing her second state board exam just 6 months after graduating from her postdoctoral program, I felt ambitious and hungry with an appetite for a new adventure that could pull me away from the confines of my 8 by 8 cubicle and throw me into the world of excitement and unpredictability. Now, don't let me get you lost in the glitz and glamour of the spectacle that Hollywood and traveling the world playing golf most definitely warrants, because as big as a no brainer this opportunity was, it came with one glaring downside, they both paid significantly less money. Which didn't mean I couldn't ever get back to making the kind of money I was currently being offered in my financial role, but for the immediate future, it meant I would be taking nearly a fifty percent pay cut. I can genuinely say without the full support and selfless deeds my wife continually showed me throughout our entire marriage, I would have never been in the right position financially, emotionally, and spiritually to take the leap of faith to move on from my financial career and start down a path where there were no promises of tomorrow and just the certainty of today. One thing that kept coming up in my head though was a quote that I had in all my email signatures which read, "In the end we only regret the chances we didn't take." If that was true, I knew from the bottom of my heart I would never forgive myself if I didn't at least make an effort to see where this sort of life could take me. I had been dreaming for a long time to find a new purpose in my career and after a desperate search to fill a void that was never there to begin with, my wife and best friend reminded me that sometimes what you think you had been looking for had actually been right under your nose this whole time. The moment I put faith in my relationship with the person I loved was when I had been rewarded with the opportunity I had been seeking and the confidence we could conquer whatever the next adventure brought along with it.

Chapter 44
Life in the Fast Lane

"People don't normally change when things are going well. But I want to see what's next and keep moving. That keeps things fresh."
– Neil Young

Awakened from the seclusion of pedestrian tasks and the ongoing mindlessness of my everyday way of thinking, I bustled with a new sense of vigor as I was handed a sufficient foundation to begin building my new life from. The instant I resigned from my position as a lead procurement officer I created a full itinerary on how I was going to successfully transition to the entertainment and hospitality industry. To start, I had to inundate myself with everything that it took to break through the barriers Hollywood and its gatekeepers laid in front of me.

Fortunately, I already had a huge head start when it came to getting my name recognized amongst the people who matter, as I had already signed with a reputable talent agency who made it their mission to get me camera ready for whenever the next job opportunity came knocking. This meant I was able to secure a whole new wardrobe, headshot, monologue, resume and of course acting lessons to help boost my overall marketability to potential suitors looking for a Caucasian male, 5'10 and 165 lbs. One thing I had to learn however, was just because you had an agent working to find you casting calls to show up from time to time didn't mean you weren't equally searching around to find your own auditions to pitch yourself. If I wanted to be taken seriously as a real professional then I needed to put in the time and work required for casting directors to say, yes, we need that guy for this specific part.

So, for the next 6 months I woke up every day with the simple mission to try and improve by any means possible on how I looked, spoke, and rehearsed lines so when I finally did stand in front of a camera it felt like I was right at home. Not to say those first few months were not hard and very humbling at times, but they were made easier knowing I had already seen some sort of success and with a little patience I knew the breaks would start to come.

In the meantime, I needed some money because Sherry was still working as an intern and even though she was getting paid to do so, it wasn't quite enough to cover all the bills and rent that was due at the end of each month. This is where working from home and scheduling golf trips around the world during my free time really began to pay off. The flexibility to work hours whenever I was not auditioning, or filming allowed me to juggle the impulsiveness of the entertainment industry while at the same time steadily making a dependable paycheck to take care of my responsibilities at home.

On top of all that, about every other month Jeff would ask me to fly out to a golf destination to help organize and run the bigger events he needed more assistance with. We were a perfect team, as he would be the face of the company that everyone knew and loved, while I would be in the background meticulously making sure none of the craziness behind the curtain ever showed to our customers.

During this time, I would get to visit some of the most beautiful places on Earth, as well as some of the best golf courses the world has to offer including Ireland, Italy, Dominican Republic, Pebble Beach, TPC Sawgrass, Old Head and Oakmont Country Club just to name a few. I was enthralled with the ease with which I was able to leave my old life behind and embrace the chaotic whims of whatever the next day brought along with it. I had even maneuvered my way into testing new golf clubs for TaylorMade twice a week and was rewarded with never having to worry about where I was going to play golf again.

Essentially, everything I had ever wanted was out there for the taking and I was doing my best to try and keep up while staying available to jump on the next big opportunity that came my way.

One of those chances came when my Uncle Mitch suddenly had to back out of a once in a lifetime white water rafting trip that involved paddling down the Colorado River for over 200 miles and camping on the banks of the Grand Canyon for 10 days. It had always been a dream of his to accomplish this feat of man vs. nature but unfortunately a camping accident a couple months before prevented him from ever achieving his life-long goal. In his stead though, he wanted my sister and me to take up the reins and enjoy a two-week bonding adventure that neither Tanya nor I would ever forget. It was right around the time I was turning 30 years old, and both my sister and I were miraculously able to carve out the required time to take on such a huge commitment.

We both said yes and packed our bags for the long trip to the blistering heat of the Arizona desert. Over the next fortnight, Tanya's and my will to go on was pushed nearly to the breaking point. Not the strength of a 4-time national water polo champion or the endurance and fortitude of a man who has been able to overcome death itself was immune to the sheer exhaustion and punishment the Grand Canyon laid upon us during those endless days and nights. Our bodies were nearly on the verge of collapsing by the time we finally were able to make the 9.5-hour hike out from the depths of the valley below. It was an experience that is quite honestly hard to put into words and might even be harder to put into perspective, but the best way I could sum up how it felt after my sister and I were able to challenge ourselves in a survival situation over a long period of time was outright invigorating.

Never before had I felt the rush of adrenaline that flowed through my veins while we soared through the unpredictable current of the Colorado river and the overwhelming pride when we reached the summit of our daily treks up to our campsites. I was hooked and from then on, I knew I would stop at nothing to try and search for the next great expedition that could test who I was and what I was made of.

If I wasn't going to put my body in harm's way anymore with regards to playing sports, then I was going to fill that lack of intensity with the combination of nature's unpredictability, entertainment adventures and my long forgotten competitive personality. For the next couple of years, I drove myself to train to acquire a complete fitness level in the categories of cardiovascular fitness, strength, and overall mobility. I would routinely assess my progress by entering into premiere athletic competitions such as Spartan races, half marathons and high endurance runs. The ecstasy of opposition in the face of defeat and somehow being able to will your mind to push through your body's pleas' to just give up is what extinguished any doubts that I had that this was not exactly what I was supposed to be doing. If it wasn't training for the next big race, traveling to the next great adventure, or transforming myself into a new identity on stage, I was back home caddying for my friends in tournaments like the US Open or playing in local competitive golf competitions. One such contest was the Randy Jones Invitational where a group of friends and I were able to take down over 1,500 competitors over 10 days' worth of qualifiers, as well as a 2-day 36-hole finale to claim our tickets on a private jet up to Northern California to play none other than the world renown Pebble Beach golf course.

My life was in a constant state of motion and everywhere I turned there seemed to be something new and exciting for me to embark on. On the flip side of what I was enjoying, Sherry's career was really starting to take off, and she was hired on as a full-time clinical psychologist at a nearby medical health center and just recently saw the dissertation she had worked on for over 4 years finally get published. As chaotic as our lives seemingly were, we had found a sense of balance between ourselves that worked, which meant, the obvious next thing we had to do was turn the whole thing upside down again.

Chapter 45
Moment of Truth

"Accept your past without regrets and face your future without fears." – Paulo Coelho

Almost exactly 2 years after I decided to bid farewell to the structure of corporate America and embrace the spontaneity of the entertainment world, I had absorbed a new sense of pride in what I was doing and who I was starting to become. No longer was I shackled to the pressure of the almighty dollar, which had become reduced to just a means to an end, but instead was supported with the freedom to carve out my own path to success.

In just 5 years of marriage Sherry and I were able to build our lives around the core values we both believed in and stuck to the conviction that as long as we had faith and trust in each other, our happiness and ultimate long-term goals would be attainable. With hard work, a sense of self-belief, perseverance, and freedom of expression 2 young adults turned the limitations that were bestowed upon them as adolescents into representations of everything the human spirit can overcome. Sherry was steadily settling into her role as a health provider who could help change the lives of people who were desperately in need of assistance, while I was doing my best to help bring a smile to people's lives with a well-deserved vacation. During this time in our life, I would say we were hard at work perfecting our crafts and enjoying the constant variety each of our professions brought along with it. We were busy and always on the go, traveling to one part of the world one month and to the total opposite the next. For those first few years we lived in a sort of controlled chaos, with the exception being we had still yet to discuss the pink elephant in the room that had been increasingly growing to a point where it was soon unavoidable.

Sherry and I had been together for over 11 years and had just entered our early 30's before it became quite apparent to both our families that time was ticking, and we weren't getting any younger. From an outside perspective we seemed to have settled into a perceived sense of normality in our everyday lives and were perfect candidates to start breeding the next generation of dreamers. To me though, the thought of having kids was terrifying. I was not ready to willingly volunteer a look back into my past for the rudimentary satisfaction of anybody else besides my wife. Reciprocally, Sherry showed no interest in putting her newfound career on hold just to shake things up once again for the off chance we were actually able to procreate. Ever since we both said, "I do," we came to a mutual understanding that because of my unique circumstances from when I was younger, we would not plan to have children until much later in life. This was a conversation that I knew I was eventually going to have to face at some point in my life and it was only fair that the person who I decided to marry was fully informed of my whole medical situation. What I had been so hesitant to share with the person I had grown to love and care most for in this entire world was the fact that I had no idea if I was ever going to be able to produce any offspring.

At that moment, the answer was looking more and more like it was going to be no. The reason for this pessimistic belief was because I had yet to show any evidence that my body was capable of manufacturing the necessary tools that were essential for creating another human being. Basically, what I'm alluding to was that I had been shooting blanks when I was in the bedroom, which actually for the first 30 years of my young life was quite a blessing. However, it was my understanding that the fun couldn't last forever as eventually it would be expected of me to start bearing fruit to all my partner and my hard work or there would be some serious questions that needed to be answered. The problem was, it wasn't just me who didn't know if children were in my future or not, but my childhood urologist and primary physicians hadn't the slightest clue either. To be fair though, I was supposed to come back and start the whole process of confirming the probability of being able to have kids after I had finished puberty but, well, who wants to do all that when they were dealing with more pressing concerns at the time? Does a kidney transplant, car crash and life-threatening intestinal surgery ring a bell? As important as it might have been to have known if parenthood was going to be a distinct possibility for me down the road, it did not take precedence over the fact that I was simply just trying to survive with the cards I had been dealt. This is why you can imagine how it became a reality that I had gone over 3 decades without knowing my future genetic outlook. So, when Sherry finally revealed that she was ready to come to terms with whatever answer we were going to be told, I was inexplicably petrified.

One of the reasons I had avoided knowing the truth was because I had grown scared of what the outcome might bring in regard to disappointing not only myself but my wife and our families. I had made it my mission not to let my shortcomings determine my stature in life but, there was nothing I could do about what god had decided to supply me with or not. When I was born, I had undergone plenty of surgeries to fix a plethora of different kinds of birth defects but one imperfection that wouldn't be found until much later was the disappearance of both my reproductive organs. It wouldn't be until I was 3 years old and undergoing my 12th surgery when the doctors would rush out of the operating room with some astonishing news.

At first my mother thought they had lost me while in surgery because she had become such a veteran of what a typical routine looked like for a child under the knife, and two surgeons running out 6 hours before the operation was due to end was not part of it. Nevertheless, she braced herself for what she was about to hear and to her amazement they said, "We found your son's testicles!"

Now, that's not generally a cause for any sort of celebration but for a child who had been perceived to have been born without any, this news came as a revelation. Not only had they found where they were, but the one doctor in the world who could perform such a revolutionary procedure to relocate them back to where they were customarily thought to be, happened to be in the building visiting from out of town.

With the permission given to extend the scope of my initial operation for the addition of being the 8th person in the world to successfully undergo a testicular auto transplantation for the intra-abdominal testis, my mom and dad put the future of their family's legacy in the hands of a doctor they had never met before. Based on your worldview, you could either see this moment as just a fortunate set of unrelated coincidences or like San Diego Children's hospital and my family would choose to recognize it, one of the single greatest miracles in medical history.

I would later be able to go on and experience the joys of adolescent puberty but was still perplexed with the notion that not every part of my reproductive system was working like all the classes and books I had so passionately done my diligence on. It wouldn't be for another 15 years before I would be able to muster up the courage to walk back into my urologist's office and find out if Sherry and I were actually going to be able to start a family. To his credit, he was absolutely thrilled to see me come back as a grown adult and did everything in his power to guide me in the right direction to finding the answers I was now desperately in search of.

This is how I would ultimately come to meet male fertility specialist Dr. Martin Bastuba, who after an initial testicular mapping examination, only gave me a 50 percent chance of having the capability of producing enough viable sperm to fertilize an egg. He would also enlighten me on the TESE procedure he would have to perform, which required him making a small incision into my testis and examining the tubules for the presence of sperm. All of this sounded quite painful and nothing that I wanted to be a part of but, when I looked over to my lovely endearing wife, I could see in her eyes that I was going to have to suck it up because this one was not up for negotiation. She had been by my side through a countless number of horrifying surgeries before, so when I went to protest how discomforting all of this was going to be, she stopped me in my tracks with a look that could only be interrupted as,

"I think you'll be able to manage one more itty-bitty cut, honey."

So just like that, I was wheeled back into the operating room, where I was to be awake for a procedure that involved slicing into the most sensitive part of my body with only a 50 percent expectation that the retrieval was going to be a success. I remember that night Sherry and I stayed up talking about everything we would do if the results came back positive or negative and how or if either result would change the way we thought of one another. Obviously, it was more about me trying to gauge how disappointed Sherry would be if we were not able to have children together and with the help of some strong pain medication, I was finally ready and willing to hear all of her reservations.

Without hesitation she grabbed both sides of my face so I was forced to look her in the eyes as she kissed me and said,

"I love you Brandon and no matter what we hear in the next 24 hours we'll still be together, and nothing will ever change that." Bewildered and a little ashamed I kissed her back and said,

"I know Share, I would just hate to let you down, as I want to be able to offer you the world and I'm not sure after tomorrow's news I would still be able to do that."

It was heart wrenching knowing that I would be solely responsible for making a dream of ours a possibility or not, but with the love and devotion from such a strong individual, I was able to condemn my thoughts of self-doubt and start focusing on embracing the fortune I had currently been given. Sometime during the early morning of the next day my phone began to ring as the caller id said it was from Dr. Bastuba and whatever he had to say next was about to change the course of our lives forever.

Part Five:
Coming Full Circle

"When you have collected all the facts and fears and made your decision, turn off all your fears and go ahead!" – George S. Patton

Chapter 46
Where Do Babies Come from Again?

My hands were shaking, my heart was pounding, and it felt like I was about ready to pass out from the sheer anticipation of the news one of the top male fertility specialists in the country was about to announce to Sherry and I. On September 20th, 2017, while we sat in my car on the side of the I-5 freeway, we received the information I had been waiting to hear for the past 31 years and counting, "You can make a baby!"

A flood of emotion instantly came over me as I fell into Sherry's arms and cried in relief that something that was once believed to be impossible was now a real possibility. After a prolonged moment of celebration, I jumped back onto the phone and began to profusely thank Dr. Bastuba for making my dreams come true. Gracious for the sentiments but still a bit puzzled by the overzealous response, Dr. Bastuba quickly elaborated on what this prognosis actually entailed. "Yes, you do have the right amount of substance to start making a baby but there's a catch." He would go on to conduct a full breakdown on how the male anatomy worked and why my reproductive system was currently in no place to start fathering children the natural way. Sometime during one of my many surgeries the "inner plumbing" of my core makeup had gotten damaged to a point where I was no longer able to conceive a child without the assistance of the very latest in new medical technology.

Then it hit me, of course I would be told I couldn't do this one natural human act the easy way, I would have to jump through a hoop of fire dangling over a pool infested with crocodiles before I was given the slightest chance at making Sherry and my dream come true. Somehow, even before he told me all of this, I instinctively knew there would be an additional surgery or operation I would have to encounter if I really wanted this to happen. However, my lack of knowledge when it came to how science and biology actually worked really showed when I was left speechless after Dr. Bastuba directed the conversation to Sherry instead of me and said, "I know a remarkable doctor who can help with the next steps in regard to your part in this process, which might include a small procedure and additional medications."

Unsettled and a bit taken back by what I had just heard, I remember cautiously waiting until we ended our phone call with Dr. Bastuba before I looked over to Sherry and asked her how she felt about everything we had just been told. With no resentment or hostility for the circumstances I had unfortunately placed us in, she radiated with delight because now we knew for sure there was still the prospect of being able to have children of our own. It didn't matter that she was going to have to put her body through a tremendous amount of stress or even that the probability of such an enormous undertaking was still highly unlikely to succeed, because all that mattered was that there was still a glimmer of hope and now the ball was finally back in our court.

As for me, I was still puzzled about my whole role in this process and exactly how I felt about asking my wife to physically endure the level of discomfort that I could only imagine was going to be required for all this.

Subtly, she took my hand in reassurance and said, "I had known all along that this was going to be the only way. I was never under the illusion my part in all of this wasn't going to come without its fair share of difficulties."

Like a true dunce, I should have known the only doctor in the family would have already done her research for all the outcomes if her partner was told he was fertile but not able to have a baby the normal way. As a true embodiment of our entire relationship, I was always the one to ride through life on the seat of my pants while Sherry patiently remained in the background until it was time for her to remind everyone once again how much more mature and intellectually savvy she truly was. For the next couple of hours, she would walk me through everything we needed to get in place before we made our visit to see reproductive endocrinologist Dr. Brooke Friedman and her team of scientists at San Diego Fertility Center.

Unified in our pursuit to explore every option available to us, we walked into Dr. Friedman's office with the determination to grow our family by one. Abruptly, as soon as we sat down the door swung open and the bright smile and calm temperament of only a woman who has been creating miracles for the past 10 years could show. Dr. Friedman shook our hands and instantly put our reservations at ease and since I had a lot of explaining to do, she kindly listened as I blabbered on about how the past 30+ years of my life had gotten us to this point. What I casually left out of the conversation though was the fact that my parents had once experienced their own set of issues when they tried to have children almost 3 decades ago.

This would turn out to be quite the misstep later on when Dr. Friedman would explain the types of necessary medications Sherry would be asked to take in order for them to ensure we could expect optimal results. One medication Dr. Friedman would go on to suggest would be none other than the drug that was proven to cause all of my life's misfortunes, Clomid. Now, let's be clear about one thing before we move on, at no point did Dr. Friedman ever know what caused my current infertility, so when she instantly noticed my eyes widen to the size of half dollar coins, she had immediately stopped her train of thought and asked if we had any concerns about what she had just said. As I quickly recovered my poise, I hurriedly explained why Clomid was not going to be an option for us and if she had any other recommendations for Sherry to try instead.

The rest of the appointment went pretty smoothly, as Sherry had some of her lab work done and went through a routine physical examination, but I was a little spooked with the realization that Sherry and I were being put in almost the same situation my parents were placed in before I was born. It was something that I was continually wrestling with in my head because even though my family and I had been tested multiple times for any genetic irregularities there was still the small nagging self-doubt in the back of my head that said, what are you doing Brandon, what if your baby comes out with the same sort of birth defects as you? Premature in my thinking I spoke up to both Sherry and the doctor and said I don't know if I could go through with this, I don't want to be responsible for bringing a child into this world who has to live with the same number of struggles and pain that I've had to overcome.

As Dr. Friedman slowly started to fade away from Sherry and my conversation, I emptied everything I had ever thought onto the table as Sherry sat in total silence. All my fears and uncertainties raced out of my head and out of my mouth as I shared how scared I was about having my wife put her body through such intense and invasive procedures. I also acknowledged my anxiety about forcing a dream into a reality even if it could sacrifice our baby's overall well-being. Finally, I argued that we had discussed possibly adopting if we were told we couldn't have kids of our own and we had both been excited for the idea of raising a child who was in need of a loving family. I knew I was contradicting what I had always conveyed to Sherry when it came to not letting my past determine the way I wanted to live my life, but I was self-destructing over the thought of not having control over the type of pain my wife was potentially going to put herself through. Finally, after I had lost my will to continue with interrogating my own partner with a relentless number of questions, I took a deep breath and anxiously awaited her response.

Overwhelmed with the avalanche of emotion that was just hurled her way Sherry took a minute before she regained her composure and let me in on a little secret she had been keeping ever since we had first started dating. "One thing I have always known about you and why I have grown to love you as much as I do is that deep down inside you cannot fathom the people around you experiencing any sort of pain or discomfort while you are stuck helpless to make it go away. Your whole life you have felt like you have carried the burden of being the one person who was always sick or hurt but never were you forced to step back and let someone else take on the responsibility for you. This time though, it's my turn to make the sacrifice in the hopes of creating something special that you and I could one day share for the rest of time."

She was right of course; she usually is about these sorts of things. I just needed to hear it again before I could commit to the idea that we were really ready to start down a path where the final destination was no guarantee. With a couple more reassuring hugs and a few more tears we asked Dr. Friedman to join us back in her office as we nodded our heads simultaneously and said as one, "We are ready to make a baby."

I had finally been confronted with the scars of my past just to be told to wash them away and trust that the people I loved the most were strong enough to overcome their own set of difficulties. This would be one of the most important lessons I would come to learn, as what comes next was news from my mom and brother that would shake my foundation to the core.

Chapter 47
On the Other Side of the Curtain

"You can't heal the people you love. You can't make choices for them. You can't rescue them. You can promise that they won't journey alone. You can loan them your map. But this trip is theirs." – Laura Jean Truman

The whole family gathered around my parents' dining room table to enjoy yet another Sunday night meal cooked by none other than Mrs. Chef herself, Linda Gandy. My dad was sitting at the head of the table as usual, while my brother and I were seated on the opposite sides of him, so we were guaranteed that all the food was filtered through us before it ever reached the never-empty plate of the "Bear." Right next to us were our lovely wives Sherry and Kristina, as well as my brother's daughter, Mackenzie, with a surprised appearance from our always elusive younger sister, Tanya and her new NorCal boyfriend, Brian Whitlock.

The house was filled with laughter and soft-hearted debate while my mother worked tirelessly in the kitchen cooking up one of her many famous dishes that I'd argue are the best that money can buy. Everybody seemed to be in a joyous mood because on this night mom was whipping up her specialty, homemade beef tacos and enchiladas with Mississippi Mud Pie for dessert. Ooooweeee, this combination was only brought out for the most important of celebrations and to our knowledge this appeared to be just another ordinary family Sunday night dinner. Then came the news after the last piece of pie was handed out that would send a shockwave through the heart of our family's soul.

My mom would end up walking over to my dads' side and holding his hand as she shared with all her kids that she had recently been diagnosed with squamous cell skin cancer and would need to undergo immediate surgery to stop the aggressively spreading disease. She would go on to explain how skin cancer has been highly prevalent on her side of the family for generations and how important it was for the rest of us to constantly apply suntan lotion whenever we went outside. Considering my sister and my livelihoods required us to constantly be in the sun for extended periods of time, she was indirectly voicing her concerns squarely at us. In that moment though, her caution for safety went in one ear and right back out the other because the only thing we heard was one of the scariest 5 letter words in the English dictionary, cancer.

Never before had I ever been forced to reckon with the fact that somebody I loved was going to have to fight for their lives like I've had to do multiple times before. I just always assumed everyone around me was going to be healthy forever and it would only be me who really had to have any life-threatening scares happen to them. As egocentric as that might seem today as I write this, that is exactly how I felt at the time because for the past 3 decades I really hadn't been put in a situation where I was the one having to empathize with the person dealing with pain. I had never known anyone in my immediate family who had to go through any kind of surgery, let alone have to visit the hospital unless it was to come and see me.

So, unsurprisingly, when my mother announced the news of her unfortunate prognosis, it was me who ended up taking it the hardest. It caught me by such surprise that I couldn't hold back the tears which poured down my cheeks and onto the floor as I mumbled out a question, I wish I could have waited to ask another time. Since I was new to all of this, I didn't really know what was the proper thing that needed to be said or done at the time, so I just blurted out the first thing that came to my mind, "How long do we have left with you?"

Without knowing it I had broken the ice in the room, as my mom started to laugh and go on to say, "Oh Brandon, I hope for a very long time. The doctors believe even though they found the cancer on the backside of my head, they can still remove 100% of the infection using a technique called Mohs micrographic surgery and I should be able to make a full recovery."

Frustrated and a little confused, I pressed on and said, "You don't have to sugarcoat anything for me mom, I have been through a lot myself and I just want to know the truth."

Apparently, I had missed the memo on how to sympathize with someone who was only looking for the people around them to provide love and support as they went through one of the toughest moments in their life. My lack of knowledge on how cancer actually worked, and my stubbornness to preach instead of listen was a direct result of only thinking about how her problem was going to affect me and not how I could help my mom in her time of need. I was unaware that the finding of cancer in someone's body didn't automatically result in certain death and even if it did, wouldn't excuse the right to demand to have that information divulged to me as my mother was still processing the news herself.

Thankfully, my family has had plenty of practice at coming to terms with bad news over the years and they were able to excuse my rash behavior by simply smiling and saying, "Stop being so cynical, mom is going to be just fine, and we just need to all be there for her while she recovers from this small set back." Stubborn and still a little annoyed, I wiped away my tears as I gradually withdrew from the table and gravitated towards another room in the house. The irony was, every time I was told I was going to have to go through surgery, I trusted in the fact that the doctors were going to be able to heal me back up and I would eventually bounce right back to being my old self again.

Contrary to that belief, I was convinced the worst was going to happen and I was going to be left without my mother if she didn't receive immediate care. A week later, my mom would go into surgery, where the size of a small pancake of cancerous skin would be removed from the back side of her skull, which would later be repaired with the help of some clever plastic surgery. For the next four months she would be in and out of the hospital checking to see if the doctors had successfully removed all the cancer that was currently attacking her body. During her long recovery our family received the next piece of devastating news, which informed all of us that my brother had been diagnosed with testicular cancer during a routine physical checkup.

Feeling like this was all a sick joke I had dismissed the notion anything bad was going to happen to my brother because he'd always been the strongest and most reliable person I had ever known. This is why I turned most of my attention inward and focused my energy towards helping Sherry with all the difficulties that came along with trying to become pregnant. A couple of those challenges included being there while my wife went under anesthesia so the fertility doctor could extract enough eggs from her ovaries that would give us the best chance at creating an embryo down the road. As luck would have it, those eggs would come to produce 4 healthy embryos, one of those would eventually be implanted into Sherry's uterus just a few months later.

During this whole process I would be required to administer 2 rounds of progesterone shots every night for the next 20 weeks with the hope that the increased level of hormones would give our new embryo the best opportunity at sticking around. Every night we would both take 10 minutes to mentally prepare ourselves for what needed to be done and it tore me up inside every time I stuck her with that needle knowing I was delivering her a dose of undesirable pain. We had become fatigued by the formality of the whole process and by the end of those 20 weeks we were just looking forward to hearing that all of Sherry's hard work was going to pay off in the end.

That year had become one of the hardest in my life as I was forced to the sidelines to watch my mom, brother and wife courageously battle through every single day of their lives without the guarantee of any extravagant reprieve. I had found solace and strength in knowing that my family was there with me as we unified around each other to help bring camaraderie to the ones that we loved. It didn't all happen at once but over time I came to realize all those years while I was sick or hurt, my parents and family members were going through the same types of emotions and sentiments I was currently experiencing now that I was sitting on the opposite side of the curtain.

My initial judgment on how I was able to overcome all the limitations I was allocated earlier on in my life had been saturated with the simple thought that with the help of some incredible doctors and my relentless pursuit to never give up, I had been able to push aside all of the pain and misfortune to come out better on the other side. Except, now that I was experiencing first-hand how the presence of myself and the rest of my family were able to be there to listen or even sometimes alleviate one another's problems and concerns, I understood for the first time what really shaped me into the person I had become today, was the never-ending love and support my family had consistently showed me. It's one thing to be the fighter constantly taking punch after punch and digging deep within yourself to persevere even when you feel like you don't have anything left to give, but it's a whole other thing when you're the coach in the corner screaming and encouraging your partner to keep fighting because you know from experience, they can beat whatever is standing in their way. It had finally become my turn to stand on the outside of the ropes looking in as there was nothing else I could do except watch and wait to see how it all played out.

The fate of both my mom and brother's extended battle with cancer, as well as Sherry and my personal journey in becoming parents of our own would all come to fruition in the later part of the year 2018. The first of three that would be divulged to our family was the successful removal of all my mom's skin cancer that was growing rapidly on the back side of her head. After 6 long months of treatment, she had finally been given the news we had all been waiting to hear, "You are cancer free." The smile on everyone's face when she broke out in tears and told us she had recovered from her long fight with cancer was contagious and we couldn't help but feel relieved that the heart and soul of our family was back and going to be ok. We had struggled through all the hardships and prayed for this day to finally come and when it did it felt like we had just seen a miracle take place and we wouldn't be surprised if a couple more were still yet to come. They don't happen often and that's probably why they are called miracles in the first place, but when you are privy to experiencing one right in front of your eyes, the thought of seeing more doesn't seem to be as far-fetched of an idea than it once was not so long ago. A short time after we all came down from the high of celebrating my mom's good bill of health, it was time for Jacob to undergo his radical inguinal orchiectomy, which in layman terms meant the removal of the tumor stuck inside him. Scared and anxious from his worrying tendency, Jacob was wheeled into Scripps Memorial Hospital but not before our whole family wished him luck and poked fun at how much ice cream he was going to be able to eat once he woke up from his short cat nap.

    Six hours later, we were told the tumor had been removed and my brother was now "cancer free." The world had once again shifted into balance, and we could all finally take a break from the continuous stress the past half a year had taken on our entire psyche. The roller coaster of 2018 wasn't quite over for Sherry and me though, as we would receive a phone call from Dr. Friedman at San Diego Fertility Center a couple weeks later with an update that Sherry was indeed 6 weeks pregnant. Not knowing if I was even capable of having children just 6 months prior, I had been given the news I was going to become a father less than 9 months from that day. A dream that I never dared to entertain had now become my new reality and with it a sense of accountability that wasn't there before. I now had another purpose to life other than the love I had for Sherry, and it was going to be someone who solely relied on me to be there to help guide them through everything the world was about to throw their way. Ignorant to all the ups and downs that were lying ahead, I would be caught off guard when on the day of delivery my world would be flipped upside down and the experience my parents had gone through just 32 years ago would come back to play itself out with their grandson clinging to life and their son and daughter in law sitting helpless just a few feet away.

Chapter 48
Rowan's Birthday

"We never know the love of a parent till we become parents ourselves." – Henry Ward Beecher

Two weeks prior to one of the most highly anticipated days of my life, I was offered a ticket to go see newly acquired basketball icon Lebron James play in his first game as a Los Angeles Laker. Considering I was a die-hard Lakers fan just like my dad was before me and his dad was before him, I found the opportunity too good to pass up and was just hoping my 38-week long pregnant wife would be able to understand. Up until that point, her pregnancy had been going pretty smoothly with no complications or cause for concern and we were even able to take a babymoon to Northern Italy during her second trimester. This is why even though Sherry was starting to get really uncomfortable with the pressure of a baby almost fully grown inside of her, I was confident she would welcome the idea of having a couple hours to herself without the presence of her high energy, sometimes loud and boisterous husband lurking around. To everyone's astonishment I was right, all my wife wanted to do was lie on the couch and watch a movie in peace. So as my dad and I were enjoying the high-flying entertainment of Lebron and Company, Sherry was relaxing at the house lost in one of her favorite Rom Coms, until a stab of pain on the right side of her ribs forced to make an unexpected visit to the hospital.

Sherry knew something was wrong, but she didn't know exactly how dangerous of a situation she was currently in until she spoke with my mom over the phone and was told she needed to get to the emergency room as soon as possible. Unbeknownst to either of us Sherry had developed a medical condition called preeclampsia which rapidly raised her blood pressure and swelling of her extremities to a point of serious concern. Unfortunately, we would not find this out until my mom drove her to Sharp Mary Birch where it would then be realized her blood pressure had skyrocketed from her normal 110/85 to an eye popping 175/110. The blood supply to her placenta also had been severely impaired, which posed a risk to our baby's lungs and birth weight. All the more worrisome, the pain she was experiencing on the right side of her abdominal was not from the baby kicking her ribs, but from elevated liver enzymes essentially causing her internal organs to shut down.

All of this was scary enough to trigger a sense of panic that both Sherry and the baby were looking at a life-or-death situation, but it wouldn't be until the doctor on call would inform her that the baby needed to come out now, when the unimaginable fear of doing this by herself really hit home.

Relishing the rare freedom away from home, I didn't notice I had missed a couple of calls from both Sherry and my mom until halftime began an hour after they had already left for the hospital. By the time I was able to reach her again, she had already been omitted to the back room of the hospital and was beginning IV treatment to help induce labor. Disoriented and filled with guilt, I ran out of the arena like my hair was on fire with only one goal in mind, how can I get to the hospital as fast as humanly possible?

Thankfully, my dad was with me and was able to calm me down just enough to help bring a little sense to the chaos that was currently swirling in my head. He intelligently proposed that I stay on the phone with Sherry while he drove the both of us to the hospital. Looking back at it, this probably saved a countless number of lives because I was no longer in the right headspace to be behind a wheel and my dad was smart enough to know it. The one thing that was working on our side was the fact that the game was being played in San Diego instead of Los Angeles and the drive from the San Diego Sports Arena to Sharp Mary Birch was less than 10 minutes away. Call it luck or call it fate but whatever you call it, the situation at that moment couldn't have been more perfect and imperfect all at the same time. I had missed being there to help Sherry get to the hospital, but I had been close enough to make it in time for when the Ob/Gyn came in to let us know the baby was on his way.

    All hands were on deck as the epidural was put in and the time for delivery was here and now. Sherry's blood pressure was being closely monitored as the risk of going into complete shock or having a stroke during labor was at an all-time high. All I could do was hold her hand and pray to anybody who'd listen to save my wife and unborn child from the terrors of a nightmare that was currently being played out right in front of my eyes.

    With the courage only a woman who was bringing a new life into the world could possess, Sherry was able to summon the strength nobody in the room, including yours truly, had thought was conceivable before we had all witnessed it first-hand. In less than 3 hours after she began her first contractions, Sherry had given birth to a 5-pound 2-ounce baby boy who in all intents and purposes was the greatest miracle I have witnessed. It felt like the whole world had come to a standstill as I stood bedside not wanting to blink in case I missed a moment I knew I would never be able to get back. The first thing I noticed when I laid eyes on my son, Rowan Brandon Gandy was his beautifully constructed tiny feet. I couldn't help but run through a checklist of everything I was bearing witness to as I shouted out to Sherry that our son had two normal looking feet, two hands, my almond shaped eyes and of course two private parts in the right place. All my doubts and fears about whether my baby would be born with the same debilitating deformities as I once had to overcome were laid to rest as I looked down at my healthy baby boy and cut the umbilical cord.

    The doctor then handed our child to Sherry to hold for the first time, and all the pain and anxiety I had kept tucked away since we started on this long journey to becoming parents broke inside of me. An intense outpouring of emotion rushed out like a dam had just been broken and everything from a sense of gratitude, reprieve and outright exhilaration began to overwhelm my entire person. As I sat next to Sherry rubbing my hand on the backside of Rowan's head, we both cuddled up next to each other and took in the moment, for what we had just created needed no additional words to describe. It will be a memory that I would cherish for the rest of my life because even though it would soon become short lived, its impact on my heart was forever changed within those few minutes I had held the meaning of life in the grasp of my hands. Nothing can last forever though because just like that, Rowan was taken away from the loving arms of his parents and transported down to the newborn intensive care unit (NICU), leaving Sherry and I alone and in utter disbelief.

Chapter 49
Perspective Realized

"There is no normal life that is free of pain. It's the very wrestling with our problems that can be the impetus for our growth." – Fred Rogers

History had repeated itself as Sherry and I sat in the delivery room without our newborn child grief stricken over the fact this misery was happening to us. Subconsciously I do remember the doctor mentioning to the both of us before he rushed out the room that Rowan had developed a late stage of newborn jaundice, which if not treated immediately could cause severe brain damage and possible death in an infant. None of this made any sense to me though because I was under the impression the doctors were only worried about Sherry's overall well-being and that there was no cause for concern when it came to Rowan's current health.

It would take several days before it would be fully explained to the both of us what exactly happened and why our baby was currently struggling just to stay alive. Sherry's unexpected development of severe pre-eclampsia, which caused high blood pressure in the final 4 weeks of her pregnancy is what ultimately set off a chain reaction that caused the problems we were currently up against. Once Sherry's blood pressure started to rise, Rowan started to experience growth restriction within her stomach, which then triggered the decision to have the baby delivered 2 weeks early.

Naturally though, Rowan was not ready to come out on his own yet, so the hospital staff proceeded to artificially induce labor with a series of oxytocin hormones. To their credit, the medicine did get the job done as Sherry was finally able to go into labor, but the side effects of the extensive use of oxytocin consequently resulted in Rowan's development of neonatal jaundice and magnesium toxicity. It's hard to say if anything else could have been done differently to prevent the outcome of what had happened during that tenuous time, but one thing was for sure, never had I felt like I understood what my parents must have gone through all those years with me, then in that moment I was looking down at my baby covered with wires and tubes from head to toe.

Surprisingly, it would be Sherry who was able to handle the terror of the unknown better than me, as she was the one who dealt with the daily prognosis from the doctors and nurses, while leaving me to wander the shallowly halls of the hospital building wondering when and if we'll ever be able to take our son home. Night after night I would sit up watching my son peacefully sleep away in his little glass tube, hoping that the next morning would be the day he would finally make the turn for the better. Then came the introduction of phototherapy where it was supposed to make it easier for Rowan's liver to break down and remove the extra bilirubin from his blood stream that was causing his skin and eyes to turn yellow.

This was when I finally broke down and reached out to my parents to ask how the hell were they able to stand watching their son go through so much discomfort and not be able to do a darn thing about it.

To this I was told, "You are doing something Brandon. Both you and Sherry are doing everything you can to make sure that baby knows you love him and when he does wake up, he'll be able to tell that you were there to greet him with a welcoming smile and a positive outlook on his future."

Before I could process exactly the meaning of what my parents were trying to let me in on, I reverted back to when I first woke up from my car accident and saw everyone who cared for me standing by my side. It wasn't anything they were able to do in particular that helped me heal up any faster, but the knowledge that they cared enough to just be there to help me recover is what made all the difference in the world. This is when I started to think, maybe I was wrong in believing that my son wouldn't have to experience the level of pain growing up like I had to all those years ago, because in truth, everyone has to overcome their own version of adversity and it's how they come out afterwards that defines who they become later on in life. This is why I've always known my parents were special, because if I've learned anything from them over the years, as the saying goes, it's not how many times you get knocked down, it's how many times you can get back up.

Somehow, Rowan knew that and after 3 days of light therapy and 7 days recovering in the NICU, he finally was able to make the turn we had all been hoping for and was released from the hospital with a full bill of health. Now it was time for the real parenting to begin and Sherry and I hadn't the slightest clue on how we were going to do that, but our initial perspective on how we thought it was going to go totally changed after we were thrown a curveball to start the first couple of weeks of parenthood.

As soon as we arrived home to our second level, 2 story condo I felt an immediate difference on how I once viewed the living quarters Sherry and I had been residing in for the past 10 years. Within a matter of hours after bringing home our newborn, the space in which we lived felt much smaller and the steps that were once so great for working out, had been transformed into an immediate death trap. I had always flirted with the idea of wanting to upgrade to a more spacious house but had never been willing to leave the comfort of what we already had. Then came the addition of Rowan and the threat to his overall safety and it had become quite obvious it was time for Sherry and me to make our move.

Frankly, I wish we had this revelation before Rowan was born, but nevertheless the market was on the upswing, and we believed we were going to be able to make a big enough profit on the sale of our property to walk right into our dream home. Sherry and I were financially in the best position we had ever been, with her being promoted as the director of behavioral health and I still working for the Friars Golf Club, while also securing a major role on the FX hit series The Passage at San Diego Comic-Con. Everything had been set up perfectly for us to make the next leap forward and discover the new home we were eager to enjoy raising our little miracle baby in. How perfect that decision was, to say goodbye to our youth and welcome in adulthood, would later be recognized as one of the smartest choices either of us had ever made, as the unthinkable was about to happen and the whole world was about to change forever.

Chapter 50
Immunocompromised

"The oldest and strongest emotion of mankind is fear, and the oldest and strongest kind of fear is fear of the unknown." – H.P. Lovecraft

Nothing can prepare you for when the world suddenly comes to an end, as once it's realized by the masses, all reasoning and rationale go out the window. On January 21, 2020, almost exactly one year after Rowan was born and our family moved into our new home, the center for disease control and prevention (CDC) confirmed the United States first coronavirus case.

At first, this historical announcement was received by many with an innate amount of skepticism, as well as some heavy eye rolling. However, within the transplant and immune compromised community our antennas sprouted up because this highly contagious disease was said to be 5 times more deadly than the influenza virus, more commonly known as the flu. Since I had been taking antirejection medications that had been weakening my immune system for the past 16 years, I fell into the category of the people who were most likely not going to survive if we were ever exposed to this terrible illness. Ever since I had been given a second chance at life (when my mom selflessly donated her kidney to me), I had been considered immunocompromised, essentially making me more vulnerable to infection than the normal healthy individual. Therefore, almost immediately after the Covid-19 virus started to spread throughout the country my family and I made the decision to quarantine together to wait out the storm. It was scary to think this unknown disease could fatally run rampant throughout our family because even though I was the one everyone was mostly concerned about; we had become keenly aware that no one was safe from this awful disease.

It was just one month earlier before the first case of Covid-19 was initially reported when I fell deathly sick with a respiratory infection that ultimately sent me to the hospital. I had given up putting my body on the line for the short-term benefit of my inflated ego, but once a year for the past 15 years, my high school friends and I would come together to throw the pigskin around on the morning of every Thanksgiving holiday. This timeless Turkey Bowl classic had been ingrained in me ever since I could remember and stubbornly even though it was forecasted to rain 6 inches on the day of our event, I decided to partake in our annual get together. Consequently, 3 days later I would come down with the pneumonia virus, which if you don't know, is extremely dangerous to anyone with a compromised immune system. It is said, "Though overall patient survival has increased, pneumonia is both the most common invasive infection in immunocompromised patients and have the highest mortality and morbidity rate." Since I was ill prepared for the aftermath of my poor decision I was left to struggle for oxygen through the help of a respirator and was just lucky enough to recover in time before this life saving machine would eventually become virtually impossible to find. After all was said and done, I would go on to spend 5 weeks in and out of the hospital until I was finally discharged for the last time on January 3rd, 2020. 2 months later the world would go into lockdown because of another more contagious and deadlier disease, leaving Sherry and I shaking our heads with the disbelief that once again I had escaped a certain disaster and was still alive to fulfill whatever prophecy that needed to be achieved.

    On edge from my previous run in with a deadly respiratory infection and feeling a little extra protective for our newborn's safety, Sherry and I desperately scavenged through articles online, while listening to news updates on how we could better prepare if the worst was to happen. We had begun to turn inward and pull away from our usual routines as we became paralyzed with fear that after everything we had just gone through to bring life into this world, it could suddenly be taken away with the contamination from either of us.

Disheveled from the quickness our lives had switched into survival mode, we made a vow that no matter what happened to either of us our number one priority was to keep 18-month-old baby Rowan safe and away from harm's way. So, we adapted to our new reality by listening to science and patiently delayed our return to normal until we were specifically told by our medical advisors the threat had been contained. No one could have ever foreseen the devastation the Covid-19 pandemic turned out to be, where grimly 1 million U.S. citizens would lose their lives within the first 2 years of its existence.

It had become surreal to think that Rowan's first few years of life would be consumed with being hidden away from the outside world only to watch the seasons go by through the plain glass window from our front living room couch. However, I wouldn't have changed anything about that first year locked away because during that time our family was given a once in a lifetime opportunity to reconnect on a deeper level and once again appreciate what really mattered in life, which was the love and support only family can provide.

With that being said though, it wasn't like we all lived harmoniously together and were not dispirited by each day that went by where we were left to play another game of Yahtzee instead of being outside enjoying the thrilling atmosphere of a live sporting event, because trust me, that surely wasn't the case. Like most families who were forced to put their lives on hold during that time, we started to grow impatient amongst each other and would have done anything to go back to how things used to be.

Unfortunately, the stakes were much too high for any of us to risk the potential of contracting a mysterious virus that for all intents and purposes could shut down a person's vital organs resulting in a quick and immediate death. No, it was well understood that this was going to be our new normal for at least the time being, as it was better to lean towards the safe side than have any regrets later down the road. Yet, the funny thing I have learned over all my years growing up as a miracle child, is that no matter how much you plan for what the future could possibly bring, life will still find a way to sneak up from behind and smack you right across the head.

For the past year and a half, I had been preparing myself for a battle that was surely going to come, but when the day finally arrived for me to summon that wolverine mentality, I was caught off guard because it would be with an opponent I never expected I'd ever have to face.

Chapter 51
Didn't See that Coming

"I hate pain, despite my ability to tolerate it beyond all known parameters, which is not necessarily a good thing." – Hunter S. Thompson

Time had slowed to an agonizing crawl as each day that passed felt like it was groundhogs' day over and over again. The world had been at a standstill for the past year and a half with only the glimmer of hope that a new vaccine could resurrect our stagnant economy and allow life to slowly trickle back out from the bunkers we had all been hiding in. For me, it didn't matter that this new experimental vaccine had been rushed into production and had bypassed many of the traditional red tape that most pharmaceutical drugs were normally forced to go through.

The simple truth of the matter was that I was not about to start questioning what my doctors were recommending now, since it was only because of their innovation and expertise over the past 33 years that I was still alive today. I had been lucky enough to make it this long without contracting the Covid-19 virus and now that there was a real opportunity to protect not only myself but the people I loved around me, I couldn't wait to finally ease the anxiety we had all been dealing with. So it was, when the executive order came down where anyone who was 65 years or older, as well as immunocompromised, was eligible to receive the highly anticipated vaccine shot, I would be the first in line to roll up my sleeve and start the journey back to the world's new normal. It had felt like a huge weight had just been taken off my shoulders and now I could finally take a deep breath of fresh air without the fear of the possible consequences for what I was breathing in. A part of my life, and for that matter all our lives, had been stripped away from us with no warning or sign of regret, but now rejuvenated with a boost of hope from the wonder of what modern medicine can provide, I was ready to travel the world again to accomplish the goals I had been forced to put on hold when this universal tragedy had first taken place.

Before I could do that though, I had one last doctor appointment, where I was to receive my 2nd vaccine shot and a full physical examination that would allow me to go back to work in any part of the United States. Consequently, this is where I would learn I had been diagnosed with the scariest 6 letter word in the English dictionary, cancer.

The shock of the announcement was so unexpected at first, I could have sworn the doctor was speaking to someone else. Never in my wildest dreams did I imagine a scenario where I would have to face the threat of what cancer can do to a person's cellular make up, as I was convinced my body and mind had already been put through enough of what the world could possibly allocate to one person.

Captivated by the ignorance of my folly, the doctor on hand assured me that it was entirely possible, and actually more likely, that of all people who would be diagnosed with basal cell carcinoma, it would most certainly be someone like me. A few reasons for this were because this type of skin cancer was found primarily in people who spend a significant amount of time in the sun and had a hereditary link with someone who has had this disease in the past. Well, this was strike one and two against me because not only did I work and play on a golf course almost every day of my life, both my mom and aunt had previously been diagnosed with an array of different forms of skin cancer. If that wasn't bad enough, he went on to educate me on the fact that because I was immunocompromised, I was at a far greater risk of developing cutaneous malignancies which inherently meant that was strike three.

I had been dealt a lot of setbacks in my life, but this one planted my butt right to the ground, as it felt like I had gone through too much these past couple of years to prevent myself from getting sick, to than just be rewarded with a prognosis that was surely going to require a surgical miracle to overcome.

Obscured from the reality of my imminent future I plunged into a desolate state of depression where I found myself pessimistic for a return to my outgoing charismatic self. In retrospect, nothing had really changed in regard to being given a hurdle that needed to be jumped, besides the fact that this time around I'd struggle with the knowledge that my son's view of his invincible father would be shattered the instant I went under the knife for the 27th time. It was an illusion that I had created in my head where I believed I could leave the ghosts of my medical fragility in the past and assume the role of the indestructible superhero I so badly sought after. It was this misconception I had of my own dad that led me to believe that this is what it meant to be a real husband and father.

If my family couldn't depend on me to even be able to take care of myself, then how could I ever expect them to trust that I would always be able to take care of them? It was an unfair attack towards my own self-worth, but this was the daunting task I was allotted once I decided to bring loved ones into my inner circle without the guarantee from disappointment and despondency. A few weeks went by as the doctors double-checked the biopsy results from the cyst they had spotted in my lower left eyelid, and I learned the gameplan on exactly how they expected to remove the exponential growth that had slowly started to take over my passion for life.

The MOHS micrographic surgery would be done in stages, which included lab work to make sure they had removed all the cancerous cells while I patiently waited in the operating room. The whole premise around this procedure was to remove a layer of tissue at a time with the hope of sparing as much healthy tissue as possible until the surgeon knew for sure there were no cancer cells remaining. The only disadvantage to this technique is that the examiner is unaware of how large of an area the cancer cells might have spread and there was no assurance once they started cutting, they would be able to extract the full amount. Nevertheless, this was my only option if I had any hope of avoiding chemotherapy and looking like the same person, relatively speaking I was before the operation.

I was told the whole process would take less than an hour and because of my age the doctor expected I would only have to have one, maybe two layers at most, removed from my lower eyelid. Once the site was clear of all cancer cells, he would then stitch the wound back up and I would be able to go home the same day. Alas, nothing could quite be that simple when it involves operating on a guy who has already had every misfortunate operational error ever conceived of happen within the past 3-decade span. Maybe that's a bit dramatic, but after the 6th layer of tissue was removed from my thinly eroding skin I was dangerously starting to contemplate if they were ever going to stop cutting away at my face.

Eventually, after the 7th round of removing the roots from the cancerous iceberg submerged under my skin in the upper part of my left cheek, I was left with a hole the size of a half dollar and without any one around who was qualified to sew it back up. Not only did my face look like it belonged in the tv show *The Walking Dead,* but I was also still scared that maybe they didn't actually get all of the cancer growing within my body. Thankfully, the head specialist was called in to help intervene and he reassured me that the good news was they had indeed removed all the cancerous cells laid hidden amongst my face. The bad news was that because of the scope of how much tissue they had to remove in such a short period of time, I was to be immediately rushed to San Diego's widely acclaimed plastic eye surgeon, Dr. Asa Morton.

There had been no time for me to fully grasp the levity of the situation I was currently experiencing because before I knew it, I was in another hospital and on a separate operating bed getting ready to be put to sleep for the 28th time. There with me and heartbroken over watching her husband go through not one but two major surgeries, Sherry clung to the belief in my ability to heal through any physical ailment solely because she had routinely seen me do it so many times before. This time around, however, would be less about my instinctual will to survive and more of the unmatched expertise from a surgeon at the top of his game. Nothing about that day would ever be misconstrued as glamorous, but there was a reason I had been recommended to Dr. Morton because the man is the absolute best at what he does for a living. Not only did I recover in less than 3 months from the nightmare that was that day, but he had miraculously saved my eye and face from being permanently deformed with his quick thinking and artistic precision. Yet, what he couldn't fix with just a scalpel and the talent only a surgeon who has been in practice for over 30 years could possibly have, was the psychological damage entrenched into my memory bank after being confronted once again with my own mortality. Yes, I had faced life and death situations on multiple occasions before, but this time I was unprepared for the solemnity I would feel after I saw the pain my possible demise had caused regarding my son's unconditional conviction in my self-preservation. When I looked into his eyes, it felt like the unbreakable aura that surrounded me had been stolen away and from here on out my son's interpretation of who his father was would be forever tainted with the knowledge that one day I wouldn't be around.

    This realization had been a hard pill for me to swallow and even though I would make a full recovery and had been declared cancer free, I had lost a part of the spark that made up my internal zest for life. I had become enamored with the notion that one day I would end up abandoning the people I loved through no fault of my own and in turn defy the promise I made to both Sherry and Rowan that I would forever be there to love and protect them to the best of my ability. These thoughts would plague me for many months after the last physical scar had faded away and it was going to take an unprompted intervention to help pull me out from beneath the psychological chasm, I had fallen into so deeply.

Chapter 52
Wolverine Mentality

"You can't wait until life isn't hard anymore before you decide to be happy." – Nightbirde

One minute you feel like you have the whole world figured out and the very next minute you can't even tell if the world has ever known you were there. My past and future had all of sudden become blurred by the distinct reminder that nothing is ever guaranteed in life, especially the promise of seeing what tomorrow can bring. After my scare with cancer and the gruesome recovery of a surgically repaired frontal orbital socket, I was starting to find it harder and harder to rest my head down at night. The thoughts of what I still needed to accomplish and what I believed still needed to be passed down to Rowan raced through my mind as an endless cycle of unfinished hopes and dreams in which I didn't know if I'd ever get a chance to live out. So, as impatience took over my ability to stay in the here and now, I threw caution to the wind and began to change the way I was living my life.

No matter how safe I played it or how reckless my actions had become in the past, I finally realized that the ultimate aftermath of what was going to happen was out of my control and I might as well start living my life to the fullest instead of worrying about the consequences that had always been unavoidable. I so badly wanted to be a great father to Rowan like my dad was to me, but I felt flawed with my own health insecurities that I started working out and training my body to be as physically fit as humanly possible. That's when I was first introduced to the new pandemic novelty of mountain biking, and I latched onto its adrenaline-fueled appeal like a full-blown adventure seeking addict. I immediately went out and spent thousands of dollars on all the top-notch biking gear, as well as a state-of-the-art full suspension Giant Stance Mountain bike. Never mind the fact that I had never been mountain biking in my life before, I was ready to test the limits of my newfound health obsession, not realizing all the risks that were ultimately involved.

    I began to hit the trails and explore the back roads of the mountain tops that rested behind my property, with each ride gaining more confidence and dialing in new lines. My riding had evolved into an escape from the pain I was experiencing while contemplating what my impact on my son's future would ultimately be if I could stay healthy long enough to be a part of it. Subconsciously, I knew I was disobeying my own instincts on the preservation of my own survival but in the moment while I was sprinting down the mountain side of some of the toughest terrain San Diego's outskirts had to offer, I felt invincible to the imminent threats that the common mortal would otherwise usually shy away from. Consumed with the belief that my wolverine mentality could prohibit any fatal outcome; I flew down the tracks that were meticulously edged into the local foothills naïve to the fact that I was about to make another appointment with my old nemesis, death itself.

    The day was like any other, where my longtime friend Jamie and I would strap on our bikes to the back of his truck and travel out to an unexplored destination in hopes of finding a true expedition worth remembering. This time however, neither of us knew exactly what we were getting ourselves into as after an hour into our voyage we had become keenly aware we were in way over our heads. The nice open trail we had started on had suddenly turned into a 5-foot-wide walking path with a 300-foot drop to the lake below. Considering I was no expert in the art of flying, I soon grew weary that it was about time we started heading back to where we had just come from. The only problem was the trail had become too tight for us to safely turn around and we agreed to press on until we found a wider opening to flip our bikes back around. As always, Jamie was leading the way as he was the more experienced rider and I trusted he could navigate his way through unknown territory way better than I could ever have done. For the most part this strategy tended to work out well because he could ride ahead and scout out where we needed to go, while I lagged behind and conserved my energy for the treacherous climbs ahead. On this specific occasion though, I was left to steer my way down a rocky hillside with no one around in case I happened to fall. As fate would have it, that was exactly what was about to happen as my front tire clipped the point of a protruding rock and I jerkily lost control as I went tumbling off the cliff's edge.

You know that moment when you say or do something you instantly regret, well this was that moment, as the weightlessness from being flung in the air sent my heart rate skyrocketing and my stomach into an absolute free fall. I only had time to think of one thing and that was how soon was I about to feel the impact from my colossal mistake? Oddly, a lot sooner than I initially anticipated as about 8 feet down I landed face up on top of a concealed sugar bush about 10 x 12 ft wide. Beyond that, laid a vast amount of open space about 250 feet down and with it, the unmistakable death for any unfortunate soul who happened to fall from that far off the cliff's edge. With a 50-pound mountain bike lying atop me and no one around to call for help, I was left alone with just my thoughts and prayers on where exactly my life had gone so terribly wrong.

Let me rephrase that, I meant to say how did I find myself hanging onto a bush, off a side of a mountain, staring up at the bright blue sky with certain death just below me? As I hung there too scared to try and move in case a branch would have suddenly given way and I dropped to my imminent doom, I refocused my attention on what I was going to do if I was lucky enough to survive this dire situation. One thing was for sure, I would never go downhill mountain biking ever again because I came to understand that this sport had just become entirely too freaking dangerous for my liking anymore.

My 2-year-old son adored me too much for me to be risking my life just so I could believe I was living my life to the fullest. Somehow along the way, I had misconstrued what it meant to live your life like there is no tomorrow because in actuality there is, and even if I'm not there to see what that tomorrow brings, my son will be and so will my wife, family, and friends. It was then when I realized it was the way in how I went about living my life that ultimately determined my lasting impact on not only the people I love, but the countless number of people I would never end up meeting but were indirectly affected by my contributions to this world. Maybe I wasn't guaranteed a long and fruitful life but who is? My dad once told me that no one is guaranteed anything when it comes to the game of life and during those last moments at the edge of the world, I had finally understood what he was trying to get through to me all those years ago. Then, out from the depths of nowhere, I saw Jamie's hand reach down from over the ridge and I knew I was being given another chance.

Chapter 53
The Price of Admission

"I cannot say whether things will get better if we change; what I can say is they must change if they are to get better." – Georg C. Lichtenberg

You'd be surprised how fast 10 years goes by, as it seemed like just yesterday Sherry, and I were saying "I do" to one another and dreaming of the future we were so eagerly awaiting to build towards. Fast forward to a couple months after I had been literally pulled back from the cliff I had fallen from, and we were once again visualizing how we wanted the next chapter of our lives to look like. I knew as a couple we were coming up to a pivotal point in our relationship where it was going to be either now or never if we were serious in trying to have a second child.

Sherry and I both were 35 years of age and if we wanted to assure a higher likelihood of a safe and healthy pregnancy, then the sooner we could start, the better. Therein lay the problem, because for three years now, since Rowan first miraculously came into our lives, we had grown accustomed to the routine a one child household fully entailed. As intriguing as it was to think Rowan could grow up with a friend and not solely have to rely on either of our full and undivided attention, we had still felt a bit hesitant about putting Sherry's body through the types of physical and mental strain she had courageously endured during her last go around. Not to mention the difficulty I'd recently had with my own psychological conflict with pain and mortality, really left us sympathetic to the idea that maybe we should just stay to the status quo. Then came the bike accident and from that point on the desire to grow our family by one revitalized our entire enthusiasm.

In a way, I had become inspired by Jamie's heroic effort to lend his hand in my time of need and sparked a fire inside of me that would change the trajectory of where my life was heading. I no longer saw myself wanting to be on the road for weeks at a time going from one work event to the next, while my family stayed back at home living their lives without me. I recognized that what I truly wanted was to find a way to be more involved in Rowan's upbringing instead of sporadically showing up here and there, envious of the people who were making a true impact in his everyday life.

This became even more evident when Sherry and I were starting to discuss adding even more responsibility to our plates with the addition of one more child. With all that being said, I still absolutely loved being on the golf course on a daily basis and meeting people from all around the world, which is why I turned to my dad for some well needed guidance on how exactly I could find my way out of this convoluted conundrum. See, my dad had retired a while back from his job as a commercial sales rep and decided to spend the rest of his days helping to produce one of the biggest nonprofit charity foundations in San Diego County. His dream had always been to create one of the most competitive 4-man scramble tournaments in the country with the premise being to help raise money for military families who needed food, education, housing, and financial assistance supporting children's personal growth.

After years of hard work and countless numbers of generous donations, Cy Young award winner Randy Jones and my parents, Curtis and Linda Gandy partnered up to create the Randy Jones Invitational, which coincided with the formation of the Randy Jones Foundation. Their unconventional way of being able to host over 1,400 free rounds of golf for every person who played in a local 501-C charity golf tournament throughout the year, directly led to their immense popularity and charitable contribution of over $1 million dollars as of 2022. In light of this success came several opportunities to expand their operations by helping other charitable organizations successfully run their own golf tournaments. Unfortunately, because of the time and energy their own tournament and foundation demanded from them, they could not in good faith take on the additional responsibility of any other foundation's event. However, in light of my newfound hunger to be home and around my family, coupled with my experience in running high profile golf outings, the timing couldn't have been more perfect for me to pivot my career from a national to a local golf events coordinator.

The transition from living out of my suitcase to the comforts of my hometown scenery by the end of 2021 was quite smooth and had allowed me to get in the right frame of mind to start considering expanding our family of 3 to a family of 4. One thing Sherry and I had going for us was the fact that we still had 3 embryos who were all deemed healthy enough to be transferred for implantation whenever we decided to turn this possibility into a reality.

After much thought and consideration, we had finally concluded that we wanted more than ever to bring home another addition to love and raise as one of our own. In the blink of an eye, the wheels were in motion, and we were scheduled for a transfer date the week before Rowan's 3rd birthday. Everything about the whole process of getting ready to create life for the second time was essentially the same from our first experience, with one minor exception, Sherry's pregnancy was considered geriatric because she was now over 35 years of age. However, the doctors reassured us Sherry was in perfect health and as long as they could keep her preeclampsia at bay, she would be just fine in delivering a second child. So, without any further delay, we showed up to the hospital ready for round 2 where we would be caught off guard as we would learn that the plan we had originally set out to do was no longer a viable possibility.

Some things in life will always be out of our control and at the top of that list of unpredictable certainties will continue to be the inner workings of the human body and more specifically nature's own reproductive system. No matter how well our scientific data gets to being able to predict the procreation cycle between two people there will never be a hundred percent certainty to being able to produce life. With that being said, this does not erase the utter sadness and disappointment a family feels when they are told their procedure has failed and the embryo that had held their dreams for the future within it has been lost forever. It's hard to put into words the emotion you feel when you are first hit with the news that everything you and your partner had been working tirelessly to make come true had fallen up short, and you were now in a position to see if you both had enough strength or even the same will to start the whole process over again. For Sherry and me this was our new reality as we had just been told Sherry was unable to get pregnant with the first of the 3 embryos we had in storage and unfortunately, the likelihood of her being able to actually get pregnant again had fallen to less than 10%. Feeling dejected and in a somber mood we had left the facility that once provided us with one of the happiest moments of our life and headed home to reevaluate our next move. Two months passed before Sherry, and I found ourselves sitting across the table watching our then 3-year-old boy enjoying the Thanksgiving holidays with all his cousins and close family. Rowan's happiness reinvigorated our spirits in wanting to provide him with a sibling he could grow up sharing those types of memories with and as bold as it might have seemed to test the futility of Sherry's reproductive cycle, we were determined to give it one last shot.

 Sherry and I waited until after the new year to try our luck at the improbable and we hoped that 2022 would bring the birth of a brand-new healthy baby. We both knew the deck had been stacked against us, but in my experience, the human mind was still the most unique and complex object in the known universe and had proven over and over again to be able to turn the truly impossible into the absolute feasible no matter what kind of physical or mental limitations a person was currently experiencing. We had become tantalized with the thought of Sherry electing to forgo taking the extra medication to help get pregnant and avoiding putting her body through another round of physical stress, that for us, didn't feel beneficial for her long-term well-being. So, unconventional by most standards, Sherry decided to cut out the daily needle pricking from her regimented routine, as we clung to the hope that her natural instincts coupled with our faith in God's plan would ultimately prevail. It would take a whole fortnight after our last embryo was transferred, before we would finally know, after 6 years from the first day we had decided we wanted to have multiple children if our wish was going to come true.

Chapter 54
Layla Joon

"You made my world stand still, and in that stillness, there was a freedom I never felt before." – Sarah McLachlan

Congratulations Mr. and Mrs. Gandy, Sherry is indeed pregnant, and you can expect to be having a baby girl." In that moment as we both sat in utter disbelief, all I could think was how for the second time we were given the miracle of life and how wrong I was to ever think this might never happen.

Out of all people, I should have known that nothing in this world is impossible, especially when it comes to the wonders of what the human body can do. It had been a long, hard adventure to get to this point, but we knew the whole process wasn't over just yet, as we still had 9 more months to go before we were to meet this little angel of ours. In the meantime, Sherry and I had a lot of work ahead of us regarding getting our jobs and family dynamics ready for our new addition that was soon to arrive. The year 2022 was setting up for a whole bunch of change as I was beginning to move away from traveling for work, Sherry was being asked to take on more responsibility at her ever-evolving company and Rowan was slowly transitioning from the baby stage right into full toddler mode. Life was coming at us fast as I was still reckoning with the fact that I was just a little over a year away from being diagnosed with skin cancer and my wife's last pregnancy resulted in her almost losing her life to a rare condition called HELLP syndrome. This is why I believe after 35 years I decided it was finally time to chronicle my own life's story, so the future of my family's legacy and all the people who have ever had to overcome any kind of adversity, could understand in my own words the journey I took that ultimately changed my entire perspective on what I thought life was all about.

Over the years, my family and I had been approached on several occasions to share my story with the world as it was seen to be unique and inspirational to many. However, it never felt like the right time for such an overwhelming undertaking because simply, I always thought I still had a lot more to learn and experience before I was ever going to sit down and write this mid-life memoir. That all changed though when I realized for the first time, I had already lived a lifetime worth of experiences and was now ready to hopefully make a difference to someone in the world who has also struggled with the ups and downs that life can throw our way. I remember in the very beginning, Sherry challenged me to take the extra time I now had at home to write about the history of my battle with chronic illness, so one day Rowan and my new unborn child could know the origin of their beginnings. What I didn't expect was the therapeutic feeling I would soon receive from the countless number of memories I had tucked away never to be brought to the forefront ever again. In a sense, it was a reminder of how resilient the human body and mind can actually be, which really helped regulate my fears for what the next chapter in my life was about to bring.

I came to recognize it was ok that some things were out of my control because the uncertainty of what tomorrow has in store is what makes all of us human and free to choose how we go about enjoying our lives. The funny thing was, the more I began to reminisce on the past, the more I came to understand that the way I perceived the world around me, as well as the outlook I chose to have after every good or bad situation that ever happened, directly impacted how I went about living my life. I started to notice through the stories I was telling that the majority of the decisions I made were a result of the physical, emotional, and spiritual trials and tribulations I routinely came to encounter. It was soon apparent that I was having a hard time grappling with not wanting to be known as a victim to my own personal shortcomings, but at the same time contradicting myself with the belief that because of my past medical circumstances I shouldn't plan for the future and instead just focus on what I was guaranteed today. This sole thought process was the driving force behind most of the reckless and sometimes selfish behavior I found myself partaking in for a good portion of my life. I once bought into the conviction that life was short and you should try and live each day to its fullest, but then two things recently happened that shifted my view on how I would forever see the world.

The first was coming to terms with the truth that even though I regularly found myself fighting to stay healthy and in good spirits after every one of my unexpecting misfortunes, I was still alive and here to tell the story. The second, and might I add the more enlightening of the two, was the recent birth of my baby girl, Layla Rose Gandy. No longer was it good enough just to live for a moment, as I realized after gazing down at my family all sleeping together on the first night, we brought Layla home, because in that moment of self-reflection, life had transformed into being about living for ALL the moments be them from the past, the present or the future. Those 2 little individuals peacefully dreaming away in a bed that resided in a home that Sherry and I had worked so hard to provide for them, didn't care in the slightest for either of our perceived shortcomings, all they cared about was that mommy and daddy were there to love and care for them as much as humanly possible. This is why after recounting the entirety of how I survived life as a miracle child, I can genuinely now say it shouldn't be because of all the wild adventures or life-saving surgeries that separates me from everyone else, because we all have a unique and distinct story of persevering through tough times, and this is why in my eyes we are all life's miracle.

Chapter 55
To Infinity and Beyond

"The challenge of our unknown future is so much more exciting than the stories of our accomplished past." – Simon Sinek

As I sit here wrapping up the last chapter of my story, I am blessed with the company of my 3-day old baby girl dreaming away in her crib just 2 feet away from my desk. When did my world of scars, broken bones and life-threatening illnesses cease to matter and were instead replaced with pride, hope, and an endless amount of cute little smiles? It's like, after witnessing the smooth pregnancy and birth of my second child, I had finally been able to reconcile with the demons of my past and come to understand that not every hospital visit had to be a scary experience.

I have always considered the doctors and nurses to be the main reason why I am still alive today and if it were not for their skill and determination during the most critical of times my whole story of survival could have turned out to be a lot different. Luckily for me, I had been surrounded by some of the best in the world, who repeatedly gave me the greatest gifts any one person could ever ask for. From the success of my very first operation, to the transfer of my mom's kidney, to the birth of my two beautiful children and everything in between I would like to thank those medical professionals for everything I have today. Together, these miracle workers also afforded me the gift of time, in which I have been able to reflect and process everything that has come my way and everything I still have to look forward to.

Currently, I am 36 years old with a wife and 2 kids under the age of 4 living in one of the most beautiful cities in the world—San Diego, California. I have been able to use my knowledge and experience to carve out a career in the sport I love most and am happier and healthier than I have ever been before. Does that mean

I no longer live with chronic illness that derives from my previous traumas? Of course not, but it does mean I have been able to refocus my energy on making the best of the circumstances I have been given, which I feel has opened the door to a safer and more appreciative way of living. I can't tell you what the future has in store for me and the rest of my life, but for now I'm making plans as if I'm going to be around for a lot longer than I originally thought my body was ever capable of providing me.

    A couple of those plans include hiking to Mount Everest base camp, first inspired after reading Bear Grylls' autobiography, *Mud, Sweat and Tears*, as well as, qualifying to play in the United States Four-Ball Championship before the age of 40. These are the goals I have set for myself as a reminder that life continues to go on and if you prepare and put in the hard work it takes to make it to the top, one day you might catch yourself accomplishing what you once had thought was impossible. I never asked to be considered a miracle child nor have I ever thought of myself as an inspiration, but with that being said, I do believe my story resonates with many parents, children, and people of all walks of life who are either going through or have gone through a difficult situation and are looking for any sign of hope. *Surviving Life as a Miracle Child* is about bringing that hope to them, through the stories I have lived and the experiences I have learned from along the way. So, these will definitely not be the last words you will hear from me, as I am filled with anticipation for what the future entails, but for now, this is Gameday Blades signing off and leaving you all with my own pearls of wisdom: It doesn't matter if you see the glass half full or half empty, all that matters is that you have a glass and you know it can always be refilled.

Acknowledgements

I first would like to start off by thanking all the doctors and nurses who helped save my life on multiple occasions and never once gave up hope. Without them I can honestly say I would not be here authoring this story today. There are two specific doctors in particular, Dr. Alberto Pena and Dr. Oscar Salvateria, who I would like to personally thank because it was their unique set of skills which allowed me to persevere through some of the most challenging times. I'd also be hard pressed not to acknowledge the sacrifice both my mom and dad made early on in my life, as I couldn't imagine the emotional and financial stress they must have gone through. They truly are my heroes, and I will forever be grateful for their love and guidance. As my parents were the rock that I leaned on for support when I needed it most, my brother Jacob and my sister Tanya were the glue that kept me grounded when I started to drift too far away from home. Their way of never making me feel like an outsider even when I was away from home for months at a time gave me the strength and reassurance that no matter what I went through, I would always be their goofy annoying brother.

Now, let me get to the people who I have come across throughout my life that honestly made such an impact on my personal growth that I would be remiss not to acknowledge them here. Curtis, Jamie, and Jon you will forever be my best friends as it was because of you that I realized what true friendship looks like. No matter how many surgeries I went through and no matter the time in between our next meeting you have always been there to answer the phone or fly across the country to make sure your buddy was doing ok. This leads me to the man, the myth and the legend Jeff Renzulli who took me under his wing when I was just a young kid from the sunny coast of Southern California and looking to make a name for himself in the game of golf. I can't thank you enough for all the support and leadership you showed me, as it was because of you that my dream of traveling the world while playing golf and meeting some of the most friendly and interesting people along the way had become a reality. You also introduced me to the world of audiobooks where I instantly fell in love with the story of Bear Grylls and his crazy adventures that tested his resolve and fortitude in trying to survive the wild. It was because of his book Mud, Sweat and Tears that I got the itch to write my own autobiography and hopefully one day be able to compare survival stories with the survival king himself.

    In the beginning, when I first sat down to write about the life I have lived up until this point, I had thought this would only be shared amongst my wife and children. It wasn't until I encountered the most amazing and hardworking agent in the writing industry, Andrea Comparato. From the very first time we met she had a belief in my story that the world needed to hear and without her unwavering conviction to see my book get published I don't know if anybody would be reading it today. One thing any writer will tell you about bringing their story into the public's eyes is that it takes an entire team of dedicated people who believe in the work you have created to truly make something special. For my team, I would like to thank my agency Inscriptions Literary, my publisher Captivate Press, the whole editing team at RB Media, as well as Ingram Content Group who is responsible for manufacturing and distributing my book for everyone's reading pleasure. I also couldn't have written nor produced such a polished version of my work without the help of a few talented beta readers, John Hendrickson, Terry Mix and Elyse Languirand. Thank you for sacrificing your time and energy in reading through the first few drafts of Surviving Life as a Miracle Child as the version you are all reading now would have sounded tremendously different without their much-appreciated literary insight.

 Finally, I would like to say to my wife Sherry and my 2 kids Rowan and Layla, you are the heart and soul of everything I do, and you have made my time on this Earth worth living every second of it. I can only hope that my story helps show you a better glimpse into the life I have lived and gives meaning to all the scars you routinely ask about. Continue to stay curious and take risks as the world is your playground and I am forever grateful that I am here to share it with you.

References

Cecka, M. J. (2005). The OPTN/UNOS Renal Transplant Registry. National Center for Biotechnology Information. Retrieved August 23, 2022, from https://pubmed.ncbi.nlm.nih.gov/17424721/

Donovan, D. (2022, May 17). The U.S. officially surpasses 1 million COVID-19 deaths. Johns Hopkins Coronavirus Resource Center. Retrieved August 23, 2022, from https://coronavirus.jhu.edu/from-our-experts/u-s-officially-surpasses-1-million-covid-19-deaths

Julie B Zhao, M. D. (2022, January 28). Pneumonia in immunocompromised patients. Overview, Causes of Pneumonia, HIV/AIDS. Retrieved August 23, 2022, from https://emedicine.medscape.com/article/807846-overview

KF, N. (2016, January 11). Organ donation and Transplantation Statistics. National Kidney Foundation. Retrieved August 23, 2022, from https://www.kidney.org/news/newsroom/factsheets/Organ-Donation-and-Transplantation-Stats

MacMillan, C. (2022, May 3). What does it mean to be 'immunocompromised'? Yale Medicine. Retrieved August 23,

2022, from https://www.yalemedicine.org/news/what-does-immunocompromised-mean.

Professional, C. M. (2022, February 28). Advanced maternal age (geriatric pregnancy): Definition & Risks. Cleveland Clinic. Retrieved August 23, 2022, from https://my.clevelandclinic.org/health/diseases/22438-advanced-maternal-age.

Reporter, R. P. H. D. (2020, December 18). Covid far more lethal than flu, data shows. WebMD. Retrieved August 23, 2022, from https://www.webmd.com/lung/news/20201218/covid-19-is-far-more-lethal-damaging-than-flu-data-shows#1.

Sobsey, D. (2004). Marital stability and marital satisfaction in families of children with disabilities: Chicken or egg? Retrieved August 23, 2022, from https://files.eric.ed.gov/fulltext/EJ848190.pdf.

Index

Amy Poehler - "Sometimes you need to know to quit while you're ahead or at least before things get much worse!" Ch. 41

Angela Wood - "If you know you're going home, the journey is never too hard." Ch. 5

Arthur Schopenhauer - "It is with trifles, and when he is off guard, that a man best reveals his character" Ch. 34

Atticus - "Never go in search of love, go in search of life and life will find you the love you seek." Ch. 30

Avinash Wandre - "Every time you are able to find humor in some difficult situation, you win!" Ch. 28

Babe Ruth - "It's hard to beat a person who never gives up." Ch. 4

Benjamin Disraeli - "There is no education like adversity." Ch. 15

Bob Marley - "Open your eyes, look within. Are you satisfied with the life you're living?" Ch. 22

Brandon Gandy - "The world can be full of challenges, so do your best to overcome the hard times and when the good times come, embrace them with everything you have." Ch. 33

Caroline Myss - "Always go with the choice that scares you the most, because that's the one that is going to help you grow." Ch. 35

Cate Blanchett - "Marriage is a risk: I think it's a great and glorious risk, as long as you can embark on the adventure in the same spirit. Interludes - Wife

Catherine Pulsifer - "Faith is unseen but felt, faith is strength when we feel we have none, faith is hope when all seems lost." Ch. 42

Conan O'Brien - "The beauty is that through disappointment, you can gain clarity, and with clarity comes conviction and true originality" Ch. 18

Confucius - "It does not matter how slowly you go as long as you do not stop." Ch. 26

Corrie Ten Boom - "Worry does not empty tomorrow of its sorrow; it empties today of its strength." Ch. 14

Dieter F. Uchtdorf - "It's your reaction to adversity, not adversity itself that determines how your life's story will develop." Ch. 29

Dr. Eben Alexander - "Those who have had near-death experiences will tell you that realm is far more real than this world, more crisp, vibrant, alive." Ch. 31

Dr. Loretta Scott - "We can't help everyone, but… everyone can help someone" Ch 8

Dr. Seuss - "When something bad happens, you have three choices. You can either let it define you, let it destroy you or you can let strengthen you." Ch. 24

Dr. T.P. Chia - "Parental love is the only love that is truly selfless, unconditional and forgiving." Pictures - Childhood

Eckhart Tolle - "Only the truth of who you are, if realized, will set you free" Ch. 9

Eleanor Roosevelt – "You gain strength, courage and confidence by every experience in which you really stop to look fear in the face." Ch. 32

Fight Club - "Without pain, without sacrifice, we would have nothing." Ch. 21

Florence Nightingale - "The very first requirement in a hospital is that it should do the sick no harm." Ch. 6

Fred Rogers - "There is no normal life that is free of pain. It's the very wrestling with our problems that can be the impetus for our growth." Ch. 49

Georg C. Lichtenberg - "I cannot say whether things will get better if we change; what I can say is they must change if they are to get better." Ch. 53

George S. Patton - "When you have collected all the facts and fears and made your decision, turn off all you're fears and go ahead!" Ch. 46

Greg Tamblyn - "On the roller coaster of life, your 21st birthday is like being at the top of the first giant hill with your hands in the air and no lap bar." Ch. 36

Henry Ward Beecher - "We never know the love of a parent till we become parents ourselves." Ch. 48

H.P. Lovecraft - "The oldest and strongest emotion of mankind is fear, and the oldest and strongest kind of fear is fear of the unknown." Ch. 50

Hunter S. Thompson - "I hate pain, despite my ability to tolerate it beyond all known parameters, which is not necessarily a good thing." Ch. 51

Jim Butcher - "When everything goes to hell, the people who stand by you without flinching – they are your family." Interludes - Family

Jim Rohn - "Your life does not get better by chance. It gets better by change." Ch. 16

John Wooden - "Do not let what you cannot do interfere with what you can do." Ch. 11

Jon Bon Jovi - "Miracles happen every day, change your perception of what a miracle is, and you'll see them all around you" Ch. 1

Krati Gupta - "If you don't do wild things while you're young, you'll have nothing to smile about when you're old." Ch. 20

Laura Jean Truman - "You can't heal the people you love. You can't make choices for them. You can't rescue them. You can promise that they won't journey alone. You can loan them your map. But this trip is theirs." Ch. 47

Marianne Williamson - "No matter what the problem, a miracle can solve it. Remember to ask for one." Ch. 25

Martin Luther King Jr. - "If you can't fly, then run. If you can't run, then walk. If you can't walk, then crawl. But whatever you do, you have to keep moving." Pictures - Adulthood

Mark Twain - "The fear of death follows from the fear of life. A man who lives fully is prepared to die at any time." Prologue

M.J. Croan - "Maturity is when your world opens up and you realize that you are not the center of it." Ch. 38

Neil Young - "People don't normally change when things are going well. But I want to see what's next and keep moving. That keep things fresh." Ch. 44

Nelson Mandela - "I never lose. I either win or learn." Ch. 19

Nightbirde - "You can't wait until life isn't hard anymore before you decide to be happy." Ch. 52

Oprah Winfrey - "As long as you're chasing the "ghosts" of your past you can never fully embrace your future." Ch. 40

Paul Di Filippo - "More than we sleep, play, or make love, we work. Yet despite – or perhaps because of – this dominant daily grind, much of our literature is biased toward other pursuits." Ch. 39

Paulo Coelho - "Accept you're past without regrets and face you're future without fears." Ch. 45

Sarah McLachlan – "You made my world stand still, and in that stillness, there was a freedom I never felt before." Ch. 54

Seneca - "Every new beginning comes from some other beginnings end." Ch. 12

Sigmund Freud - "Out of your vulnerabilities will come your strength." Ch. 43

Simon Sinek - "The challenge of our unknown future is so much more exciting than the stories of our accomplished past." Ch. 55

Susan David - "Discomfort is the price of admission to a meaningful life" Ch. 7

Ted Nugent - "Ignorance is indeed bliss, but it is also dangerous and embarrassing" Ch. 23

Terrell Owens - "If you align expectations with reality you will never be disappointed" Ch. 10

Tim McGraw - "I guess somethings never change" Ch. 17

Tommy Cotton - "The only reason a true friend won't be there to pick you up is because they are lying beneath you from trying to break your fall." Ch. 13

Unknown - "I have laid my child in a surgeon's arms, I have slept upright in a hospital chair, I have listened to the beeping of machines and been thankful, I have found strength when there wasn't any left. A parent's love is the fuel that enables a normal human being to do the impossible." Ch. 3

UNOS - "Without the organ donor, there is no story, no hope, no transplant. But when there is an organ donor, life springs from death, sorrow turns to hope, and a terrible loss becomes a gift." Ch. 27

William Barclay - "There are two great days in a person's life – the day we are born and the day we discover why." Ch. 2

Winston Churchill - "Success consists of going from failure to failure without loss of enthusiasm." Ch. 37

About the Author

Brandon C. Gandy was born with 15 birth defects and has accumulated over 28 total surgeries throughout his life but never allowed his hardships to define who he is and how he went about pursuing his dreams. Today, Brandon helps organize and run multiple charity golf events, while also assisting in the success of several foundations that he feels have made a meaningful impact on his life and others. Brandon currently lives with his wife Sherry in the San Diego Area with their two young children Rowan and Layla.

Brandon C. Gandy
brandoncg55@hotmail.com
https://www.facebook.com/Gandyman55
https://twitter.com/TheGandyMan55
https://www.instagram.com/thegandyman55/
https://brandongandy.site/

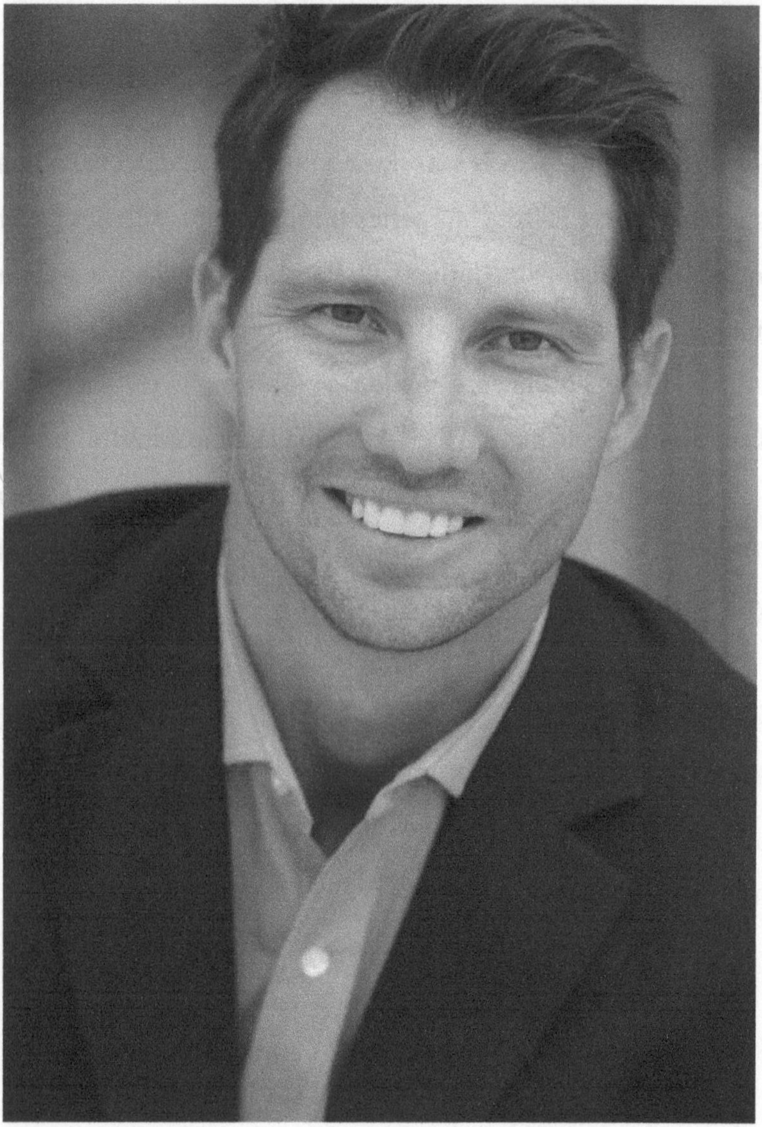